Educational Documents

This collection of documentary material illustrates the main themes of educational history from the Middle Ages to the beginning of the nineteenth century.

In covering this earlier history, Mr Sylvester's book adds an important perspective to the study of educational development. Full weight is given to the curricula and discipline of the various educational institutions over this period, as well as to the legal and constitutional framework in which they were founded.

This book was first published in 1970.

Educational Documents

ENGLAND and WALES · 800–1816

Edited by
D. W. Sylvester

Routledge
Taylor & Francis Group
London and New York

First published 1970 by Routledge

This edition published 2006 by Routledge
2 Park Square, Milton Park, Abingdon, Oxon, OX14 4RN

Simultaneously published in the USA and Canada
by Routledge
270 Madison Ave, New York, NY 10016

Routledge is an imprint of the Taylor & Francis Group

Typeset in 10/12 Imprint by TechBooks New Delhi, India
Printed and bound in Great Britain by MPG Books Ltd, Bodmin, Cornwall

British Library Cataloguing in Publication Data
A catalogue record for this book is available from the British Library

Library of Congress Cataloging in Publication Data
A catalog record for this book has been requested

ISBN 0-415-38287-4 (set)
ISBN 0-415-38288-2 (volume 1)

Publisher's Note

The Publisher has gone to great lengths to ensure the quality of this reprint but points out that some imperfections in the original book may be apparent.

Educational Documents 800–1816

Educational Documents 800–1816

D. W. Sylvester
Department of Education, University of Leeds

Methuen & Co Ltd
11 NEW FETTER LANE LONDON EC4

First published 1970 by
Methuen & Co. Ltd

Printed in Great Britain by
Butler & Tanner Ltd,
Frome and London

SBN 416 13720 2 hardbound
SBN 416 13730 X paperback

Distributed in the U.S.A. by
Barnes & Noble Inc.

Contents

Acknowledgements

The author and publishers wish to thank the following for permission to reproduce extracts from the books listed below: The Borthwick Institute of Historical Research for *Educational Records* edited by J. S. Purvis; Cambridge University Press for *Sir John Fortescue: De Laudibus Legum Angliae* edited and translated by S. B. Chrimes, *Hannah More* edited by M. G. Jones, *Dissenting Academies in England* by I. Parker, *Medieval English Nunneries* by E. Power and *Scholae Academicae: Some Account of the Studies at the English Universities in the Eighteenth Century* by C. Wordsworth; The Clarendon Press, Oxford, for *Statua Antiqua Universitatis Oxoniensis* edited by Strickland Gibson and *A Fifteenth-Century School Book* edited by William Nelson; Columbia University Press for *Chaucer's World* by E. Rickert and *University Records and Life in the Middle Ages* by Lynn Thorndike; J. M. Dent & Sons Ltd for *Tudor School Boy Life* edited by Foster Watson; J. M. Dent & Sons Ltd and Dutton & Company Inc. (New York) for *The Governour* by Sir Thomas Elyot; Burt Franklin (Publishers) for *Inedited Tracts* edited by W. C. Hazlitt; The Masters and Wardens of the Worshipful Company of Grocers for *A History of the Oundle Schools* by W. G. Walker; University of Illinois Press for *William Shakespere's Petty School* by T. W. Baldwin; L. Stanley Knight for *Welsh Independent Grammar Schools to 1660* by L. Stanley Knight, published by the Newtown Welsh Outlook Press; Liverpool University Press for *John Brinsley: Ludus Literarius or The Grammar Schoole* edited by E. T. Campagnac and *John Dury: The Reformed School* edited by H. M. Knox; Macmillan & Co. Ltd for *Documents Illustrative of the History of the English Church* edited by Gee and Hardy; Manchester University Press for *English Education under the Test Acts* by H. McLachlan and *The Household of Edward IV* by A. R. Myers; Thomas Nelson and Sons Limited for *The Chronicle of Jocelin of Brakelond* edited by H. E. Butler and *The Norwich Subscription Books* by E. H. Carter; Penguin Books Ltd for *Castiglione: The Book of the Courtier* translated by George Bull; the Regents of the University of California for *The Metalogicon of John of Salisbury* edited by Daniel D. McGarry; The Royal Historical Society for *The Stonor Letters and Papers, 1290–1483* edited by C. L. Kingsford.

Preface

This book offers a selection of documentary material illustrative of the main themes of educational history from the Middle Ages to the beginning of the nineteenth century. It is intended for use in Colleges and Departments of Education as an introduction for students to these earlier periods of the history of education. It may also be of general interest to teachers, administrators and others concerned with the development of education.

While it is true that this earlier history has not often figured in courses of education, its importance in adding perspective to studies of educational development is now being more widely acknowledged. This book attempts to fill a need for an introductory documentary text, for not only has A. F. Leach's *Educational Charters and Documents* been long out of print but many other standard texts on these earlier periods are also difficult to acquire.

An attempt has been made to provide, as far as space would allow, a balanced selection of material on the curriculum and discipline of various educational institutions, and on the legal and constitutional framework in which they were founded. The extracts are prefaced by short commentaries but, although these draw attention to certain points, they by no means exhaust the use which teachers and students might make of the documents in their reading and analysis. Similarly the suggestions for further reading have been kept to the minimum and readers requiring more detailed bibliographies will find that the books mentioned here will lead them on to other relevant reading.

Extracts from documents in Latin are given in translation. Further, the English of some of the early documents has been modernized, though others are left so that the reader has some of the full flavour of the original.

The book includes material up to about 1816 and in this way it may be seen as a companion to Stuart Maclure's *Educational Documents, England and Wales, 1816–1967*. This termination point has however meant that no more than mere intimations of the work of the National and British and Foreign School Societies could be included.

Anglo-Saxon Schools

Throughout the Middle Ages the Church was the main agent in the preservation of learning and the provision of schools. Cardinal Newman once said that there was 'not a man in Europe who talks bravely against the Church but owes it to the Church that he can talk at all', and certainly, after the fall of the Roman Empire and the Anglo-Saxon invasions of Britain, it was the Church which reintroduced schools and learning. The reason is not far to seek. Christianity is an intellectual and a teaching religion, and above all it is a religion of a book, the Bible. Readings from the Bible are the foundations of both its liturgy and its doctrines and consequently a literate priesthood is a necessity. It is not surprising then that the early missionaries who followed St Augustine to England after A.D. 597 began to establish schools. Throughout the Anglo-Saxon period the Church, and more particularly the monasteries, were centres of learning and education, and in the following centuries, bishops, clergy and religious laymen continued to provide schools in order to keep up the supply of educated clergy. However, our knowledge of schooling in Anglo-Saxon times is very tenuous.*

EARLY SCHOOLS IN EAST ANGLIA AND CANTERBURY

This extract from Bede's *Ecclesiastical History* gives evidence of early Church schools and it is notable that the school in East Anglia was to teach Latin grammar.

After Erpwald (A.D. 635), the successor to Redwald, his brother Sigbert ruled the kingdom of East Anglia. A good and religious man he had been baptized long before in Gaul where he had been living in exile to escape the hostility of Redwald. On his return home and when he became king he wished to follow the good practices of Gaul, and he established a school in which boys could learn grammar. He was helped in this by Bishop Felix, who had come to him from Kent and who provided him with teachers and masters from the school at Canterbury.

BEDE *Hist. Eccl.* Bk III, 18

**Further reading:*
A. F. LEACH *The Schools of Medieval England* (London: Methuen, 1915, reprinted 1969)
E. S. DUCKETT *Alcuin, Friend of Charlemagne* (New York: Macmillan, 1951)
D. KNOWLES *The Monastic Order in England* (Cambridge Univ. Press, 1949)

THE EDUCATIONAL WORK OF THEODORE AND HADRIAN

Theodore of Tarsus was Archbishop in England from 669 to 690 and Hadrian who accompanied him became Abbot of the monastery of St Peter and St Paul outside Canterbury. This extract indicates their work in transmitting both theological learning and Greek and Roman literature (sacred and profane) and in teaching the clergy the knowledge appropriate to their calling.

Theodore arrived in his see in the second year after his consecration on Sunday, 27 May (669), and lived in it twenty-one years, three months and twenty-six days. Soon after he visited all those parts of the island where the English had settled, and he was well received and listened to everywhere. Accompanied and helped everywhere he went by Hadrian, he taught the true way of life and the canonical rite for the keeping of Easter. He was the first archbishop whom the whole English Church obeyed and, as I have said, because both he and Hadrian were men of learning both in sacred and profane literature, they collected a large group of students, pouring into their minds rivers of saving knowledge day after day, teaching them the art of metre, astronomy and the calculation of the Church's feast days as well as the Scriptures. A proof of this is that some of their students who are alive today (c. A.D. 731) know Latin and Greek as well as their native tongue.

BEDE *Hist. Eccl.* Bk IV, 2

ALCUIN, SCHOOLMASTER AND LIBRARIAN AT YORK MINSTER 776–782

In his poem *Of the bishops and saints of the Church of York* Alcuin described the teaching of Ethelbert and then how Alcuin himself was made schoolmaster and librarian, when in 776 Ethelbert retired from the archbishopric he had been given in 766. The extract describes the curriculum of the school, mainly in terms of the seven liberal arts, and concludes with what amounts to a catalogue of York Minster library at that time. In 782 Alcuin went to Charlemagne's Palace school at Aachen and was largely instrumental in producing that revival of learning known as the Carolingian renaissance. He died in 804 as Abbot of St Martin at Tours.

Then pious and wise, both teacher and priest, he (Ethelbert) joined Bishop Egbert, to whom he was related by right of blood, and was appointed advocate of the clergy and at the same time preferred as schoolmaster in the city of York. There he watered thirsty minds with different streams of doctrine and various dews of learning, giving to these the arts of grammatical method, and pouring on those the rivers of rhetorical language. Some he took care to polish on the whetstone of the law, others he taught to sing together in Aeonian chant, instructing others to play on the pipe of Castaly, and run with lyrical feet over the hills of Parnassus. The aforesaid master made others know the harmony of heaven, the labours of the sun and moon, the five zones of the sky, the seven wandering planets, the laws of the stars, their rising and setting, the movements of the air, the quaking of sea and earth, the nature of men, cattle, birds and beasts, the different kinds of number and the various shapes. He gave certainty for the return of Easter, opening wide the mysteries of the sacred scriptures and making clear the abysses of the primitive and old law. Whatever youths he saw of outstanding talents, those he joined to himself, he taught, he fed, he loved; as a result the doctor had many pupils in the sacred volumes, skilled in various arts. More than once he went rejoicing abroad in foreign by-ways, led by love of wisdom, to see if he could find in those lands new books or studies which he could bring home with him. Also he went devoutly to the city of Romulus, rich in the love of God, wandering widely through the sacred places. Then returning home, he was received everywhere by kings and rulers with honour as the most outstanding of doctors, whom great kings wished to retain so that he should water their lands with Divine dew. But the master hurrying to the work appointed for him, returned to his homeland by God's will. For as soon as he was brought to his own shores he was compelled to take on the pastoral care and by popular demand made high priest . . . But his former fervent industry for reading the scriptures was not decreased by the weight of his duties, and he was made both a wise doctor and a pious priest . . . .

Then the most eminent minister in holy orders, the prelate having accomplished his work and full of days, happily handed over the episcopal ornaments to his beloved disciple Eanbald, and for himself he sought a secret cloister where he could be free to serve God alone. But he handed over the treasures of his books, dear above all, to the other son, who was always near to his father, ever thirsty to drink the streams of learning, whose name if you care to know it, these present verses on the front will show at once. Between them he divided his wealth in different kinds: to the one the rule of the church, the ornaments, lands and money; to the other the symbols of learning, the school, the master's chair, and the books which the famous master had collected from all sides, accumulating a notable collection of treasures under one roof. There you will find the footsteps of the old fathers, whatever the Roman has on behalf of himself in the Latin sphere, or which famous Greece transmitted to the Latins, or which the Hebrew people drink from the shower above, or which Africa has spread abroad with light-bringing lamp. What father Jerome, what Hilarius, bishop Ambrose, Augustine and Saint Athanasius felt, what old Orosius published, whatever the great Gregory teaches, and Pope Leo, what Basil and Fulgentius, and Cassiodorus and John Chrysostom also shine. Whatever Aldhelm taught and Bede the master, what Victorinus and Boethius wrote; the ancient historians, Pompeius, Pliny, keen Aristotle himself, and also the great orator Tully. What also Sedulius, and Juvencus himself sings, Alcimus and Clemens, Prosper, Paulinus, Arator; what Fortunatus and Lactantius publish, what Virgilius Maro, Statius and Lucan, and what the masters of the art of grammar have written, Probus and Phocas, Donatus, Priscian, Servius, Euticius, Pompeius, Comminianus. You will find there, reader, many other eminent in learning, masters in both art and discourse, who have written many volumes of sound sense, but to write their names in this verse would take too long.

A. F. LEACH *Educational Charters and Documents*, pp. 10–16
(Cambridge Univ. Press, 1911)

The Liberal Arts Curriculum

The education the Church introduced was based on the 'liberal arts' curriculum of the Romano-Greek world into which the Church had been born. It provided instruction in seven subjects: the *trivium* consisting of grammar, rhetoric, and dialectic (logic) and the *quadrivium* consisting of arithmetic, geometry, music and astronomy. Before pupils could begin these studies, however, they had to learn the elementary skills of reading and writing. First learning by heart the letters of the alphabet, the *Credo* (the Creed) and *Pater Noster* (Our Father), they would go on to learn to read in the Psalter. Then the study of Latin Grammar would begin using the *Grammar* of Priscian, a sixth-century teacher at Constantinople; and perhaps a book like Aelfric's *Colloquy*, the constant aim throughout being to teach the pupil not only to read and write in Latin but also to dispute and converse in Latin. In theory the teaching of the *trivium* was the function of the grammar schools and the *quadrivium* that of the universities, though in practice the grammar school, as its name implies, probably did little more than teach grammar and provide some first readings in classical texts, logic – though possibly introduced in some schools – becoming a university subject.*

AELFRIC'S *COLLOQUY* c. 1005

Aelfric's *Colloquy* was the last of three educational books which he wrote when he was master of the oblates at Cerne in Dorset, the other works being a *Grammar*, a translation of Priscian, and a *Glossary*. Aelfric became abbot at Eynsham sometime after 1005.

The *Colloquy* is a dialogue between a schoolmaster and his pupils, and it was a common way of teaching boys how to speak Latin correctly. Because some of the characters in the dialogue are ploughmen, merchants, etc., some commentators have taken this as evidence of a monastic school where the pupils were drawn from varied classes of life. However such an interpretation is difficult to maintain since the class is addressed as 'pueri' (boys) and it seems most likely that the characters in the dialogue are imaginary, introduced and assigned to the pupils as a means of making their task of learning Latin easier and more pleasant. Nevertheless, it is possible that the monastic schools of later Anglo-Saxon times did take pupils from outside the monastery.

**Further reading:*

R. W. SOUTHERN *The Making of the Middle Ages*, particularly Chapter IV (Hutchinson's University Library, 1953). Also in paperback

G. LEFF *Medieval Thought* (Harmondsworth: Pelican Books, 1958)

M. L. W. LAISTNER *Thought and Letters in Western Europe 500–900* (London: Methuen, 1957)

THE TOWER OF KNOWLEDGE

The Tower of Knowledge, taken from *Margarita Philosophica*, an encyclopædia written in the sixteenth century by a German, Gregorius Reisch, gives a graphic summary of medieval education through the seven liberal arts.

Wisdom, the teacher, offers the child a hornbook with the alphabet on it, as she leads him to the tower. Grammar is begun on the ground floor with Donatus, a fourth-century Roman grammarian, and then continued upstairs on the next floor with Priscian, a sixth-century teacher and writer of the most important of all medieval Latin grammars. On the next floor the *trivium* is completed with rhetoric, taught from Cicero, and logic from Aristotle. At the same level a start is made on the *quadrivium*, with arithmetic taught from the book written by Boethius, the sixth century Roman scholar. At the next stage, the study of music under Pythagoras, geometry under Euclid, and astronomy under Ptolemy completes the *quadrivium*. Higher still are more advanced studies as natural philosophy (sciences), taught by Pliny, and moral philosophy taught by Seneca – and so to the 'queen of the sciences', theology and metaphysics, taught by Peter Lombard.

The following extract from the *Colloquy* makes it clear that the aim was to teach Latin as a spoken language and the method, with its use of material relevant to the boys' interests, is very much like modern methods of language teaching.

This dialogue in Latin was composed by Abbot Aelfric, who was my master; but I, Aelfric Bata, afterwards made many additions to it.

BOYS Master, we children ask you to teach us to speak correctly for we are unlearned and speak corruptly.

MASTER What do you want to say?

BOYS What do we care what we say so long as we speak correctly and say what is useful, not old-womanish or improper?

MASTER Will you be flogged while learning?

BOYS We would rather be flogged while learning than remain ignorant; but we know that you will be kind to us and not flog us unless you are obliged.

MASTER I ask you what you were saying to me. What work have you?

1ST BOY I am a professed monk and I sing seven times a day with the brethren and I am busy with reading and singing; and meanwhile I want to speak Latin.

MASTER What do these companions of yours know?

1ST BOY Some are ploughmen, others shepherds, some are cowherds, some too are hunters, some are fishermen, some hawkers, some merchants, some shoemakers, some salters, some bakers of the place.

MASTER What do you say, ploughboy, how do you do your work?

PLOUGH BOY Oh, sir, I work very hard. I go out at dawn to drive the oxen to the field, and yoke them to the plough; however hard the winter I dare not stay at home for fear of my master; and having yoked the oxen and made the ploughshare and coulter fast to the plough, every day I have to plough a whole acre or more.

MASTER Have you anyone with you?

PLOUGH BOY I have a boy to drive the oxen with the goad, and he is now hoarse with cold and shouting.

MASTER What more do you do in the day?

PLOUGH BOY A great deal more. I have to fill the oxen's bins with hay, and give them water, and carry the dung outside.

MASTER Oh, it is hard work.

PLOUGH BOY Yes, it is hard work, because I am not free.

A. F. LEACH *Educational Charters and Documents*, pp. 37–41
(Cambridge Univ. Press, 1911)

A THIRTEENTH-CENTURY ACCOUNT OF THE LIBERAL ARTS

In 1480 or 1481 William Caxton printed a translation in English of a popular French encyclopaedia, the *Image du Monde*, which had been widely read since its production in 1245. It gives an illustrated account of the seven liberal arts and particularly noteworthy is the definition which it gives for the term 'liberal'.

The first of the seven sciences is grammar . . . without which all other sciences are of little recommendation . . . for grammar is the foundation and the beginning of learning (clergye); and it is the gate by which in infancy is begun and in continuing men attain the wisdom of learning. This is the science to form the speech, be it in Latin, French or English, or in any other language that men speak with. And whoever could understand all grammar could make and construe every word and pronounce it by example. God made the world by word and the word gives meaning to the world.

The second science is logic which is called dialectic. This science proveth the 'pro' and the 'contra': that is to say the verity or truth, and otherwise. And it proveth whereby shall be known the true from the false and the good from the evil, so verily that for the good was heaven created and on the contrary for the evil was hell made and established, which is horrible, stinking and redoubtable.

The third of the seven sciences is called rhetoric, which containeth in substance, righteousness, reason and the ordering of words. And it ought not to be held as foolishness, for the rights and laws by which judgements are made, and that by reason and according to right have

been kept and maintained in the court of kings, of princes and of barons, come and proceed of rhetoric . . .

The fourth science is called arithmetic . . . and without her may none of the seven sciences be perfectly and entirely known . . . And for this reason was she set in the middle of the seven sciences . . . for from arithmetic proceed all numbers, and by means of numbers all things run, come and go. And nothing is without number. But few perceive how this may be, unless they have been master of the seven

arts for so long that they can see this truth. But we may not now recount nor declare all the reasons for this; for whoever would dispute upon such matters . . . must know many things and much of the commentaries.

Whoever knows well the science of arithmetic may understand the ordering of all things. By law was the world made and created, and by law of the Lord it shall be ended (defeated).

The fifth is called geometry, which is of greater help to astronomy than any of the other seven; for by her is compassed and measured astronomy. Thus by geometry is measured all things where there is measure. By geometry may be known the course of the stars . . . and the greatness of the firmament, of the sun, of the moon and of the earth. By geometry may be known all things and also the quantity; however far they may be, if they can be seen with the eye they can be measured.

The sixth of the seven sciences is called music . . . of this science . . . cometh all temperance, and from this art comes some medicine, for as music makes harmony from all things which have discord in them . . . so medicine works to bring Nature to stop what is unnatural in man's body, when any malady or sickness oppresses it. But medicine is not of the number of the seven sciences of philosophy. But it is an occupation or craft which attends to the health of man's body . . . and therefore it is not liberal, for it serveth to heal man's body which otherwise might perish. And there is nothing liberal nor free that groweth from the earth; wherefore the science which serves to heal man's body is

devoid of freedom, but the sciences which serve man's soul deserve in this world the name of 'liberal'; for the soul ought to be free as a thing that is of noble being, as she that cometh of God, and to God will and ought to return; and therefore are the seven sciences liberal, for they make the soul all free . . . By this science of music have been made all the songs that are sung in holy church, and all the concords of all the instruments which have diverse harmonies and diverse sounds . . .

The seventh and last of the liberal sciences is astronomy, which is the end of all learning. By this science enquiry may and ought to be made of things of heaven and of earth, and especially of those that

have been made by nature and how far distant they are. And whoever knoweth well and understandeth astronomy can see reason in all things; for Our Creator made all things by reason and gave his name to everything.

OLIVER H. PRIOR (ed.) *Caxton's Mirrour of the World*, pp. 33–40 (Early English Text Society, 1913)

Medieval Grammar Schools

Education in the Middle Ages was primarily vocational. A boy or girl was given the education appropriate to his or her job in life. If a boy was to be an agricultural worker, as most were, then he acquired the necessary vocational skills on the job and his religious and moral education he learned from his parish priest in church; going to school never entered into the matter. If he was to be a tradesman or craftsman he was educated as an apprentice of a master under gild rules, and again it was unlikely that he would go to school. If he was the son of a knight he was educated as one of the feudal landed aristocracy, not in school but in some noble's household and in courtly manners and the arts of war rather than letters and book learning. It was not thought necessary that all mankind should have a common education in literacy, and schools were only for those whose job in life necessitated the ability to read and write Latin; they were for potential clerics and lawyers, administrators and schoolmasters.

Medieval society was a static society and education was not seen as a means of social mobility. It is true that a villain's son could receive a literary education and become a priest, but such a pattern of life was not common. In the later Middle Ages the opportunities for social movement increased, but on the whole a class-stratified society was accepted, with each class having its appointed role to play and receiving the education most suited to that role.

It is unwise to generalize about the provision of schools in the Middle Ages for the evidence is very scanty. Bishops might promulgate edicts periodically that priests should provide educational facilities, but there was no system to ensure that this happened and the provision of schools depended more upon the consciences and wills of individuals, either cleric or lay, who gave of their money and land to endow a school or employ a priest as a schoolmaster.

Grammar schools were provided in a variety of ways. Some were cathedral schools kept by the cathedral chapters as at Salisbury and York. Some were schools run by collegiate churches of secular priests, as at Howden in Yorkshire, founded in 1266. The monasteries had schools for their oblates and novices and in some cases they also provided almonry schools run by the almoner for choir boys and other poor boys, as at Westminster Abbey and St Albans. Other monasteries aided town grammar schools as at Bury St Edmunds. Individual bishops might endow schools as, for example, did Archbishop Thomas Rotherham of York when he founded Jesus College, Rotherham, in 1483. At the universities grammar schools appear in connection with college foundations. In 1264 Walter of Merton, Chancellor of England, founded 'the House of the Scholars of Merton' with additional provision for a grammar school. There were also the two large joint foundations of Winchester College and New College, Oxford, in 1378 by William of Wykeham, Bishop of Winchester, and of Eton College and King's College, Cambridge, in 1440 by King Henry VI. Some grammar schools were chantry schools as, for example, that founded by Lady Katherine of Berkely at Wotton-under-Edge in Gloucestershire. Other schools were endowed by gilds, as at Stratford-on-Avon, where the Gild of the Holy Cross from 1400 onwards provided for a schoolmaster and a schoolroom, or by private benefactors, as at Sevenoaks, where in 1432 William Sevenoaks, a London grocer, made provision for a grammar school. Records survive of grammar schools founded in all these various ways, but they have to be treated cautiously, and in particular the assumption of the continuity of a school must be guarded against, since a reference to a school in the thirteenth century, for example, is no guarantee that it continued to teach grammar in the fifteenth century.*

THE LATERAN COUNCIL AND THE PROVISION OF SCHOOLS 1179

This extract shows the attempts made by the church to encourage educational provision, first by ordering cathedrals and large churches to provide grammar school masters and secondly by granting licences to teach freely. In 1215 Innocent III confirmed this ruling.

By the Lateran Council:

Since the church of God, like a loving mother, is bound to provide for the needy both the things which concern the maintenance of the body and which tend to the profit of souls, in order that the poor, who cannot be assisted by their parents' means, may not be deprived of the opportunity of reading and proficiency, in every cathedral church a competent benefice shall be bestowed upon a master who shall teach the clerks of the same church and poor scholars freely, so that both the necessities of the teacher shall be relieved and the way to learning laid open for the learners.

In other churches, too, or monasteries, if anything shall have been in times past assigned for this purpose, it shall be restored.

For a licence to teach no one shall exact money, even if on pretence of any custom he ask anything from those who teach, nor when a licence is asked shall he prevent any one, who is fit, from teaching. Whoever presumes to contravene this shall be put out from any ecclesiastical benefice.

For it seems to be right that none should have the fruits of his labour

**Further reading:*

J. LAWSON *Medieval Education and the Reformation* (London: Routledge & Kegan Paul, 1967)

A. F. LEACH *The Schools of Medieval England* (London: Methuen, 1915, reprinted 1969) in the church of God, who in the greediness of his mind, by selling a licence to teach, endeavours to prevent the proficiency of churchmen.

A. F. LEACH *Educational Charters and Documents*, p. 123
(Cambridge Univ. Press, 1911)

SALISBURY CATHEDRAL SCHOOL 1091

This extract from the foundation statutes of Salisbury Cathedral makes reference to the office of Chancellor as the Schoolmaster.

These are the dignities and customs of the church of Salisbury, which I, Osmund, bishop of that church, in the name of the Holy Trinity, in the year of our Lord 1091, established and granted to the persons and canons of the same church . . .

The dean presides over all canons and vicars (choral) as regards the cure of souls and correction of conduct.

The precentor ought to rule the choir as to chanting and can raise or lower the chant.

The treasurer is pre-eminent in keeping the treasures and ornaments and managing the lights. In like manner the chancellor in ruling the school and correcting the books.

The archdeacons excel in the superintendence of parishes and the cure of souls.

The schoolmaster ought to hear and determine the lessons, and carry the church seal, compose letters and deeds and mark the readers on the table, and the precentor in like manner the singers . . .

A. F. LEACH *Educational Charters and Documents*, pp. 73–5
(Cambridge Univ. Press, 1911)

SCHOOLS IN LONDON C. 1170–1180

The following extract is from William Fitz-Stephen's *Description of the City of London*, written as a preface to his biography of his former master, Thomas Becket, in the latter part of Henry II's reign. It gives information about the London schools of that time, namely those attached to the churches of St Paul's, St Mary-le-Bow and St Martin's-le-Grand, and also about the academic and recreational pursuits of their scholars. The passage is noteworthy in that it provides evidence for the teaching of logic and rhetoric as well as grammar in the schools of that time.

The three principal churches in London are privileged by grant and ancient usage with schools, and they are all very flourishing. Often however through the favour of persons noted in philosophy, more schools are allowed. On feast days the masters call their scholars together at the churches. The scholars hold disputations, some in demonstrative argument, some in dialectic. These churn out enthymemes, those use more perfect syllogisms. Some dispute just to show themselves off, as they do at collections (examinations); while others dispute to establish the truth, which is the grace of perfection. The would-be sophists are judged happy because of the amount and flood of their words; others play upon words.

The orators with rhetorical speeches speak to the point so as to persuade you, taking care to observe the precepts of their art and to omit nothing that is relevant. The boys of different schools compete with each other in verse; or they contend about the principles of Grammar, or the rules of the perfect tenses and supines. Others in epigrams, rhymes and metres employ the common sayings of old, lashing their schoolfellows with Fescennine licentiousness, without ever mentioning names, and hurling abuse and sarcasm at them; with Socratic salt they touch upon the vices of their schoolfellows, and sometimes of their elders, or in audacious dithyrambics they bite them more keenly with the tooth of Theon. The audience, ready for a laugh, with turned up noses, groan with their raucous cackling . . .

We may begin with the boys' games, for we have all been boys. Annually on Shrove-Tuesday the boys from the schools bring to their masters each one his fighting-cock and all the morning they watch their cocks fight in the schools. After dinner the whole youth of the city go into the suburban plain (Smithfield) to play the famous game of football. The scholars from each school have their own ball and most of the holders of civic offices have a ball each too. The adults, the fathers, and the wealthy of the city come on horseback to watch the contests of the young, and grow young with them, getting hot with excitement as they watch so much movement and share in the enjoyments of the free-born adolescents. Every Sunday in Lent, after dinner a band of youth on warlike horses go out into the fields . . . The sons of the lay citizens rush out of the gates, armed with lances and shields, the younger ones with javelins, pointed but without their steel tips, and they have mock battles . . . On holidays in summer the youth exercise themselves in playing with archery, running, jumping, wrestling, throwing stones and missiles to certain distances, and in duelling. The girls, as soon as the moon rises, dance to the stringed instrument and with their steps shake the ground. In the winter before dinner . . . there are boar fights or tusked pigs . . . or bulls and large bears are baited with dogs. And when that great lake which flows near the walls of the city to the north is frozen, crowds of youth go out on the ice.

SAMUEL PEGGE *Fitz-Stephen's Description of London* (London, 1772)

ABBOT SAMSON AND BURY ST EDMUNDS SCHOOL

This extract shows the work of Abbot Samson of the monastery of St Edmund in providing education in the neighbouring town of Bury St Edmunds, which in fact belonged to the Abbey. Samson was Abbot from 1182 until his death in 1212.

The Abbot bought some stone houses in the town of St Edmund and assigned them to the master of the schools, in order that the poor clerks might be quit of hiring houses – for which each scholar, whether he could or could not, was forced to pay a penny or halfpenny twice a year . . .

After Abbot Samson and Robert de Scales had come to an agreement about half the advowson of the church of Wetherden, and the said Robert had recognized the right of St Edmund and the Abbot, the latter, though no compact or promise had previously been made, gave that part of the church which belonged to him to Master Roger de Scales, the brother of the said knight on this condition, that he should through the Sacrist pay a yearly pension of three marks to the master of the schools, whoever he might be, that was teaching in the town of St Edmund. Now this the Abbot did, being moved by a spirit of memorable piety that, just as he had formerly bought stone houses for the school that the poor clerks might be quit of hiring houses, so now for the future they might be quit of all the fees, which the master of schools used according to the custom to exact for his teaching. But if God will, and if the Abbot lives, the whole half of the said church, which is said to be worth a hundred shillings, should be turned to such use.

H. E. BUTLER (ed.) *The Chronicle of Jocelin of Brakelond*, pp. 45, 95 (London: Nelson, 1949)

ALMONRY SCHOOL AT WESTMINSTER

The following extract is from the rules for conduct at Westminster School, an almonry or chorister's school attached to the Abbey in the thirteenth century, and under the jurisdiction of the monastery almoner. Note the references to corporal punishment and to the insistence that those who are learning Latin grammar must speak Latin and not French or English.

In the morning let the boys upon rising sign themselves with the holy cross, and let each one say the creed . . . and the Lord's Prayer three times, and the salutation to the Blessed Virgin five times, without shouting and confusion; and if anyone neglects these good things, let him be punished.

Then, after they have made up the beds properly, let them leave their room together quietly, without clattering, and approach the church modestly with washed hands, not running or skipping, or even chattering, or having a row with any person or animal; not carrying bow or staff, or stone in the hand, or touching anything with which another could be harmed, but marching along simply and honestly and with ordered step . . . Whether they are standing or sitting in the choir, let them not have their eyes turned aside to the people, but rather toward the altar; not grinning, or chattering, or laughing aloud; not making fun of another if he does not read or sing psalms well; not hitting one another secretly or openly, or answering rudely if they happen to be asked a question by their elders. Those who break the rules will feel the rod without delay . . . As they go out let them take pains to keep the same manner and bearing as upon entering; and let them conduct themselves upon returning home from church or school in the same way as has been said before. Those who break this rule shall be punished in the same way as for the other transgressions.

Likewise if anyone who knows Latin dares to speak English or French with his companion, or with any clerk, for every word he shall have a blow with the rod.

Likewise for rudeness in word or deed anywhere and for any kind of oath let not the rod be spared . . .

Again, whoever at bedtime has torn to pieces the bed of his companions or hidden the bedclothes, or thrown shoes or pillows from corner to corner, or roused anger, or thrown the school into disorder, shall be severely punished in the morning.

In going to bed let them conduct themselves as upon rising, signing themselves and their beds with the sign of the cross.

Quoted in E. RICKERT *Chaucer's World*, pp. 116–17
(New York: Columbia Univ. Press, 1948)

GRAMMAR TEACHING AT MERTON COLLEGE, OXFORD

Walter de Merton, who had been Chancellor to Henry III, founded Merton College at Oxford around 1264. The foundation was for a Warden and twenty fellows, but it also included provision for a master of grammar.

The following extract from the statutes of Merton explains his position and duties. Evidently he was to be available to teach the older university students as well as younger pupils, if the former found that their Latin was deficient.

The form, therefore, which I enact and decree to be for ever observed, is, that in the house which bears the name of the Scholars of Merton, there shall be a constant succession of scholars devoted to the pursuits of literature, who are bound to employ themselves in the study of arts or philosophy, the canons or theology, the majority of whom are to continue engaged in the liberal arts and philosophy until they are passed on to the study of theology, at the award of their Warden and Fellows in consequence of their meritorious proficiency in the former studies. Still, four or five persons, whom their Head is to appoint, and whom he adjudges to be of ability and aptness for the purpose, may, if they choose, become students in canon law; and the Head is empowered to enable these persons to give their attention for a while to the civil laws, for any period of time which he deems proper. Also, some single individual, being a member of the collegiate body, is to be a grammarian, and must entirely devote himself to the study of grammar; and he is to be furnished, at the expense of the house, with a proper supply of books and other requisites: he is to have the care of the students in grammar, and to him too the more advanced in years may have recourse without a blush, when doubts arise in their faculty; and under his tuition the scholars themselves who are suited to the purpose, and in all cases where it may seem expedient in order to give them a facility, may obtain instruction in the Latin language, or in English, and he must teach them all effectively and to the utmost of his abilities.

E. F. PERCIVAL (ed.) *The Foundation Statutes of Merton College, Oxford*, pp. 15–16 (London, 1847)

This next extract, from the Ordinances of Archbishop Peckham, suggests that Walter of Merton's desire that a teacher of grammar should be appointed has been neglected, for here, in 1284, Archbishop Peckham reminds the college of its duty in this respect. Together the two extracts illustrate the danger of assuming the continued existence of a school from a foundation document. Also noteworthy is the reference to the chaining of books.

Furthermore, the founder of your college, perceiving that the clergy of England, for the most part, expressed themselves very inaccurately in the learned languages, decreed that you should educate scholars under a grammatical tutor, and that the works of grammatical authors should be kept in the library to perfect you in the learned languages. But as this has hitherto been neglected, we prescribe, under the penalty imposed on disobedience, that so far as possible the transgress must be corrected according to rule. And we will that the works of Papia and Hughico, together with the summary of Brico, be procured and fastened on a public table, that all who frequent the library may have facility of consulting them.

E. F. PERCIVAL (ed.) *The Foundation Statutes of Merton College, Oxford*, p. 56 (London, 1847)

THE APPOINTMENT OF GRAMMAR SCHOOL MASTERS IN LINCOLNSHIRE 1329

This memorandum illustrates the extent of Church control over the provision of grammar schools in certain areas.

Memorandum, that on 13th June, in the year aforesaid (1329), the reverend men and masters, the Lord Dean of the church of Lincoln, and Giles of Redmere, and John of Schalby, Canons of the church of Lincoln, as vicegerents and in the name of the Chapter, sitting in a certain low room below the Lord Dean's Chapel in his house, and discussing the collation of the Grammar Schools in the county of Lincoln which were vacant, the Chancellorship of the said church of Lincoln being vacant and then in their hands, and as to the persons to be admitted to such schools; finally they conferred the Grammar School of Barton on William of Gurney, the school of Partney on John of Upton, the school of Grimsby on William of Coleston, the school of Horncastle on John of Beverley, the school of St Botolph (i.e. Boston) on Robert of Muston, and the school of Grantham on Walter Pigot, clerks, from Michaelmas, 1329, to the same feast in the following year, in the above title and by way of charity; expressly granting that they and each of them should be inducted into the bodily possession of the said schools in accordance with their respective collations . . .

A. F. LEACH *Educational Charters and Documents*, pp. 281–3
(Cambridge Univ. Press, 1911)

A BOARDING SCHOOL C. 1380

The following letter from a chaplain, Brother Edmund, to his master, Sir Edmund de Stonor, gives interesting glimpses of boarding school education. The chaplain has evidently been to see how his master's son is getting on at school. Note the references to the Grammar of Donatus.

My Lord and God's servant, know, if it please you, that I have seen your son Edmund and observed his condition for two nights and a day. His illness grows less from day to day, and he is not in bed. But when the fever comes on he rests a little upset for two hours, after which he rises and according to the demands of the time, goes into school and eats and goes around healthy and cheerful, so that it seems there is no danger in his condition. He himself of his own accord sent his greetings to you and his mistress, and to all the others. He is beginning to learn *Donatus* slowly and so far does well. He has that copy of *Donatus* which I feared had been lost. Truly, I have never seen such care given a boy as he had had during his illness. The master and his wife prefer that some of his clothes be left at home for he has too many and fewer would suffice, and it is possible, though they would not wish it, that some clothes might easily be torn and spoilt. I send you the names of the books contained in one volume which the owner will not sell under twelve shillings, and in my opinion and others also it is worth it. If he sells it to us, he wants payment made promptly. So, if it pleases you, send me a reply by your boy of your wishes in the matters mentioned.

Farewell, in the strength of Christ and in the merits of the Virgin and Mother, Mary,

From your devoted Brother Edmund.

C. L. KINGSFORD (ed.) *The Stonor Letters and Papers 1290–1483*, Vol. I, p. 21 (Royal Historical Society: Camden Third Series, Vol. 29, 1919)

A CHANTRY SCHOOL AT WOTTON-UNDER-EDGE, GLOUCESTERSHIRE, 1384

The Catholic belief in prayers for the souls of the dead inspired many rich men and women to provide for a priest who would perform this service of intercession for them on their decease. In the fourteenth century it became common for founders of chantries – as such foundations were called – to require the priest not only to pray for their souls but also to teach grammar in a school.

This extract from the foundation deeds describes the chantry founded by Lady Katharine Berkeley in 1384 at Wotton-under-Edge in Gloucestershire. Here the priest is to celebrate mass, either in the manor-house chapel or in the parish church, for Lady Katharine and her relations, and also teach grammar in a purpose-built house provided in the endowment. The rest of the endowment is sufficient to provide the priest and two scholar-clerks with a living, so there is no need to charge fees and the grammar school is thus a free one.

Ordinance of the House of Scholars of Wotton-under-Edge [*Gloucestershire*]. *Deed of Lady Katharine of Berkeley.*

To all the sons of holy mother church, I Katharine, who was wife of Sir Thomas of Berkeley, late lord of Berkeley, Walter Burnet, chaplain, William Pendock, chaplain, health in Him who is the true health of all.

We the said Katharine, closely and attentively considering that the purpose of many wishing to be taught grammar, which is the foundation of all the liberal arts, is daily diminished and brought to naught by poverty and want of means, therefore and for the maintenance and exaltation of holy mother church and increase of divine worship and of the other arts and liberal sciences, out of the goods bestowed on us by God, caused the said Walter and William to acquire to them and their heirs in fee the lands and tenements underwritten, that they might newly build a school-house in Wotton-under-Edge for the habitation and foundation and likewise dispose of them for the maintenance of a master and two poor scholars on the art of grammar; which master and his successors shall govern and teach all scholars coming to the same house or school for instruction in such art, without taking anything for their pains from them or any of them . . .

On the first foundation of the House we have made certain ordinances and statutes for its rule which we will shall be for ever observed.

First we will and ordain that the Master of the said House of Scholars for the time being shall be a priest and shall always celebrate in St Katharine's chapel in the manor-house of Wotton when I the said Katharine or other the lord or lady of the said manor of Wotton shall be there; and when I or the Lord of the said manor shall be elsewhere, then in the parish church of the said town, for the healthy estate of us and of the said Sir Thomas of Berkeley, now lord of Berkeley, and the lady Margaret his consort, also for Sir John of Berkeley, knight, and the lady Elizabeth his consort, and for our souls when we shall have passed from this light, and likewise for the souls of Thomas late of Berkeley, lord and husband of me Katharine aforesaid, and of Peter of Veel likewise, formerly the lord and husband of the said Katharine, of John of Clyvedon knight and Emma his consort, father and mother of me the said Katharine, and of all the progenitors and parents of the said Sir Thomas now lord of Berkeley and of me the aforesaid Katharine, without taking any stipend or salary from anyone besides the rents and profits by us bestowed and given to the same in the first foundation and endowment of the said schoolhouse or hereafter to be bestowed by gift of the faithful, or otherwise lawfully acquired in augmentation of the income of the house aforesaid.

Also we will that Master John Stone, M.A., the first master to be given a title to the rule of the said house and governance of the said scholars, and the two poor and needly scholars, namely, John Beenly and Walter Morkyn, wishing to learn the art of grammar and to become proficient in it, joined to the master of the said house and placed and gathered together college-wise in the said house, shall stay together and remain in the same, as is provided below, and shall live college-wise on the lands, rents and other possessions, which we assigned and gave them on the foundation of the said house for their maintenance . . .

And the said masters and their successors shall keep the school faithfully, and usefully govern it after their power, and shall kindly receive all scholars whatsoever, howsoever and whencesoever coming for instruction in the said art of grammar, and duly instruct them in the same art, without exacting, claiming or taking from them any advantage or gain for their labour in the name of stipend or salary, so that the master aforesaid could be accused of solicitation . . .

We will also and ordain that the said two scholars now placed in the said house, as is before-mentioned, and all those who shall be afterwards admitted there in their place, whose age on their first admission shall not exceed ten years (though we do not intend absolutely to forbid such admission before that age, supposing the persons admitted are of sufficient ability), shall be of good behaviour attending school and obedient to their master, and shall not be set by the master for the time being to do any office or service, but shall be compelled continually to devote their time to learning and study.

Also we will that the aforesaid two poor young scholars thus added to the said master of the House of Scholars, as aforesaid, after they have been in the same school for six years continuously shall be wholly removed and others put in their place nominated by the master and admitted by the lord aforesaid; and if any of them within the said six years shall be undisciplined, and shall be unwilling to devote his time to learning, and shall after due warning and chastisement refuse to amend, they shall be expelled by the master under the supervision of the lord or his steward, and others put in their places.

A. F. LEACH *Educational Charters and Documents*, pp. 331–41
(Cambridge Univ. Press, 1911)

FOUNDATION DEED OF WINCHESTER COLLEGE 1382

William of Wykeham's foundation of Winchester College in 1382 was seen by A. F. Leach as a significant new step, establishing a school as 'a sovereign and independent corporation existing by and for itself', and not dependent upon a chantry or cathedral chapter. It was also new in that it was part of a joint-foundation of a grammar school at Winchester preparing pupils for further studies at New College, Oxford – a pattern which Henry VI followed in 1440 when he founded Eton College and King's College, Cambridge. In both these cases there was provision for seventy 'poor and needy scholars', but soon Winchester and Eton began to attract the sons of the nobility and in this way developed into their present-day existence as large and influential public schools.

To all the sons of holy mother church to whom these our present letters shall come, William of Wykeham, by divine permission bishop of Winchester, health in Him who is the true health of all.

Our most glorious and almighty God, the leader of the triumph of the everlasting empire, who by His ineffable power and the decree of His heavenly council has deigned to bring us miserable and naked from our mother's womb to this vale of misery, who sometimes places the lowly on high, has in His infallible providence and by His overflowing grace enriched us, though unworthy, with ample honours and beyond our deserts raised us to divers degrees and dignities. Weighing these things in our inmost thoughts we, by the Lord's grant, have lately erected and founded a perpetual college of seventy poor scholars, clerks, to study theology, canon and civil law and arts in the University of Oxford, to the praise, glory and honour of the name of the Crucified and the most glorious virgin Mary His mother. But whereas experience, the mistress of all things, plainly teaches that grammar is the foundation, gate and source of all the other liberal arts, without which such arts cannot be known, nor can anyone arrive at practising them; considering moreover that by the knowledge of grammar justice is cultivated and the prosperity of the estate of humanity is increased, and that some students in other sciences, through default of good teaching and sufficient learning in grammar, often fall into the danger of failing where they had set before themselves the desire of success: whereas too there are and will be, it is believed, hereafter many poor scholars intent on school studies suffering from want of money and poverty, whose means barely suffice or will suffice in the future to allow them to continue and profit in the aforesaid art of grammar. For such poor and needy scholars, clerks, present and to come, in order that they may be able to stay or be busy at school . . . we propose from the means and goods bestowed on us by God, with the aid of the clemency of God, to hold out helping hands and give the assistance of charity in manner underwritten.

Therefore, we, the aforesaid William of Wykeham, bishop of Winchester, having acquired for us and our successors bishops of Winchester divers messuages, lands and a meadow, with their appurtenances, in the soke of Winchester in our diocese of Winchester, and near the city itself . . . actually and effectually institute, found, establish and also ordain a perpetual college of poor scholars clerks by the city of Winchester.

And this college we will and it ought for ever to consist in and of the number of seventy poor and needy scholars clerks living college-wise in the same, studying and becoming proficient in grammaticals or the art faculty or science of grammar, by the grace of God for ever to endure.

And wishing further to give effect to the institution, foundation and ordinance of our said college, we appoint Master Thomas of Cranley, bachelor in theology, a man prudent and discreet in spiritual and circumspect in temporal matters, and of approved life and learning, warden of our same college; and we admit seventy poor and indigent scholar clerks who are to study in grammaticals or the art faculty or science of grammar and join them to the same warden; and we place actually in our same college, and assemble college-wise, the same scholars clerks, whose names are more fully written in the muniments of our said college; and wishing to give a name to the same college, as is proper, we name and also call it 'Sancte Marie Collegium', in the vulgar tongue 'Seinte Marie College of Wynchestre', and will that it shall be for ever named and also called by the same name or title.

A. F. LEACH *Educational Charters and Documents*, pp. 321–5
(Cambridge Univ. Press, 1911)

FOUNDATION OF SEVENOAKS GRAMMAR SCHOOL 1432

In the fifteenth century lay provision of schools increased. This extract from the will of William Sevenoaks, 'citizen and grocer of London', is an example of such provision. Particularly noteworthy is the reference to a lay-schoolmaster, for the founder is not at all concerned that the master should be in Holy Orders.

First, (to pay an annuity of twenty marks to Margaret Walton for life and after her death) do find and maintain for ever one Master an honest man, sufficiently advanced and expert in the science of grammar, B.A., by no means in holy orders, to keep a Grammar School in some convenient house within the said town of Sevenoaks with my goods having obtained the licence of the King or by other lawful means according to the discretion of my executors, and to teach and instruct all poor boys whatsoever coming there for the sake of learning, taking nothing of them or their parents or friends for the teaching and instructing them. For I will that the said rector (etc.) and their successors for the time being out of the issues and revenues of all the lands and tenements aforesaid with their appurtenances, do pay yearly to the aforesaid Master of Grammar by way of salary or stipend for his service and labour to be done and exercised as aforesaid, ten marks sterling at the four principal terms of the year by equal portions. Moreover I will and order that if any, and as often as it happens that any such master or teacher in grammar decease, depart or for the least time voluntarily cease from such determination, that then within at least the next quarter following another such master, if any such can conveniently be found, be newly elected and chosen by the said rector or vicar, wardens and parishioners and their successors to inhabit and keep school and determine in the same house in ways, manner and form aforesaid.

A. F. LEACH *Educational Charters and Documents*, pp. 401–3
(Cambridge Univ. Press, 1911)

STRATFORD-ON-AVON GRAMMAR SCHOOL, ENDOWED 1482

Gilds were societies of laymen and women formed for some spiritual or social purposes, sometimes employing a chaplain to teach in a school as well as perform priestly functions for them. At Stratford-on-Avon the Holy Cross Gild kept a school and this extract refers to its endowment by Thomas Jolyffe, himself a gild-priest.

That whereas the aforesaid Thomas Jolyffe of mere devotion and for the special praise of God Almighty and the health of his soul and the souls of his parents John and Jane and for the souls of all the brethren and sisters and benefactors of the said Gild has given and granted to the said Gild all and singular his lands . . . on the conditions following, namely,

That the aforesaid Thomas Clopton, master of the said Gild, and the Aldermen and proctors of the same and their successors shall find a priest fit and able in the science to teach grammar freely to all scholars coming to him to school in the said town, taking nothing of the scholars for their teaching; and the aforesaid priest shall be one of the five priests of the said Gild at the next vacancy when one falls vacant, receiving meanwhile for his salary till the next vacancy £8 of money of England to be paid by the hands of the said Master, Aldermen, Proctors and their successors . . .

And the grammar priest aforesaid shall, when he shall by God's grace be so disposed, celebrate mass in the chapel of the said Gild, and on feast days shall celebrate mass in the parish church of Stratford aforesaid at the altar of St John the Baptist for the good estate of the lord bishop of Worcester for the time being and the souls of the said Master Thomas Jolyffe and of his parents John and Jane and the souls of all the benefactors of the said Gild and the souls of all the faithful departed . . .

And the aforesaid Master Warden and the aforesaid Thomas Clopton, master of the Gild, and their successors shall name a priest to teach grammar as often as there shall be a vacancy.

A. F. LEACH *Educational Charters and Documents*, pp. 381–5
(Cambridge Univ. Press, 1911)

FEES AT IPSWICH GRAMMAR SCHOOL 1477 AND 1482

These extracts provide evidence of the existence of various kinds of schools in Ipswich with fees charged according to the level of education given. Note also the reference to the connection of the grammar schoolmaster with the Gild of Corpus Christi.

1477

Ordinance. And that the Grammar School-master shall henceforth have the jurisdiction and government of all scholars in the liberty and precinct of this town, except the petties called ABCs and Song, taking only for the fees, from every grammar scholar, psalter scholar and primer scholar according to the scale fixed by the lord Bishop of Norwich, viz. for a grammarian 10d., psalterian 8d. and primarian 6d. for quarterage.

1482

And that every burgess, being in the town of Ipswich, shall pay to the Grammar School-master for his son 8d. a quarter and not above; and that the said Grammar School-master shall celebrate for the gild of Corpus Christi for the whole term of his life.

A. F. LEACH *Educational Charters and Documents*, p. 423 (Cambridge Univ. Press, 1911)

FOUNDATION OF JESUS COLLEGE, ROTHERHAM, 1483

This extract from the foundation deed of Jesus College, Rotherham, which Archbishop Thomas Rotherham of York provided for in 1483, is interesting in several respects. Noteworthy are the reference to a wandering teacher of grammar, who provided Thomas Rotherham with teaching in his youth; the religious purposes of the foundation; the foundation of three kinds of school, grammar, song and writing; and the influence of social and economic factors on the founder, shown in his concern to provide teaching for secular business-world occupations.

To all the sons of Holy Mother Church who inspect these present letters, Thomas, by divine permission Archbishop of York, primate of England and legate of the apostolic see, health in the embraces of the Health-giver.

Whereas we, the Archbishop aforesaid, thinking over and considering that in the town of Rotherham of our diocese of York, where we were born and by the bath of holy regeneration re-born, where, too, passing our tender age we remained without letters, and should have so stood untaught, unlettered and rude for many years, if there had not come there by the grace of God a man learned in grammar, from whom as from a spring we drew our first instruction, God willing and as we believe lending His guidance, and so arrived at the state in which we now are, while many others too arrived at great things.

Desiring, therefore, in the first place to render thanks to the Saviour, and that we may not seem ungrateful and be accused of being unmindful of God's benefits and of whence we came, we have determined to make such a spring flow there for ever, in other words to establish a teacher of grammar there;

And in the second place, considering that many parishioners belong to that church and many hill-men flock to it, that they may better love

Christ's religion and oftener visit, honour, and love His church, we have thought fit to establish for ever another fellow learned in song and six choristers or children of the chapel, that divine service may be more honourably celebrated;

In the third place, because that county produces many youths endowed with the light and sharpness of ability, who do not all wish to attain the dignity and elevation of priesthood, that these may be better fitted for the mechanical arts and other concerns of this world, we have ordained a third fellow, learned and skilled in the art of writing and accounts.

But as the art of writing, music, and indeed grammar itself are subordinated to the divine law and the Gospel, above these three fellows we have established a theologian, who shall be at least a Bachelor in Theology, who shall be called Provost or Placed over, because he is placed over the other three fellows in the management and policy of the house; and he shall be bound to preach in my province the ladder of Jacob, the word of Jesus, the shortest and surest way to heaven, and to rule the college.

A. F. LEACH *Educational Charters and Documents*, pp. 423–5
(Cambridge Univ. Press, 1911)

A TEACHER TRAINING COLLEGE AT CAMBRIDGE c. 1439

This extract shows the decay of grammar schools owing to the shortage of teachers, though it is also evidence that grammar school provision was extensive by the fifteenth century. God's House provided the first teacher training college building in England.

Unto the king our sovereign lord

Beseecheth full meekly your poor priest and continual bedeman William Byngham, person of St John Zachary of London, unto your sovereign grace to be remembered, how that he hath divers times sued unto your Highness shewing and declaring by bill how greatly the clergy of this your Realm, by the which all wisdom, knowledge, and governance standeth in, is like to be impaired and feebled, by the default and lack of Schoolmasters of Grammar, in so much that as your said poor beseecher hath found . . . over the East part of the way leading from Hampton to Coventry, and so forth no father north than Ripon, seventy schools void or more that were occupied all at once within fifty years past, because that there is so great scarcity of masters of Grammar, whereof as now be almost none, nor no more to be had in your Universities over those that needs be occupied still there; Wherefore please it unto your most sovereign highness and pleanteous grace to consider how that for all liberal sciences used in your said universities certain livelihood is ordained and endowed, saving only for grammar, the which is root and ground of all the said other sciences, and there upon graciously to grant licence to your foresaid beseecher that he may give . . . a mansion called God's House the which he hath made and edified in your town of Cambridge for the free abode of poor Scholars of Grammar, and also that he and whatsoever other person or persons to that well-being willed and disposed may also give without fine or fee, livelihood as lands, tenements, rents and services such as is not holden of you immediately by Knight service, or advowsons of Churches . . . unto the master and scholars of Clare Hall in your university of Cambridge and to their successors . . . to the intent that the said Master and Scholars may find perpetually in the foresaid mansion called God's House twenty three Scholars for to commence in grammar, and a Priest to govern them, for reformation of the said default, for the love of God, and in the way of Charity.

A. F. LEACH *Educational Charters and Documents*, pp. 402–3
(Cambridge Univ. Press, 1911)

THE TEACHING OF ENGLISH IN THE FOURTEENTH CENTURY

The following extracts show that three languages competed for a place in the curriculum of later medieval schools – Latin, French and English. However, it seems that English began to gain in importance as the fourteenth century passed, becoming increasingly the language of the upper classes.

According to Ranulph Higden's *Polychronicon*, 1327, the reasons for the decay of the English Language

today come mainly from two things: boys in school, unlike the custom of other nations, are compelled to leave their own tongue and construe their lessons in French, as they have done since the Normans first came; and also gentlemen's sons are taught to speak French from their cradles and country men, wishing to be thought gentlemen, try with much effort to speak French.

John Trevisa, translator of Higden's *Polychronicon*, added the following comment on the subject, c. 1385.

This manner (of translating Latin into French) was much used before the first murrain (Black Death, 1349) and is since somewhat changed. For John Cornwall, a master of grammar (at Merton College School, Oxford) changed the lore in grammar school, and construction of French into English; and Richard Pencrych learned that manner of teaching from him, and other men of Pencrych, so that now, the year of our Lord a thousand three hundred four score and five . . . in all the grammar schools of England, children leave French and construe and learn in English, and have thereby advantage on one side and disadvantage on the other. Their advantage is that they learn their grammar in less time than children were accustomed to do; and the disadvantage is that now children of grammar school know no more French than their left heel, and that is harm for them, if they shall pass the sea and travel in strange lands and in many other places.

RANULPHUS HIGDEN *Polychronicon*, Vol. II, pp. 159–61. Edited by CHURCHILL BABINGTON (Rolls Series, 1869)

Song Schools

'Elementary' education – that is, reading and perhaps writing – might be gained in schools of various origins: a parish priest might run such a school at the back of his church; a chantry-priest might hold a school as part of his endowed duties; a bell-ringer might give elementary schooling; a grammar school might have a reading school attached to it, as a sort of preparatory school; and song schools or choir schools at cathedrals, large churches and abbeys might provide opportunities for elementary education. As the origin of these elementary schools varied so did their names, for in such documentary evidence of their existence which survives, they are known variously as ABC schools or 'abseys', as 'reading' schools, 'writing' schools and 'song' schools, and collectively as 'petties'.

CHAUCER'S SONG SCHOOL

Chaucer in his *Prioress's Tale* gives us a description of a song school making its main features quite clear – the instruction in singing and reading (in that order of importance) and not in grammar, the learning by rote and with little understanding, the discipline by beating, the use of a primer.

A litel scole of Cristen folk ther stood
Doun at the ferther ende, in which ther were
Children an heep, y-comen of Cristen blood,
That lerned in that scole yeer by yere
Swich maner doctrine as men used there,
This is to seyn, to singen and to rede,
As smale children doon in hir childhede.

Among thise children was a widwes sone,
A litel clergeon, seven yeer of age,
That day by day to scole was his wone,
And eek also, wher-as he saugh th'image
Of Cristes moder, hadde he in usage,
As him was taught, to knele adoun and seye
His *Ave Marie*, as he goth by the weye.

This litel child, his litel book lerninge,
As he sat in the scole at his prymer,
He Alma redemptoris herde singe,

As children lerned hir antiphoner;
And as he dorste, he drough him ner and ner,
And herkned ay the wordes and the note,
Til he the firste vers coude al by rote.

Noght wiste he what this Latin was to seye,
For he so yong and tendre was of age;
But on a day his felaw gan he preye
T'expounden him this song in his langage,
Or telle him why this song was in usage;
This preyde he him to construe and declare
Ful ofte tyme upon his knowes bare.

His felaw, which that elder was than he,
Answerde him thus: 'this song, I have herd seye,
Was maked of our blisful lady free,
Hir to salue, and eek hir for to preye
To been our help and socour whan we deye.
I can no more expounde in this matere;
I lerne song, I can but smal grammere.'

'And is this song maked in reverence
Of Cristes moder?' seyde this innocent;
'Now certes, I wol do my diligence
To conne it al, er Cristemasse is went;
Though that I for my prymer shal be shent,
And shal be beten thryes in an houre,
I wol it conne, our lady for to honoure.'

His felaw taughte him homward prively,
Fro day to day, til he coude it by rote,
And than he sang it wel and boldely
Fro word to word, according with the note;
Twyes a day it passed thurgh his throte,
To scoleward and homward when he wente;
On Cristes moder set was his entente.

CHAUCER *The Canterbury Tales: The Prioress's Tale*

THE PROVISION OF SONG SCHOOLS AT LINCOLN 1305

This extract illustrates the existence of song schools taught by parish priests and the jealous control a mother church could exert over education

Be it remembered that on Saturday next after the feast of the Conversion of St Paul all the parish clerks of the churches of the city of Lincoln were teaching boys in the churches singing or music; and being present in chapter before Masters Robert de Lacy and William of Thornton, who charged them that they had held adulterine schools to the prejudice of the liberty of the mother church, they firmly denied that they were keeping any schools in the churches, or teaching boys singing; but as they could not deny that they had at some time done so, the said Masters Robert and William made them swear, holding the most holy Gospels, that they will not henceforward keep any adulterine schools in the churches, nor teach boys song or music, without licence from the [Song] Schoolmaster.

A. F. LEACH *Educational Charters and Documents*, p. 236
(Cambridge Univ. Press, 1911)

Corporal Punishment for Schoolboys in the Fifteenth Century

Throughout the Middle Ages schoolmasters employed beating as the main incentive to learning. This was accepted as an appropriate pedagogic method, and when a man became a Master of Grammar at the University he was given a birch as a symbol of his office and his profession.

The Birched Schoolboy

The following late fifteenth-century poem, *The Birched Schoolboy*, gives a graphic description of the thoughts and feelings of an unwilling, and indeed truant, schoolboy who has been birched for his misdeeds.

Hay! Hay! by this day!
What availeth it me though I say nay?

I would fain be a clark
But yet it is a strange work,
The birchen twiggis be so sharp,
It maketh me have a faint heart.
What availeth it me though I say nay?

On Monday in the morning when I shall rise
At vi. of the clock, it is the gise
To go to school without a-vise
I had rather go twenty mile twice!
What availeth it me though I say nay?

My master looketh as he were mad:
'Where hast thou been, though sorry lad?'
'Milking ducks, my mother bade:'
It was no marvel that I were sad.
What availeth it me though I say nay?

My master peppered my arse with well good speed:
It was worse than fennel seed;
He would not leave till it did bleed.
Much sorrow has been for his deed!
What availeth it me though I say nay?

I would my master were a wat (hare)
And my book a wild cat,
And a brace of greyhounds in his top.
I would be glad for to see that!
What availeth it me though I say nay?

I would my master were an hare,
And all his bookis houndis were,
And I myself a jolly hunter:
To blow my horn I would not spare!
For if he were dead I would not care.
What availeth it me though I say nay?

F. J. FURNIVALL (ed.) *The Babees Book*, pp. 403–4
(Early English Text Society, 1868)

A MOTHER EXHORTS A SCHOOLMASTER TO BEAT HER SON

This extract from the *Paston Letters* gives the message which in 1458 Agnes Paston sent by messenger to a schoolmaster in London, by name Greenfield, who had recently taken charge of her son, Clement.

To pray Greenfield to send me faithfully word by writing how Clement Paston hath done his duty in learning. And if he has not done well, nor will not amend, pray him that he will truly belash him till he will amend. So did his last master, and the best that ever he had at Cambridge. And tell Greenfield that if he will take upon himself to bring him into good rule and learning, and that I may verily know he does his duty, I will give him ten marks for his labour, for I had rather he were fairly buried than lost for default (of correction).

J. GAIRDNER (ed.) *Paston Letters*, No. 311 (London: Constable, 1896)

The Education of Knights

The children of the nobility and landed classes received a vocational education which fitted them for social and military leadership and for the management of the estates of land they would eventually inherit. Until the age of seven the children would be educated at home. They would be taught to read with the help of a Primer or ABC book, and also led into the ways and practices of religion. They would be introduced to the moral standards expected of them by society, and taught courtesy, manners, and obedience to their elders. From the age of about seven, it was common for both boys and girls to be boarded out in the household of some lord or lady, or in a nunnery, where this early education was extended and reinforced together with additions appropriate to the sex of the child.

A boy would serve as page to some nobleman for some seven years until he was about fourteen. Under the supervision of the lord and his wife and tutored by the chaplain and men-at-arms in the household, he would prepare for knighthood. He would learn to ride and to joust, how to sing and dance and how to play on the harp or pipe. He would probably be taught French and perhaps a little Latin. He would continue to practise his religion and also learn the conventions of knightly courtesy – for example, how to serve at table, how to behave before visitors, and how to prepare his lord's bedchamber. After this on reaching his teens he would become a squire, learning more of the military skills of a knight by helping his master at tournaments, the medieval equivalent of twentieth century manœuvres, or actually on military service abroad.*

CHAUCER'S SQUIRE

Chaucer's portrait of the Squire shows us a man educated in both courtly and military pursuits, the product of his training in some household and his service in a military expedition overseas.

A lovyere, and a lusty bacheler,
With lokkes crulle, as they were leyd in presse.
Of twenty yeer of age he was, I gesse.
Of his stature he was of evene lengthe,
And wonderly deliver, and greet of strengthe.
And he had been somtyme in chivachye,
In Flaundres, in Artoys, and Picardye,

**Further reading:*

A. B. FERGUSON *The Indian Summer of English Chivalry* (Durham, N.C.: Duke University Press, 1962)

C. P. MCMAHON *Education in Fifteenth Century England* (Baltimore: The John Hopkins Press, 1947)

And born him wel, as of so litel space,
In hope to stonden in his lady grace.
Embrouded was he, as it wore a mede
Al ful of fresshe floures, whyte and rede.
Singinge he was, or floytinge, al the day;
He was as fresh as is the month of May.
Short was his goune, with sleves longe and wyde.
Wel coude he sitte on hors, and faire ryde.
He coude songes make and wel endyte,
Juste and eek daunce, and wel purtreye and wryte.
So hote he lovede, that by nightertale
He sleep namore than dooth a nightingale.
Curteys he was, lowly, and servisable,
And carf biforn his fader at the table.

CHAUCER *The Canterbury Tales: Prologue*

EDUCATION AT THE COURT OF EDWARD IV

The following extract from the Black Book of the Household of Edward IV, refers to the education of the sons of the highest nobility at the Court. Known as Henxmen, they were in the charge of a Master of Henxmen and the extract in describing his duties, gives an account of the education provided for the sons of the nobility.

to shew the scoolez (scholars) of urbanitie and nourture of Englond, to lern them to ride clenely and surely; to drawe them also to justes; to lern them were theyre harneys; to have all curtesy in wordes, dedes, and degrees; dilygently to kepe them in rules of goynges and sittinges, after they be of honour. Moreover to teche them sondry languages, and othyr lernynges vertuous, to harping, to pype, sing, daunce, and with other honest and temperate behaviour and patience; and to kepe dayly and wekely with these children dew convenitz, with corrections in theyre chambres, according to suche gentylmen; and eche of them to be used to that thinge of vertue that he shall be moste apt to lerne, with remembraunce dayly of Goddes servyce accustomed. This maistyr sittith in the halle, next unto these Henxmen, at the same boarde, to have his respecte unto theye demeanynges, howe manerly they ete and drinke, and to theyre communication and other formes curiall, after the booke of urbanitie.

A. R. MYERS (ed.) *The Household of Edward IV*, pp. 126–7
(Manchester Univ. Press, 1959)

MANUALS OF INSTRUCTION IN COURTLY BEHAVIOUR

There were various books written in the fifteenth and sixteenth centuries instructing children how to behave before elders, how to lay a table, how to carve and serve, how to prepare a lord's bed, etc. Examples of these books may be found in *The Babees Book* edited by F. J. Furnivall for the Early English Text Society, from which the following extracts are taken.

The Babees Book c. 1475

But amonge alle that I thenke of to telle,
My purpos ys first only forto trete
How yee Babees in housholde that done dwelle
Shulde have youre sylf whenne yee be sette at mete,
And how yee shulde whenne men lyste yow Rehete,
Have wordes lovly, swete, bleste, and benynge.
In this helpe me O Marie, Modir dyngne! . . .

(I must first describe how you Babies who dwell in households should behave at meals, and be ready with lovely and benign words when you are spoken to.)

A, Bele Babees, herkne now to my lore!
Whenne yee entre into your lordis place,
Say first 'god spede'; and alle that ben byfore
Yow in this stede, salue withe humble Face;
Stert nat rudely; komme inne an esy pace;
Holde up youre heede, and knele but on oone kne
To youre sovereyne or lorde, whedir he be . . .

(Fair Babies, when you enter your lord's place, say 'God speed' and salute all there. Kneel on one knee to your lord.)

Take eke noo seete, but to stonde be yee preste;
Whils forto sytte ye have in komaundement,
Youre heede, youre hande, your feet, holde yee in reste;
Nor thurhe clowyng your flesshe loke yee nat Rent;
Lene to no poste whils that ye stande present
Byfore your lorde, nor hanylle ye no thyng
Als for that tyme unto the hous touching . . .

(Stand till you are told to sit: keep your head, hands and feet quiet: don't scratch yourself, or lean against a post, or handle anything.)

Oute overe youre dysshe your heede yee nat hunge,
And withe fulle mouthe drynke in no wyse;
Youre nose, your teethe, your naylles, from pykynge,
Kepe at your mete, for so techis the wyse.
Eke or ye take in youre mouthe, you avyse,
So mekyl mete but that yee rihte welle mowe
Answere, and speke, whenne men speke to you . . .

(Don't hang your head over your dish, or eat with a full mouth, or pick your nose, teeth and nails, or stuff your mouth so that you cannot speak.)

Kutte nouhte youre mete eke as it were Felde men,
That to theyre mete have suche an appetyte
That they ne rekke in what wyse, where ne when,
Nor how ungoodly they on theyre mete twyte;
But, swete children, have alwey your delyte
In curtesye, and in verrey gentylnesse,
And at youre myhte eschewe boystousnesse.

(Don't cut your meat like field labourers, who have such an appetite they don't care how they hack their food. Sweet children, let your delight be courtesy and eschew rudeness.)

F. J. FURNIVALL (ed.) *The Babees Book*, pp. 2–7
(Early English Text Society, 1868)

The following extract is from *The Boke of Nurture* by John Russell, who was Usher and Marshal to Humphrey, Duke of Gloucester (1391–1447).

The Wardrobes

In the warderobe ye must muche entende besily
the robes to kepe well & also to brusche them clenly
with the ende of a soft brusche ye brusche them clenly,
and yet over muche bruschynge were the cloth lyghtly.
Lett never wollyn cloth ne furre passe a senenyght
to be unbrosshen & shakyn tend therto aright,
for moughtes be redy ever in them to gendur & alight
therefore to drapery & skynnery ever have ye a sight.

(Brush clothes at least once a week for fear of moths.)

Whan youre soverayne hathe supped & to chambur takithe his gate,
then sprede forthe youre fote shete like as y lere yow late;

than hos gowne ye gadir of, or garment of his estate,
by his licence & ley hit upp in suche place as ye best wate.

(Spread out the foot sheet. Take off your Lord's robe.)

uppon his bak a mantell ye lay his body to kepe from cold,
set hym on his fote shete made redy as y yow told;
his shon, sokkis & hosyn to draw of be ye bolde;
the hosyn on youre shuldyr cast on uppon your arme ye hold;

(Pull off his shoes, socks and hose.)

youre sovereynes hed ye kembe but furst ye knele to ground;
the kercheff and cappe on his hed hit wolde be warmely wounde;
his bed y-spred the shete for the bed the pelow prest that stounde,
that when youre sovereyn to bed shall go to slepe there saaf & sounde,

(Comb his head, put on his kerchief and nightcap.)

The curteyns let draw them the bed round about
se his morter with wax or perchere that it go not owt
dryve out dogge and catte, or els geve them a clout;
Of youre soverayne take no leve; but low to hym alowt.

(Set his night-light or candle. Bow to your lord.)

Looke that ye have the bason for chamber & also the urinalle
redy at alle howres when he wille clepe or calle:
his nede performed, the same receve agayn ye shalle,
& thus may ye have a thank & reward when that ever hit falle.

F. J. FURNIVALL (ed.) *The Babees Book*, pp. 180–2
(Early English Text Society, 1868)

Education in Nunneries

From the beginning of the fourteenth century some nunneries provided schooling not only for novices but also for children from the upper and wealthy classes. Their main motive in providing schools was financial and they accepted children, mainly girls but also young boys up to the age of ten, in return for cash payments of on average 6d. to 10d. a week for each child. Bishops did not regard teaching the young as part of a nun's vocation but provided that the children, and in particular the male boarders, were not too old, they were prepared to countenance it. These nunnery schools were never large; they educated only a small proportion of the upper classes and in no way provided an education for the poor.

The education they gave was stronger in the dissemination of piety, manners and morality than booklearning, for after the Anglo-Saxon period, nunneries were never centres of learning. For example, it is likely that the majority of nuns in the fourteenth century and after knew no Latin, but sang the services by rote. Some might know French, as Chaucer's Prioress who spoke French

> 'after the scole at Stratford atte Bowe,
> For French of Paris was to hir unknowe',

but in the fifteenth and sixteenth centuries even this seems to have disappeared. There would be no teaching of Latin then, though the children would be taught the *Credo*, the *Ave* and the *Pater Noster* in Latin. They would be taught to read English, perhaps to write, and the girls would probably have been taught spinning and needlework, with perhaps a little French in some nunneries.*

EPISCOPAL RULING ON BOARDERS IN NUNNERIES C. 1431–6

This reference to the nunnery at Burnham, Buckinghamshire, illustrates the general attitude of bishops to the presence of boarders whether child or adult in nunneries. It is a ruling from William Gray, Bishop of Lincoln, issued c. 1431–6

... that henceforward no secular women who are past the fourteenth year of their age, and no males at all, be admitted in any wise to lie by night in the dorter or be suffered so to lie ... That you henceforth admit or suffer to be admitted and received to lodge in the said monastery no women after they have completed the fourteenth year of their

**Further reading:*

E. POWER *Medieval English Nunneries* (Cambridge Univ. Press, 1922)

age and no males after the eighth year of their age . . . That you remove wholly from the said monastery all . . . secular folk, male and female, who, being lodgers in the said monastery, have passed the ages aforesaid.

Linc. Visit. I, p. 24. Quoted in E. POWER *Medieval English Nunneries*, p. 569 (Cambridge Univ. Press, 1922)

LETTER FROM ABBESS OF ST MARY'S WINCHESTER c. 1535

The following letter written c. 1535 from Elizabeth Shelley, Abbess of St Mary's Winchester to Honor, Viscountess Lisle, gives the latter news of her stepdaughter, the lady Bridget Plantagenet, who was at school at the nunnery together with some twenty-five other young ladies, all children of the aristocracy. It is noticeable that the letter has only one small reference to book learning, in the remark about matins books.

After due recommendation, pleaseth it your good ladyship to know that I have received your letter, dated the 4th day of February last past, by which I do perceive your pleasure is to know how mistress Bridget your daughter doth, and what things she lacketh. Madam, thanks be to God, she is in good health, but I assure your ladyship she lacketh convenient apparel, for she hath neither whole gown nor kirtle, but the gown and kirtle that you sent her last. And also that she hath not one good partlet to put upon her neck, nor but one good coif to put upon her head. Wherefore, I beseech your ladyship to send to her such apparel as she lacketh, as shortly as you may conveniently. Also the bringer of your letter shewed to me that your pleasure is to know how much money I received for mistress Bridget's board, and how long she hath been with me. Madam, she hath been with me a whole year ended the 8th day of July last past, and as many weeks as is between that day and the day of making this bill, which is thirty three weeks; and so she hath been with me a whole year and thirty three weeks, which is in all four score and five weeks. And I have received of mistress Katherine Mutton 10s., and of Stephen Bedham 20s.; and I received the day of making this bill, of John Harrison, your servant, 40s.; and so I have received in all, since she came to me, toward the payment of her board, 70s. Also, madam, I have laid out for her, for mending of her gowns and for two matins books, four pair of hosen, and four pairs of shoes, and other small things, 3s. 5d. And, good madam, any pleasure that I may do your ladyship and also my prayer, who shall be assured of, with the grace of Jesus, who preserves you and all yours in honour and health. Amen.

M. A. E. WOOD *Letters of Royal and Illustrious Ladies of Great Britain*, 3 vols (1846). Quoted in E. POWER *Medieval English Nunneries*, pp. 279–80 (Cambridge Univ. Press, 1922)

The Education of Girls

Girls of wealthy parents were educated like their brothers in the households of the nobility or, as has been indicated, in nunneries. They were trained in some of the domestic arts as well as such social pursuits as singing and dancing. Moral and religious training was imbibed in an informal way through the habits of the household.

The most notable manual of behaviour for girls was *The Book of the Knight of La Tour-Landry* and extracts from it are given below.

For girls as for boys corporal punishment was a common means of bringing them to order and in this respect there was then no differentiation in the treatment of the sexes.

The Book of the Knight of La Tour-Landry

In 1371–2 a French noble, Geoffroy de La Tour-Landry, compiled a book for the instruction of his daughters and from then until the sixteenth century it was widely used in France, England and Germany for the education of girls of noble birth. It aimed to give girls an understanding of the need for chastity, for wifely obedience to husbands, for piety and charity, for courtesy, modesty and temperance. It warns women against the dangers of using too much powder and paint on their faces, of trying to keep up with all the latest fashions in dress, of extra-marital sexual relations and, amongst other things, of over-indulgence in drink, making its meaning clear with apt and earthy examples drawn from the Bible, from classical literature and from legend and history. The following extracts indicate the books purpose and range.

This first extract explains how the book came to be written.

In the year of the incarnation of Our Lord MCCCLXXI, as I was in a garden, all heavy and full of thought, in the shadow, about the end of the month of April, I rejoiced a little with the melody and song of the wild birds . . . and they made me to think of the time that is passed of my youth, how love in great distress had held me . . . but my sorrow was healed . . . for he gave me a wife that was both fair and good . . . and I delighted me so much in her that I made for her love songs, ballads, rondells . . . in the best way that I could. But death, that on all maketh war, took her from me . . . And so it is more than twenty year that I have been for her full of great sorrow . . . And as I was in the said garden, thinking of these thoughts, I saw come towards me my four daughters, of the which I was joyful, and had great desire that they should turn to good and . . . I departed and went out of the garden and found in my way two priests and two clerks that I had. And I said to them that I would make a book of examples, for to teach my daughters . . . and so I made them extract for me examples of the Bible and other books that I had, as the deeds of kings, the chronicles of France, Greece, of England, and of many other strange lands . . . and then I made this book. But I would not set it in rhyme, but in prose . . . that it might be better and more plainly to be understood.

T. WRIGHT (ed.) *The Book of the Knight of La Tour-Landry*, pp. 1–4 (Early English Text Society, 1906)

The over-riding importance of education into the ways of religion is made clear in this next extract.

And, therefore, the first work of labour that a man or a woman should begin is to serve God; at every time he awaketh he ought to give God thanks, by thought or prayer, that he is his lord, creator and maker. And when he ariseth, to say his matins, or orisons . . . and to say prayers and things that is praising and thanking to God. For it is an higher and more worthy thing to praise and thank God than to request him for gifts or rewards.

ibid., p. 5

A cautionary tale on the dangers of pre-marital sex follows.

It is contained in a tale of Constantinople, there was an emperor had two daughters, and the youngest had a good disposition, for she loved well God, and praised him, at all time that she awaked, for the dead. And as she and her sister lay a bed, her sister awoke, and heard her in her prayers, and scorned and mocked her, and said, 'hold your peace, for I may not sleep for you.' And so it happened that youth constrained them both to love two brethren, that were knights and were goodly men. And so the sisters told her counsel each to the other. And at the last they set a time that the knights should come to lie by them at night privately at a certain hour. And one came to the youngest sister, but he thought he saw a thousand dead bodies about her in sheets; and he was so sore afraid that he ran away . . . and caught the fevers and great sickness through the fear he had, and laid him in his bed and might not stir for sickness. But that other knight came into that other sister . . . and begat her with child. And when her father knew she was with child, he cast her into the river and drowned her and her child, and flayed the knight. Thus, for that delight, they were both dead; but that other sister was saved. And I shall tell you on the morrow it was in all the house how that one knight was sick in his bed; and the youngest sister went to see him, and asked him whereof he was sick. 'As I went to have entered between the curtains of your bed, I saw so great a number of dead men that I was nigh mad for fear, and still I am afraid of the sight.' And when she heard that she thanked God humbly, that had kept her from shame and destruction; and from that forward she worshipped and praised God devoutly at all times that she awaked, and always (kept) herself clean and chaste. And not long after, a king of Greece wedded her, and was continued a good woman and a devout, and had a good name . . . And therefore daughters, be-think you on this example when you wake, and sleep not till you have prayed for the dead, as did the youngest daughter.

ibid., pp. 5–6

The next extract contains exhortations to learn courtesy and humility.

After, daughters, you must be meek and courteous, for there is none so great a virtue to get the grace of God and the love of all people; for humility and courtesy overcometh all proud hearts, as a sparrow-hawk, be he never so untamed, you may overcome him with goodly and courteous demeanour, you may make him come from the tree to your hand. And if you are rude and be cruel with him, he will fly his way and never come at you. And since that courtesy and softness may overcome a wild bird, that hath no reason, of necessity it ought to refrain the felonious proud heart of man and woman . . . And therefore I advise you to be courteous and humble to both great and small . . . for to the great you do courtesy which is due to them as of right, but the courtesy that is made to poor gentlemen, or to other of less degree, it cometh of a free and gentle courteous and humble heart . . . as it happened as I was not long since with a company of knights and ladies, a great lady took off her hood and bowed to a tailor. And one of the knights said, 'Madame, you have doffed your hood to a tailor.' And she said that she was gladder that she had taken it off to him than to a lord. And they all saw her meekness and wisdom, and held her wise.

ibid., pp. 14–15

In this final extract the virtues of wifely obedience are taught.

And here is a good example . . . a woman ought not to strive with her husband, nor give him no displeasure, (nor) answer her husband before strangers, as did once a woman . . . with great insolent words, dispraising him and setting him at nought; of the which he was oft ashamed and bade her hold her peace, but the more fair he spoke, the worse she did. And he that was angry of her governance, smote her with his fist down to the earth; and then with his foot he struck her in the face and brake her nose, and all her life after she had her nose crooked, the which spoilt her face after, that she might not for shame show her face, it was so foully blemished. And this she had for her evil and great language, that she was wont to say to her husband. And therefore the wife ought to suffer and let the husband have the words, for that is her duty; for it is shame to hear strife between them, and especially before folk. But I say that when they are alone, she may tell him with goodly words, and counsel him to amend if he do amiss. And if he know any good, then he will acknowledge her much thanks, and say she doth as she ought to do.

ibid, pp. 25–6

TREATMENT OF GIRLS IN THE *PASTON LETTERS*

The *Paston Letters* contain some interesting comments upon the education and treatment of girls, and the following extracts illustrate the putting out of girls into other households and the corporal punishment of girls.

In 1470 Margaret Paston wrote to John Paston about his sister, Anne.

My cousin Calthorp sent me a letter complaining in his writing that for asmuch as he cannot be paid of his tenants as he hath before this time, he purposeth to lessen his household . . . wherefore he desireth me to purvey for your sister Anne: he saith she waxeth high, and it were time to purvey her a marriage.

J. GAIRDNER (ed.) *Paston Letters*, No. 660 (London: Constable, 1896)

The previous year in 1469 Margaret Paston had been trying to find a place to board out her daughter Margery, and wrote to her son, John.

Also I would that you should purvey for your sister to be with my Lady of Oxford, or with my Lady of Bedford, or in some other worshipful place, where you think best, and I will help to her finding, for we be either of us weary of the other.

ibid., No. 601

A letter c. 1449 from Elizabeth Clere to her cousin John Paston, describes the harsh treatment Elizabeth Paston was receiving from her mother Agnes Paston, and suggesting that John finds Elizabeth a husband quickly so that she can leave home.

She (Elizabeth) was never in so great sorrow as she is now-a-days, for she may not speak with no man, whosoever come, ne not may see nor speak with my man, nor with servants of her mother's but that she beareth her on hand otherwise than she meaneth; and she hath since Easter the most part been beaten once in the week or twice, and sometimes twice a day, and her head broken in two or three places.

ibid., No. 71

The Education of Craftsmen

The medieval craft gilds were associations of skilled workers who, pursuing the same craft within the walls of the same town, joined together to protect and monopolize their trade and enjoy the social benefits that such an association could offer. In their concern to secure quality in the work produced, they organized a highly effective system of vocational education. Parents who wished their child to be taught a craft found a willing and competent master and entering into a contractual relationship with him, put their child under his care, the master becoming *in loco parentis*. The indentures of apprenticeship, which were usually drawn up and signed in the gild hall in the presence of the wardens of the gild, involved rights and obligations on the side of both the master and the apprentice. Usually an apprenticeship was to last seven years, and the master was to provide food and clothes for the apprentice for most of that period. The boy on the other hand had to work for his master, learning the craft and keeping its secrets.

Gilds were unwilling to allow masters to take on more than one or two apprentices at any one time. They did not want to flood the market and so cause a cut in their standard of living. Their regulations accordingly forbid the engagement of too many apprentices. On the other hand the regulations show a concern that masters should teach their craft well and not misuse their apprentices. In this connection it is noteworthy that while indentures often allow a master to administer corporal punishment, there are cases on record of masters being found guilty before the law courts of excessive beating of apprentices.

It was always possible for the sons of the labouring class to have a literary education and so rise into one of the professions as a priest or an administrator. William Langland in *Piers Plowman* tells how 'a beggar's brat can become a bishop, and sit among the peers of the realm and lord's sons and knights crouch to him.' However, though possible, it was not easy and the social mobility which Langland describes was always very limited. Similarly, it was difficult for the son of an agricultural worker to escape from his manorial lord and become an apprentice to some craft. With the gradual break-up of manorial organization in the fourteenth century, however, the chances to change occupational prospects in life increased. The governing classes passed legislation to prevent ploughmen's children learning a craft but it was ineffective and eventually repealed. The expanding economic life demanded changes in society which no legislation could resist.

LEGISLATION TO LIMIT APPRENTICESHIPS

These enactments to limit apprenticeships, one of which is quoted here, were often evaded and eventually repealed under Henry VI. Note the freedom given to every man to send his children to school if he could. Whether this was at all possible for the ordinary parent is, of course, another matter.

1405–6

And Whereas in the Statutes made at Canterbury (1388) among other Articles it is contained that he or she that useth to labour at the Plough or Cart, or other Labour or Service of Husbandry, till he be of the age of Twelve Years, that from the same time forth he shall abide at the same Labour, without being put to any Mystery or Handicraft: and if any Covenant of Bond be made from that time forth to the contrary it shall be holden for none: Notwithstanding which Article, and the good Statutes afore made through all parts of the Realm, the Infants born within the Towns and Seignories of Upland, whose Fathers and Mothers have no Land nor Rent nor other Living, but only their Service or Mystery, be put by their said Fathers and Mothers and other Friends to serve, and bound Apprentices, to divers Crafts within the Cities and Boroughs of the said Realm sometime at the age of Twelve Years, sometime within the said Age, and that for the Pride of Clothing and other evil Customs that Servants do use in the same; so that there is so great Scarcity of Labourers and other Servants of Husbandry that the Gentlemen and other People of the Realm be greatly impoverished for the Cause aforesaid: Our Sovereign Lord the King considering the said mischief, and willing thereupon to provide Remedy, by the advice and assent of the Lords Spiritual and Temporal, and at the request of the said Commons, hath ordained and stablished, That no Man nor Woman, of what Estate or Condition they be, shall put their Son or Daughter, of whatsoever Age he or she be, to Serve as Apprentice to no Craft nor other Labour within any City or Borough in the Realm, except he have Land or Rent to the Value of Twenty Shillings by the Year at the least, but they shall be put to other labours as their Estates doth require, upon Pain of one Year's Imprisonment, and to make Fine and Ransom at the King's Will. And if any Covenant be made of any such Infant, of what Estate that he be, to the contrary, it shall be holden for none. Provided Always, that every Man or Woman, of what Estate or Condition that he be, shall be free to set their Son or Daughter to take Learning at any manner School that pleaseth them within the Realm.

Statutes 7 Henri IV, Cap. xvii. *The Statutes of the Realm*, Vol. 2, pp. 157–8 (1816)

GIRL APPRENTICE BEATEN

The following London court record shows that misuse of apprentices and failure to enrol apprentices in the proper way could lead to legal action.

John Catour of Reading brought a bill of complaint against Elis Mympe, broudurer (embroiderer) of London, to whom his daughter Alice had been apprenticed for five years, for beating and illtreating the girl, and failing to provide for her.

The parties were summoned to appear on March 3, when they announced that they had come to an agreement on terms that the defendant should pay the complainant 13s. 4d. and release the girl from her apprenticeship. Thereupon he released her.

The defendant was then asked why he took the girl for less than seven years, and had not enrolled the indentures, according to the custom of the city and his oath. He put himself on the mercy of the mayor and the aldermen, who gave judgement exonerating the said Alice from her apprenticeship. By order of the court the indentures were surrendered for cancellation.

Quoted in E. RICKERT *Chaucer's World*, p. 108
(New York: Columbia Univ. Press, 1948)

RULES FOR APPRENTICESHIPS, GILD OF THE TAILORS OF EXETER, c. 1480

These extracts illustrate the terms and methods of enrolling apprentices and the duties expected of any master who took apprentices.

Also it is ordained, by the Master and Wardens and all the whole craft, that every person of the said craft that taketh an apprentice, shall bring him before the Master and Wardens, and there to have his Indenture enrolled, and the Master to pay 12d. for the enrolment; and this to be done within twelve months and a day, or else to lose his freedom of the craft for evermore. Also it is ordained, the Master and Wardens and the craft aforesaid, that every apprentice of the said craft that is enrolled and truly serveth his covenant shall pay a spoon of silver . . . and shall give a breakfast to the foresaid Master and Wardens, before the day that he is able to be made freeman of the City aforesaid (and if he pay not a spoon worth 4s. or else 4s. in money for the same).

TOULMIN SMITH (ed.) *English Gilds*, p. 316
(Early English Text Society, 1892)

The Oath for the teaching of any person that shall be admitted You shall swear that you shall well and truly behave yourself, in teaching (abelling) of this person in all such skill as belongeth to the craft of Tailors that cometh to your mind, and in all such knowledge as you find him able to show to the Master and Wardens; and that you shall not delay in this, for love, favour, friendship, nor any other hatred, neither malice of no person. So God help you and holiness and by this book.

ibid., p. 319

ORDINANCES OF THE CRAFT OF BARBERS, BRISTOL, 1418

This extract illustrates the control a Gild attempted to assert over its masters and apprentices.

First that no manner of person henceforth shall poll or shave any person, citizen or stranger, within the franchises of Bristol unless he be a burgess and master of the said craft, their servants and apprentices, on pain of paying 6s. 8d., that is to say 40d. to the common profit, and 40d. to the contribution of the said craft each time that he be convicted thereof . . . Also that no master of the said craft, henceforth take an apprentice to the same craft for less than the term of seven years, and if anyone do the contrary that he be presented to the surveyors of the same craft for the time being, and be amerced in 20s. that is to say 10s. to the common profit, and 10s. to the contribution of the craft above said without any pardon . . . Also that no manner of person hereafter shall keep any house, shop or chamber of the said craft before he be accepted in the liberties of Bristol, and that he holds and exercises his trade openly in a shop and not in chambers halls or in other privy places, and that he be able and sufficiently learned in the said craft, on pain of paying everytime that he does the contrary as is contained in the last article to pay as is before said.

FRANCIS B. BUCKLEY (ed.) *The Little Red Book of Bristol*, Vol. II, pp. 137–40 (Bristol, 1900)

Medieval Universities

In Carolingian times Benedictine monasticism had been the main agent of learning and education in Western Europe. However, the reforming orders of the eleventh and twelfth centuries, such as the Cluniacs and the Cistercians, had the effect of turning the monasteries towards a more ascetic life in which learning figured less. The immediate successors to monasticism in providing education were the Cathedral schools, and in certain towns these became centres of learning great enough to become known and accepted as universities. No simple explanation can be offered for the growth of universities. The revival of trade, the growth of towns, a widespread intellectual restlessness and the appearance of a student population able and willing to wander in search of knowledge – all these factors need to be considered in attempting to explain the rise of the universities.

In England the two universities which eventually established themselves did not rise from cathedral schools as the University of Paris did. Nevertheless Oxford and Cambridge were part of that European revival of learning which by 1500 had become institutionalized in the foundation of over seventy universities. The extracts which follow attempt to illustrate the general origins and features of universities as well as those peculiar to England.*

PETER ABELARD (1079–1142)

The personality and teaching of Abelard were both a cause and a symptom of that upsurge of intellectual enquiry which eventually became institutionalized in the universities of the Middle Ages. The following extract, from a letter of Abelard, indicates his own studies and his climb to eminence as a teacher.

. . . Moreover I had a father who had some training in letters before he put on the trappings of war. Wherefore later he grew so fond of literature that he was disposed to have all his sons instructed in letters before they were trained in arms. And so 'twas done. As therefore he held me his firstborn the more dear, so much the more pains did he take with

**Further reading:*

C. H. HASKINS *The Renaissance of the Twelfth Century* (Cambridge, Mass: Harvard Univ. Press, 1927)
C. H. HASKINS *The Rise of Universities* (New York: Cornell Univ. Press, 1957)
H. WIERUSZOWSKI *The Medieval University* (London: Van Nostrand, 1966)
H. RASHDALL *The Universities of Europe in the Middle Ages*, 3 vols. Edited by F. M. POWICKE and A. B. EMDEN (Oxford: Clarendon Press, 1936)
H. WADDELL *Peter Abelard* (novel) (London: Constable, 1933). Also in paperback
H. WADDELL *The Wandering Scholars* (Harmondsworth: Pelican Books, 1954)

my education. For my part, the more extensively and readily I progressed in literary studies, the more ardent became my devotion to them, and I was allured into such a passion for them that, surrendering to my brothers the pomp of military glory and my hereditary prerogative as firstborn, I totally abdicated the court of Mars to be received into the bosum of Minerva. And since I preferred the panoply of dialectical arguments to all the documents of philosophy, I exchanged other arms for these and esteemed the conflict of disputation more than the trophies of war. Whereupon traversing various provinces, disputing wherever I had heard that the pursuit of this art was flourishing, I became an emulator of the Peripatetics.

Finally I came to Paris, where already this discipline was accustomed to flourish most, to William forsooth of Champeaux as my teacher, who was then prominent in this field actually and by reputation. Tarrying with him a time I was at first welcomed but later cordially disliked, when I tried to refute some of his opinions and often ventured to argue against him and sometimes seemed superior in disputation. Which indeed those who were esteemed chief among our fellow scholars received with so much the greater indignation as I was considered their junior in years and time of study. Hence the first beginnings of my calamities which have lasted until now, and envy of others has multiplied against me, the more my fame has been extended. Finally it came about that presuming upon my ability beyond the strength of my years, I, a mere youth, aspired to instruct classes and selected a place where I should do so the then celebrated town of Melun and royal seat. My aforesaid teacher got wind of this and tried to remove my classes from his as far as he could and schemed secretly in every way he could to carry off my classes and the place provided for me before I should leave his. But since he had there some enemies among the powers that be, relying on their aid I stuck by my purpose, and his manifest jealousy won me the support of many.

From the very beginning of my teaching my name began to be so magnified in the dialectical art that not only the reputation of my fellow students but even of the master himself gradually contracted and was extinguished. Hence it came about that, becoming more confident of myself, I transferred my classes to Corbeil which is nearer Paris and so gave opportunity for more frequent assaults of disputation. But not long afterwards I had a breakdown from over-studying and had to go home, and, for some years removed from France, I was desired the more ardently by those whom the study of dialectic attracted. Moreover after a few years, when finally I had recovered my health, that teacher of mine, William, archdeacon of Paris, had changed his former habit and joined the order of regular clergy with this intention, as they said, that as he was believed more religious he would be promoted to a higher degree of prelacy, as soon happened, he being made bishop of Châlons. But this changed mode of life recalled him neither from the city of Paris nor from his accustomed study of philosophy, but in the monastery too, to which he had betaken himself for religion's sake, he straightway instituted public classes in the wonted manner. Then I, returned to him in order to hear rhetoric from him, among other aims of our disputations compelled him by the clearest line of argument to alter, nay to destroy, his old view as to universals. Moreover, he was of such opinion concerning the community of universals that he held that the same whole thing essentially was at once present in its single individuals, of which there would be no diversity in essence but variety only in the multitude of accidents. Then he so corrected his opinion that he said henceforth the same thing not essentially but indifferently. And since the main question among dialecticians regarding universals has always been on this very point – so that even Porphyry in his *Isagoge*, when he wrote of universals, did not venture to define it, saying, 'For this is a very difficult business' – when William had corrected, nay rather abandoned, this opinion, his lectures became so neglected that he was hardly permitted to lecture on logic, as if the whole sum of that art consisted in this opinion as to universals. As a consequence my teaching acquired such strength and authority that those who before were violent adherents of that master of ours and who most attacked my teaching poured into my classes, and the successor of our master in the schools of Paris offered his place to me, in order that there with others he might sit under my teaching, where once his master and my master had flourished.

Therefore within a few days after I began to teach dialectic there, with what envy our master began to grow green with what grief to rage, is not easy to express in words. And not long enduring the tide of woe, he cannily set about to get rid of me even then. And because he had nothing which he could bring openly against me, by advancing most disgraceful charges he plotted to take away the classes from him who had yielded his teaching to me, substituting in his place another person hostile to me. Then I went back to Melun and held classes there as before, and the more clearly his envy had me as its object, so much the more authority it conferred upon me.

PETER ABELARD *Historia Calamitatum.* Quoted in
LYNN THORNDIKE *University Records and Life in the Middle Ages*, pp. 3–6 (New York: Columbia Univ. Press, 1944)

ABELARD'S *SIC ET NON*

Peter Abelard's particular strengths as a teacher were his attractive personality, his ability to clarify issues and his concern to foster the spirit of free enquiry among his students. This last characteristic is apparent in his *Sic et Non* (*Yes and No*). The book contains a hundred-and-fifty-eight questions for debate on various theological, ethical and metaphysical topics, and each question is followed by a collection of conflicting opinions drawn from the writings of the Fathers on the Scriptures. The opinions are merely stated, and no attempt is made to reconcile them, the aim being to stimulate readers to seek the truth for themselves. Abelard's method, modified and developed, became known as the scholastic method and was widely used in medieval university studies. The 'disputation' or debate which became a common requirement for all degrees developed directly from Abelard's method. Similarly the medieval method of lecturing by comment on collected texts followed the form of *Sic et Non* as did the main university text-books in Canon Law and Theology – namely the *Decretum* of Gratian and the *Liber Sententiarium* of Peter Lombard.

Abelard's demand for intellectual independence may be usefully compared with that of Anselm in the preceding century. Anselm had stated: 'I do not seek to know in order that I may believe, but I believe in order that I may know.' Abelard's view was, 'by doubting we are led to inquiry, and by inquiry we attain the truth.' The following extract from the prologue to the *Sic et Non* sets forth Abelard's attitude.

In truth, constant or frequent questioning is the first key to wisdom; and it is, indeed, to the acquiring of this [habit of] questioning with absorbing eagerness that the famous philosopher, Aristotle, the most clear sighted of all, urges the studious when he says: 'It is perhaps difficult to speak confidently in matters of this sort unless they have often been investigated. Indeed, to doubt in special cases will not be without advantage.' For through doubting we come to inquiry and through inquiry we perceive the truth. As the Truth Himself says: 'Seek and ye shall find, knock and it shall be opened unto you.' And He also, instructing us by His own example, about the twelfth year of His life was to be found sitting in the midst of the doctors, asking them questions, exhibiting to us by His asking of questions the appearance of a pupil, rather than, by preaching, that of a teacher, although there is in Him, nevertheless, the full and perfect wisdom of God.

Now when a number of quotations from [various] writings are introduced they spur on the reader and allure him into seeking the truth in proportion as the authority of the writing itself is commended . . .

In accordance, then, with these forecasts it is our pleasure to collect different sayings of the holy Fathers as we planned, just as they have come to mind, suggesting (as they do) some questioning from their apparent disagreement, in order that they may stimulate tender readers to the utmost effort in seeking the truth and may make them keener as the result of their seeking.

A. O. NORTON *Readings in the History of Education*, pp. 19–20 (Harvard Univ. Press, 1909)

This next extract lists some of the questions Abelard proposed for debate. That Abelard should dare to raise some of these topics for debate was a sign of independence of thought in itself.

1 That faith is based upon reason, *et contra.*
5. That God is not single, *et contra.*
6. That God is tripartite, *et contra.*
8. That in the Trinity it is not to be stated that there is more than one Eternal being, *et contra.*
13. That God the Father is the cause of the son, *et contra.*
14. That the Son is without beginning, *et contra.*
32. That to God all things are possible, *et non.*
36. That God does whatever he wishes, *et non.*
37. That nothing happens contrary to the will of God, *et contra.*
38. That God knows all things, *et non.*
53. That Adam's sin was great, *et non.*
84. That man's first sin did not begin through the persuasion of the devil, *et contra.*
55. That Eve only, not Adam, was beguiled, *et contra.*
79. That Christ was a deceiver, *et non.*
85. That the hour of the Lord's resurrection is uncertain, *et contra.*
122. That everybody should be allowed to marry, *et contra.*
153. That a lie is never permissible, *et contra.*
154. That a man may destroy himself for some reasons, *et contra.*
155. That Christians may not for any reason kill a man, *et contra.*
156. That it is lawful to kill a man, *et non.*

ibid., pp. 20–1

This final extract illustrates how Abelard brought out the conflict of opinions on one particular topic.

That it is lawful to kill a man, and the opposite thesis.

Jerome on Isaiah, Bk V: He who cuts the throat of a man of blood, is not a man of blood.

Idem, On the Epistle to the Galatians: He who smites the wicked because they are wicked and whose reason for the murder is that he may slay the base, is a servant of the Lord.

Idem, on Jeremiah: For the punishment of homicides, impious persons and poisoners is not bloodshed, but serving the law.

Cyprian, in the Ninth Kind of Abuse: The King ought to restrain theft, punish deeds of adultery, cause the wicked to perish from off the face of the earth, refuse to allow parricides and perjurers to live.

Augustine: Although it is manslaughter to slaughter a man, a person may sometimes be slain without sin. For both a soldier in the case of an enemy and a judge or his official in the case of a criminal, and the man from whose hand, perhaps without his will or knowledge, a weapon has flown, do not seem to me to sin, but merely to kill a man.

Likewise: The soldier is ordered by law to kill the enemy, and if he shall prove to have refrained from such slaughter, he pays the penalty at the hands of his commander. Shall we not go so far as to call these laws unjust or rather no laws at all? For that which was not just does not seem to me to be a law.

Idem, on Exodus, ch. xxvii: The Israelites committed no theft in spoiling the Egyptians, but rendered a service to God at his bidding, just as when the servant of a judge kills a man whom the law hath ordered to be killed; certainly if he does it of his own violition he is a homicide, even though he knows that the man whom he executes ought to be executed by the judge.

Idem, on Leviticus, ch. lxxv: When a man is justly put to death, the law puts him to death, not thou.

Idem, Bk I of the 'City of God': Thou shalt not kill, except in the case of those whose death God orders, or else when a law hath been passed to suit the needs of the time and express command hath been laid upon a person. But he does not kill who owes service to the person who gives him his orders, for he is as it were a mere sword for the person who employs his assistance.

ibid., pp. 21–3

JOHN OF SALISBURY ON LECTURING IN LOGIC

John of Salisbury (c. 1120–1180) was one of the students drawn to Paris by Abelard's fame as a teacher. His *Metalogicon*, completed about 1159, is the best contemporary account of education in France in the twelfth century. The extracts here illustrates the importance and attraction of Logic in the studies of those schools which eventually grew into universities. Logic was eagerly pursued by students who felt perhaps that it was a means of bringing order into a world of chaos. In the twentieth century Sociology has exerted an appeal for university students similar to that which Logic had in the twelfth century. The work of Porphyry (d. 304) referred to here, the *Isagoge*, was an introduction to Aristotle's *Categories*. Boethius (c. 470–525) had translated and commented on this work and it became very influential as a basic text in the early study of Logic. It raised the question of Universals – that is, the relation of genera and species to individuals – a question which dominated medieval philosophical thought. The extract is also notable for its description of Abelard as a teacher.

CHAPTER I. *How one should lecture on Porphyry and other books*

It is my conviction that one should lecture on any book in such a way as to make the comprehension of its contents as easy as possible. Instead of searching for loopholes, whereby we may introduce difficulties, we should everywhere endeavour to facilitate understanding. Such was, as I recollect, the practice of the Peripatetic of Pallet. I believe that this was why, if I may so speak with the indulgence of his followers, he [Abelard] favored a somewhat childish opinion concerning genera and species, for he preferred to instruct his disciples and expedite their progress by more elementary explanations, rather than to lose them by diving too deep into this question. He very carefully tried to observe what Augustine laid down as a universal rule: he concentrated on explaining things so that they could be easily understood. According to this principle, [the *Isagoge* of] Porphyry should be taught in such a way that the author's meaning is always preserved, and his words accepted on their face value. If this rule be followed, Porphyry's work will remain the right kind of introduction, remarkable for easy brevity. It thus suffices for introductory purposes to know that the word 'genus' has several meanings. In its original sense 'genus' refers to the principle of generation, that is one's parentage or birthplace . . . Subsequently the word 'genus' was transferred from its primary meaning to signify that which is predicated in answer to the question 'What is it?' concerning a number of things that differ in species. The word 'species' likewise has several senses . . . The same method (which I have recommended for the discussion of genus and species) should also be followed in discussing differences, properties, accidents. What the words mean should be explained in a simple way. Terms that are pertinent should be pinned down by very definite descriptions, and their divisions given in each case. Finally, the differences between words, as they occur, should be designated in a clear manner. With this, one has completed his treatment of Porphyry. That which is written should be studied with sympathetic mildness, and not tortured on the rack, like a helpless prisoner, until it renders what it never received.

JOHN OF SALISBURY *Metalogicon.* Bk III, Chap. I (c. 1159).
Translated by D. D. MCGARRY, pp. 146–8
(Univ. California Press, 1962)

THE ORIGINS OF THE UNIVERSITIES OF OXFORD AND CAMBRIDGE

It is impossible to be certain about the origins of the universities of Oxford and Cambridge. However, for Oxford there are a few pieces of evidence to suggest that there were important schools there between 1130 and 1150, and that after Henry II's edict of about 1165, recalling all English clerks from abroad, a full university developed there. By about 1231 a university had also developed at Cambridge, though it is not at all clear whether this was due entirely to the migration of scholars there from Oxford in 1209, following the hanging of three Oxford scholars for murder.

This first extract gives evidence of theological lectures at Oxford in 1133.

1133. Master Robert Pullein began to lecture at Oxford on the Scriptures, which had gone out of fashion in England. Afterwards when both the English and the French church had greatly profited by his teaching, he was summoned by Pope Lucius II, and promoted to be chancellor of the Holy Roman church.

A. F. LEACH *Educational Charters and Documents*, p. 101 (Cambridge Univ. Press, 1911)

The next extract mentions the lectures of Vacarius on Roman Law at Oxford c. 1150.

Theobald (the archbishop) was indignant, and through the instrumentality of Thomas of London (Becket), a clerk, prevailed on Pope Celestine, Innocent's successor, to remove Henry (de Blois) and let Theobald be legate in England. Thereupon great disputes arose, and suits and appeals before unheard of. Then the Roman law and lawyers were first invited to England, the first of them being Master Vacarius. He taught law in Oxford, while at Rome Master Gratian and Alexander Roland, who was to be the next Pope, compiled the Canons.

ibid., p. 109

About 1165 Henry II issued the following edict bringing back scholars to England.

Let all clerks who have revenues in England be warned to come back to England, as they love their revenues, there to enjoy the same; and, if they return not within this term, let their said revenues be confiscated to the royal treasury. Let this be done throughout all the countries of our realm.

J. C. ROBERTSON (ed.) *Materials for History of Archbishop Thomas Becket*, Vol. I, p. 54 (Rolls Series, 1875)

The following extract gives one chronicler's account of the dispersion from Oxford to Cambridge.

About this same time (1209) a certain clerk who was studying in Arts at Oxford slew by chance a certain woman, and, finding that she was dead, sought safety in flight. But the mayor and many others, coming to the place and finding the dead woman, began to seek the slayer in his lodging which he had hired with three other fellow-clerks. And not finding the guilty man, they took his three fellow-clerks aforesaid, who knew nothing whatsoever of the killing, and cast them into prison; and, after a few days, at the King's bidding but in contempt of all ecclesiastical liberties, these clerks were led out from the city and hanged. Whereupon some three thousand clerks, both masters and scholars, departed from Oxford, so that not one of the whole University was left; of which scholars some pursued their study of the liberal arts at Cambridge, and others at Reading, leaving Oxford completely empty.

H. HEWLETT (ed.) *Roger of Wendover*, Vol. II, p. 51
(Rolls Series, 1887)

PUNISHMENT OF BURGESSES OF OXFORD FOR HANGING CLERKS 1214

In 1208 the burgesses of Oxford had hanged two clerks ignoring the custom of 'benefit of clergy' which left judicial proceedings against clerks to the ecclesiastical authorities. However, in 1213 King John ended his quarrel with the Church and so the burgesses also had to submit to the judgement of the Papal Legate. He imposed various conditions upon them, but the whole episode illustrates the insecurity of the early academic settlement in Oxford.

Nicholas, by the Grace of God Bishop of Tusculum, Papal Legate, to the beloved sons in Christ, the burgesses of Oxford, greeting in the Name of the Lord.

Since because of your hanging of clerks . . . we wishing to deal with you compassionately, decree that from Michaelmas A.D. 1214 for the next ten years following, there shall be remitted to the scholars studying in Oxford one half of the rent of all Halls let to clerks in the town, of the rent that is which was assessed by the common counsel of clerks and burgesses before the Withdrawal of the Scholars, on account of the hanging of the aforesaid clerks. At the end of this ten years, for the next ten years following the Halls are to be let at the full rents assessed as aforesaid. Thus for Halls built and assessed before the Withdrawal of the Scholars: for those built afterwards or built before but not previously assessed, they are to be assessed by arbitration of four Masters and four Burgesses and let in the manner aforesaid for both periods of ten years. Also the townsmen are to give annually fifty two shillings for the use of poor scholars . . . and also feed a hundred poor scholars with bread, cereals, drink and a fish or meat course each year on St Nicholas' day . . . They shall also swear to sell to the scholars all necessary provisions at a just and reasonable price . . . If indeed it happen that you arrest a clerk, immediately you are requested by the Bishop of Lincoln, or the Archdeacon of the place, or his official . . . you are to give up the prisoner to him.

H. ANSTEY (ed.) *Munimenta Academica*, Vol. I, pp. 1–2
(Rolls Series, 1868)

ROYAL LETTER TO THE MAYOR AND BAILIFFS OF CAMBRIDGE 1231

This letter is evidence that the University of Cambridge was thriving by 1230, whatever view one takes of its origins. It also shows the way in which royal support could help a university in such things as fair rents for lodgings. Then, as now, the problem of student accommodation was a pressing one.

The king to the mayor and bailiffs of Cambridge, greeting.

You are aware that a multitude of scholars from divers parts, as well from this side the sea as from overseas, meets at our town of Cambridge for study, which we hold a very gratifying and desirable thing, since no small benefit and glory accrues therefrom to our whole realm; and you, among whom these students personally live, ought especially to be pleased and delighted at it.

We have heard, however, that in letting your houses you make such heavy charges to the scholars living among you, that unless you conduct yourselves with more restraint and moderation towards them in this matter, they will be driven by your exactions to leave your town and, abandoning their studies, leave our country, which we by no means desire.

And therefore we command and firmly enjoin you that in letting the aforesaid houses you follow University custom and allow the said houses to be valued by two masters and two good and lawful men of your town assigned for the purpose, and allow them to be let according to their valuation, so conducting yourselves in this matter that no complaint may reach us through your doing otherwise, which may compel us to interfere.

A. F. LEACH *Educational Charters and Documents*, pp. 151–3
(Cambridge Univ. Press, 1911)

ROYAL SUPPRESSION OF NORTHAMPTON UNIVERSITY 1265

The following letter illustrates the great power which medieval students had in dispersion to another town whenever they had conflict with town or university authorities. Such a dispersion inevitably meant a serious loss of income to the university townspeople. The extract also illustrates the importance of royal support in the establishment of a university, either to protect it against the greed of the townsmen or, as in this case, to prevent a rival university being established.

The king to his mayor and citizens of Northampton, greeting.

On account of a great contest which arose in the town of Cambridge three years ago some of the clerks studying there unanimously left that town and transferred themselves to our said town of Northampton and desired, with a view to adhering to their studies, to establish a new University there: we, believing at the time that town would be benefited by this, and that no small benefit would accrue to us therefrom, assented at their request to the wishes of the said clerks in this behalf. But now, as we are truly informed by the statements of many trustworthy persons that our borough of Oxford, which is of ancient foundation, and was confirmed by our ancestors kings of England, and is commonly commended for its advantage to students, would suffer no little damage from such University, if it remained there, which we by no means wish, and especially as it appears to all the bishops of our realm, as we learn from their letters patent, that it would be for the honour of God, and the benefit of the Church of England, and the advancement of students that the University should be removed from the town aforesaid; we, by the advice of our great men, firmly order that there shall henceforth be no University in our said town, and that you shall not allow any students to remain there otherwise than was customary before the creation of the said University. Witness, the king at Westminster, 1st February in the 49th year of his reign.

A. F. LEACH *Educational Charters and Documents*, p. 163
(Cambridge Univ. Press, 1911)

THE RIGHT OF TEACHING EVERYWHERE (*JUS UBIQUE DOCENDI*)

As the universities developed the notion grew that the hallmark of a university was the acceptance of its degrees elsewhere as a qualification to teach without further examination. At first, universities as Paris, Bologna and Oxford gained this privilege by common consent but later, universities obtained the right by a Bill issued by the Pope or the Emperor of the Holy Roman Empire. In 1292 even Paris and Bologna received the privilege formally from the Pope. The granting of the privilege marked the rank of a school as a *Studium Generale*, or place of higher education in which instruction was given by masters in one or more Faculties of Arts, Theology, Law and Medicine and which consequently could attract students from all countries.

The following extract is from the Bill issued by Pope Nicholas IV in 1292, granting the *jus ubique docendi* to Paris.

Desiring, therefore, that the students in the field of knowledge in the city of Paris, may be stimulated to strive for the reward of a Mastership, and may be able to instruct, in the Faculties in which they have deserved to be adorned with a Master's chair, all those who come from all sides – we decree, by this present letter, that whoever of our University in the aforesaid city shall have been examined and approved by those through whom, under Apostolic authority, the right to lecture is customarily bestowed on licentiates in said faculties, according to the custom heretofore observed there – and who shall have from them license in the Faculty of Theology, or Canon Law or Medicine, or the Liberal Arts – shall thenceforward have authority to teach everywhere outside of the aforesaid city, free from examination or test, either public or private, or any other new regulation as to lecturing or teaching. Nor shall he be prohibited by anyone, all other customs and statutes to the contrary notwithstanding; and whether he wishes to lecture or not in the Faculties referred to, he shall nevertheless be regarded as a Doctor.

A. O. NORTON, *Readings in the History of Education*, pp. 97–8
(Harvard Univ. Press, 1909)

UNIVERSITY HALLS

At the beginning of the thirteenth century there were at least fifteen hundred students at Oxford, a number equal to that of the townsmen, and the consequent problems of accommodation and of fights between students and townsmen became pressing. To provide residence, graduates established boarding houses, which gradually developed into Halls under Principals. It was through the Halls that the university effected a closer supervision over the students and their studies, insisting on daily attendance at lectures. The university also used the Principals to help them discover and discipline students guilty of affrays, either with townsmen or with other students in the 'nation' fights between Northerners and Southerners. Halls were numerous but they lacked formal founders or benefactions and, by the middle of the sixteenth century, had been superseded by the Colleges. The latter had greater stability and wealth, having been well endowed by their founders to ensure that they provided permanent centres where scholars could pursue university studies. At first they had been for postgraduate studies, but when they began to take in fee-paying undergraduates in the latter part of the fifteenth century, the less financially secure Halls could not compete and declined. An additional cause of their decay was their inability, as compared with the colleges with their resident graduates, to provide a tutorial system at a time when the university lecture system was in decline. Of the fifty Halls thriving in the middle of the fifteenth century, only eight survived a century later.

Concerning Principalships of Halls c. 1250

Because sometimes in the University there has been a shameful trade in Principalships, buying and selling for money . . . it is decreed by the congregation of Masters, that no Master or Bachelor shall hereafter buy or sell the Principalship or the right of taking in scholars or a Hall, and if anyone does so and is convicted, he shall be punished as an excommunicate, and both, buyer as well as seller shall lose the School or the house. Also the buyer shall give to the University chest the price which he had agreed to pay for the Principalship.

It is by custom agreed that no Principal can be expelled from his house or his School, if before six o'clock on the morning after the Feast of the Nativity of the Blessed Virgin (9 September) he has shown security to the landlord or in his absence to the Chancellor or his deputy, unless the landlord shall have given notice to the Principal before the Nativity of St. John the Baptist (24 June) that he wishes himself to live in the house with his family or that he needs to let the house on a ten year lease, having already received money for this.

H. ANSTEY (ed.) *Munimenta Academica*, Vol. I, pp. 14–15
(Rolls Series, 1868)

Oath for Principals 1313

Because the names of delinquents will be better known to the Principals of houses, who live continuously among their students, it is decreed that every resident Principal, or his deputy, both of Halls and lodgings, within fifteen days or sooner of the beginning of each year, as it seems expedient to the Chancellor and Proctors, should come to swear on oath that if they should know of anyone from their society who is organizing meetings, or showing agreement with those organizing them, or going to gatherings, or in common with others is often calling the different nations with malicious jealousy, or disturbing the peace of the University, or practising 'bucklery', or holding a brothel in their house, or carrying arms, or causing in whatever way discord between Southerners and Northerners, they should within three days of learning about it, report it to the Chancellor or to one of the Proctors, who shall punish all the disturbers of the peace with imprisonment. At the same time every maniple (lodging house keeper) shall be bound to take the same oath.

ibid., pp. 92–3

Statute enforcing residence in Halls 1421

That all scholars and their servants shall be under the government of Principals, sufficient and provident men, properly approved and admitted by the Chancellors and Regents, and shall not live in the houses of laymen, under pain of punishment for the first offence loss of academic privilege, for the second offence imprisonment, and for further contumacy, banishment.

ibid., p. 279

STATUTES OF MERTON COLLEGE, OXFORD, 1270

Detailed evidence about the foundation of colleges and their essential difference from halls is provided in the Statutes of Merton College, Oxford. A college was an endowed self-governing community, ruled as at Merton by a Warden and with Deans to watch over the Fellows (see Chapters 5 and 7). Dress, daily life and church-going are supervised and regulated (see Chapters 8–11). Regulations for admission to the college favour the founder's kin (see Chapter 13) but that entrants should be of good behaviour and intent upon learning is made quite explicit and the penalty for failure in these respects is expulsion (see Chapter 13).

Though University College and Balliol College were endowed earlier, Merton College was the first to be formally constituted, and its statutes became a pattern for other colleges, notably Peterhouse, the first college to be founded at Cambridge in 1284. Merton was originally founded for a warden and twenty fellows, but this number later increased to about forty and in addition undergraduate students were attached to the college, foreshadowing the future role of colleges in the developments of the universities at Oxford and Cambridge.

The extract on 'Oaths of Bachelors' shows how a college could supervise university studies and ensure that its Fellows took their Masterships or 'incepted' in the proper manner.

Chapter 1

In the name of the most glorious and undivided Trinity, the Father, Son, and Holy Ghost, Amen: I, Walter de Merton, clerk, and formerly Chancellor of the illustrious Lord the King of England, trusting in the goodness of the Sovereign Creator of the world, and of its blessings, and confidently reposing on the grace of Him who at his pleasure orders and directs to good the wills of men, and after I had frequently and anxiously considered how I might make some return in honour of his name, for the abundance of his bounty towards me in this life, did formerly, and before the troubles which have of late arisen in England, found and establish a house which I willed and commanded to have the title and name of Merton School. This House was founded and settled before the troubles which arose lately in England on my own property, which I had acquired by my own exertions: it was situated at Maldon in the county of Surrey, and was destined for the constant support of scholars residing in schools, and in behalf of the salvation of my own soul, and of the souls of the Lord Henry, formerly King of England, that of his brother Richard, the renowned King of the Romans, and those of their progenitors, and heirs, and of all my own parents and benefactors, and to the honour and glory of the Most High. But now that peace is restored in England, and our old troubles are allayed, I approve with firm purpose of mind, establish, and confirm the former grant; and I limit, grant, and assign that the local habitation and site of the school shall be at Oxford, in the University, and on that freehold and inheritance of mine which abuts upon St John's Church; and it is my will that it should be called the House of the Scholars of Merton, and I decree that it shall be devoted to the residence of scholars for ever.

Chapter 5: Of the Office of Warden

The house is to have a Superior, who is always to be denominated the Warden, and who must be a man of circumspection in spiritual and temporal affairs; he is to have the pre-eminence and superiority over all the scholars who reside there, and over the ministers of the altar, and over all the other brethren and managers or bailiffs, or by whatever other name they go, who are appointed to the external or domestic administration and government of the house; and all persons, as well scholars as ministers of the altar, brethren, managers, and bailiffs, are to obey and look up to him as their Superior.

Chapter 7: Of the Office and Salary of the Deans

Some of the discreetest of the scholars are to be selected; and they, in subordination to the Warden, and in the character of his coadjutors, must undertake the care of the younger sort, and see to their proficiency in study and propriety of manners: so that every class of twenty or ten, should such further division be necessary, may have a superior of its own; and these superiors, so long as they devote a diligent attention to the rest, are in some particulars to have a more liberal allowance than the others, as fairness requires. Notwithstanding this regulation, there is to be one person in every chamber, where scholars are resident, of more mature age than the others, who is also to have a superintendence over the other fellows, and who is to make his report of their morals and advancement in learning to the Warden of the house itself, and also to the other parties who have authority in this particular, as well as to the general meeting of the scholars, in case it becomes necessary.

Chapter 8: Of the Common Table of the Fellows, and of uniformity in Dress

Moreover the scholars who are under the Head himself, and the other twenty superiors, and also the Deans who are appointed to the duty of studying in the house, are to have a common table – and a dress as nearly alike as possible.

Chapter 9: Of Church-going, and of the Number of the Ministers of the Altar

The members of the College must all be present together, as far as their leisure serves, at the canonical hours and celebration of masses on holy and other days. And in order that these duties may be performed with the greater comeliness and decency, I have resolved and I decree that four ministers of the altar, or three at fewest, who are to be in priests' orders, and who must adopt a respectable and suitable attire, shall be appointed from among the members of the house, to be in constant residence.

Chapter 10: Of the Table-reader

The Scholars are also to have a reader at meals, and while eating together they are to observe silence, and to listen to what is read.

Chapter 11: Of the conduct to be observed in the Chambers

While in their chambers they must abstain from noise, and interruption to the fellows, and apply themselves with all diligence to study, and when they speak they must use the Latin language.

Chapter 13: Of the admission of the Scholars

There is another rule also, which I would have and decree to be particularly observed in this house, and it regards those persons who shall hereafter be admitted to these alms, and it is this – that care and a diligent solicitude shall be taken that no persons be admitted but those who are chaste, of good conduct, peaceful, humble, indigent, of ability for study, and desirous of improvement; and in order to make trial of these qualifications, at the time when they become candidates for admission into the society a gratuitous support for one year, for the purpose of probation, is to be allowed them in the first instance, that in case they fairly make good the above-mentioned qualifications they may eventually be admitted into the body. Among those, however, who are to be admitted and to receive this gratuitous support, those persons who are of my own kin are to be the chief and first, because of the succession which by the custom of the realm is their due in my fee-simple estates; and next to them are to come the persons who are from the diocese of Winchester and from other dioceses and other places where the benefices or estates in fee and the other possessions appointed for the support of the college are situated.

All the individuals, during the period of this admission to the house, are to be paid the above-mentioned yearly sums for their support, so long as they act in obedience to their superiors, and live with their fellows in peace, forbearance, and modesty, and while they employ themselves diligently in the studies appointed for them, and behave in a praiseworthy and reputable manner.

E. F. PERCIVAL (ed.) *The Foundation Statutes of Merton College, Oxford*, pp. 14–20 (London, 1847)

REGULATIONS FOR THE DEGREE OF BACHELOR OF ARTS AT OXFORD 1267

The basic principle of medieval university study and learning was one of apprenticeship. A student learned the art of study under a master, became a pupil-teacher still under a master, and finally a master himself. The Determination referred to in this extract, was the point at which a student became, as it were, a pupil-teacher, for here he becomes a Bachelor in the Faculty of Arts and begins a period of lecturing prior to receiving his licence to teach. The final step would be Inception, some two or three years after Determination, when after a solemn disputation, the receiving of his symbols of office – a cap on his head, a ring and an open book – and an inaugural lecture, he would be admitted to the mastership and in celebration entertain his fellow masters to a banquet in a tavern.

Before Determination a student would have spent some four years hearing lectures on the various books here mentioned and engaging in a number of disputations. The Old Logic consisted of books studied up to the end of the twelfth century such as Capella's Logic from his Encyclopedia, Augustine's *Principia dialectica*, Cassiodorus's *De Dialectica* and Boethius. The New Logic consisted of Aristotle's works as listed in the extract.

Since it seems expedient and right to the Masters and Bachelors of the University of Oxford that a certain form should be provided under which Bachelors of Arts who are about to determine shall be admitted to determine in the future, an ordinance was provided in the following form, viz: Every year in the week before Ash Wednesday, in the congregation of masters, four Masters of Arts, that is two northerners and two southerners, shall be chosen by the proctors, and shall promise in the presence of the masters by the trust by which they are bound to God and the University that they shall not admit anyone who is not suitable to determine according to the form provided, and also that as quick as they can, they will admit those who are about to determine for themselves, and if in any way they can, finish it all within three days. The Bachelors who are to determine that same year shall come before the Masters with the favourable approval of Masters or Bachelors, and if they are going to determine for themselves, shall swear on the scriptures, that they have heard all the books of the old logic at least twice, with the exception of Boethius which it is sufficient to have heard once, and the Fourth Book of Boethius *Topica* (*Topics*) which they need not hear at all. However in the new logic they shall swear that they have heard the book *Posteriora Analytica* (*Posterior Analytics*) at least once, and *Priora Analytica* (*Prior Analytics*), *Topica* (*Topics*) and *Sophistici Elenchi* (*Sophistical Refutations*) twice.

They shall swear they have heard for grammar Priscian's *De Constructionibus* (*Constructions*) twice and Donatus' *Barbarismus* (*Barbarisms*) once, and in science, the *Physica* (*Physics*), *De Anima* (*Of the Soul*) and

De Generatione et Corruptione (*of Birth and Decay*). And may it be known, that if they first answer publicly in the schools, they must have answered in sophistry for a whole year, no part of the year in which they have answered to the question being reckoned in the said whole year. To one question they ought to have answered at least once in the summer before the Lent in which they are going to determine. But if they have not answered publicly in sophistry they shall swear that they have heard all the books aforesaid, with this addition, that they have heard the *Posteriora Analytica* twice. They ought also to make a longer stay in hearing them than if they have publicly answered in sophistry. If, however, there are any who have not before determined on their own account and want to determine for others, they are bound to swear that they have heard all the before-mentioned books as aforesaid, and also have heard in their own time Priscian's *Magnum* (*Great Grammar*) once; the three books on *Meteorica* (*Meteors*) they shall anyhow swear that they have heard. The masters or bachelors too who are going to give such evidence shall come and say in good faith that the candidates are reasonably exercised in answering according to the above manner; and that those who have not before determined have studied suitably and that in the year before they were in such a stage that they could have suitably determined for themselves according to the form aforesaid. And may it be known that if any of those who are going to determine have heard the books, which according to the aforesaid rule they are held to have heard twice, only once and not all twice, or have not heard properly all those which according to the aforesaid rule they ought to have heard once, as long as they have heard other books which are not in the rule, and those books are, in the opinion upon oath of the masters elected to examine, sufficient compensation, they shall be admitted to the office of determiners, but otherwise shall be entirely refused.

This ordinance was made by ten masters elected for the purpose, Master Nicholas of Ewelme being chancellor, and Master Roger of Plumpton . . . then proctors of the University of Oxford, on Thursday next before the feast of St Matthew the Apostle A.D. 1267, and confirmed, and all who contravene it denounced excommunicate, and sealed with the chancellor's seal, the same Nicholas remaining chancellor and the same proctors A.D. 1267, on the eve of the Purification of the Blessed Virgin Mary [i.e. 1 Feb.].

H. ANSTEY (ed.) *Munimenta Academica*, Vol. I, pp. 34–6 (Rolls Series, 1868)

METHODS PRESCRIBED FOR LECTURES IN LIBERAL ARTS AT PARIS 1355

Though this extract refers to the University of Paris, it has a general interest as an indication of teaching methods in medieval universities.

In the name of the Lord, amen. Two methods of lecturing on books in the liberal arts having been tried, the former masters of philosophy uttering their words rapidly so that the mind of the hearer can take them in but the hand cannot keep up with them, the latter speaking slowly until their listeners can catch up with them with the pen; having compared these by diligent examination, the former method is found the better. Wherefore, the consensus of opinion, warns us that we imitate it in our lectures. We, therefore, all and each, masters of the faculty of arts, teaching and not teaching, convoked for this specially by the venerable man, master Albert of Bohemia, then rector of the university, at St Julien le Pauvre, have decreed in this wise, that all lecturers, whether masters or scholars of the same faculty, whenever and wherever they chance to lecture on any text ordinarily or cursorily in the same faculty, or to dispute any question concerning it, or anything else by way of exposition, shall observe the former method of lecturing to the best of their ability, so speaking forsooth as if no one was taking notes before them, in the way that sermons and recommendations are made in the university and which the lectures in other faculties follow. Moreover, transgressors of this statute, if the lecturers are masters or scholars, we now deprive henceforth for a year from lecturing, honors, offices and other advantages of our faculty. Which if anyone violates, for the first relapse we double the penalty, for the second we quadruple it, and so on. Moreover, listeners who oppose the execution of this our statute by clamor, hissing, noise, throwing stones by themselves or by their servants and accomplices, or in any other way, we deprive of and cut off from our society for a year, and for each relapse we increase the penalty double and quadruple as above.

LYNN THORNDIKE *University Records and Life in the Middle Ages*, p. 237 (New York: Columbia Univ. Press, 1944)

STATUTE ON COLLEGE GOWNS, OXFORD, 1358

The following extract provides an interesting comment on the origin and purpose of academic dress.

On Sunday, the vigil of the visitation of St Frideswyde (October 18) in the year of our Lord 1358, Master John Reygham, chancellor, and Masters Richard Sutton and Walter Wandefforde, proctors at the same time, in the congregation of regent masters, all being present, it was ordained unanimously by each and all of the then regents, that any tailor cutting and making gowns in the University should make and cut it generously so that the master and beadles should not have narrow or short gown, but full and reaching to the ankles, as they were accustomed to wear in times past. For it is decent and reasonable that those to whom God has given preference beyond the laity with internal mental gifts, should also be different outwardly in dress from the laity. If however any tailor contravenes this ordinance, he shall be punished with imprisonment and shall not go out of prison until he has made good any part he cut off in order to cut and make a gown too small and against the honour of the university.

H. ANSTEY (ed.) *Munimenta Academica*, Vol. I, pp. 212–13 (Rolls Series, 1868)

THE GRADUATION OF A MASTER IN GRAMMAR

The Master's degree in Grammar was a teacher's professional qualification, forerunner of the present B.Ed. Both Oxford and Cambridge had faculties of grammar and the mode of creating masters in grammar was similar in both universities. The following extract is taken from *Stoky's Book*, the work of Matthew Stokys or Stokes who was Bedel and Registrary at Cambridge, c. 1530. It is noteworthy that the medieval practice of conferring an office symbolically by the gift of some visible sign, is followed here, for the Master of Grammar receives a 'palmer' (for use on a boy's hands) and a birch, which in turn provide a significant comment upon the place corporal punishment held in pedagogic practice in the Middle Ages. The extract also makes it clear that degree ceremonies, then as now, had their theatrical stages or platforms and ceremonial ritual.

The Bedel shall set the Masters of Grammar to the Fathers place at vii of the clock, or between vii or eight. Then the Father shall be brought to Saint Mary's Church to the Mass beginning at viii of the clock: he shall come behind, and his eldest son next him on his right hand, like as is said afore of the Inceptors in Arts. When mass is done, first shall begin the act in Grammar. The Father shall have his seat made before the Stage for Physic. The Proctor shall say *Incipiatis*. When the Father has argued as shall please the Proctor, the Bedel in Arts shall bring the Master of Grammar to the Vice-chancellor, delivering him a Palmer with a Rod, which the Vice-chancellor shall give to the said Master in Grammar and so create him Master. Then shall the Bedel purvey for every Master in Grammar a shrewd boy, whom the Master in Grammar shall beat openly in the Schools, and the Master in Grammar shall give the boy a groat for his labour and another groat to him that provideth the rod and the palmer . . . and thus endeth the Act in that Faculty.

Note, that the Bell-Ringer shall provide a Rod and a Palmer for the Masters in Grammar, and he shall have of every Master in Grammar for his labour 4d.

Note, that the Inceptor in Grammar shall give to the Vice-chancellor a Bonnet, and to the Father and to each of the Proctors a Bonnet; and if there be but one Inceptor, he shall do this, and if there be more than one, then to pay this among them.

Quoted in G. G. COULTON *Social Life in Britain from the Conquest to the Reformation*, pp. 55–6 (Cambridge Univ. Press, 1918)

STUDENT FEES AND TEACHERS' PAY, OXFORD, 1333

From the following extract it would seem that university teachers' pay has been a perennial problem.

Although no one it is held should fight against proper pay, and although those who sow spiritual seeds reap little material rewards, nevertheless Masters of Arts willingly undergo and acknowledge various heavy labours in reading and disputation for the profit and use of their scholars, and yet on account of the more than usual meanness which has grown in everybody in these modern times, they are not paid generously for their labours, as would be fitting and as used to be done in the past.

It is decreed that every Scholar of the faculty of arts, placed in hall on weekly commons, shall be bound to pay for the old logic or the new at least twelve pence a year, dividing the sum in proportion for each term, and to the Masters from whom they usually hear the books of physics at least eighteen pence a year . . .

It is decreed also that every master of arts, whatever his status or condition, shall be bound to collect (his pay) every year by the authority of this statute, except sons of Kings, or knights or barons. For otherwise this absurdity follows, that if the rich Masters who are not hard up, do not collect their pay, the poor and needy Masters in the faculties, who need to collect their pay, will lose the audiences which they have been accustomed to have.

H. ANSTEY (ed.) *Munimenta Academica*, vol. I, pp. 128–9 (Rolls Series, 1868)

CHAUCER'S CLERK OF OXENFORD

A Clerk ther was of Oxenford also,
That un-to logik hadde long y-go.
As lene was his hors as is a rake,
And he was nat right fat, I undertake;

But loked holwe, and ther-to soberly.
Ful thredbar was his overest courtepy;
For he had geten him yet no benefyce,
Ne was so worldly for to have offyce.
For him was lever have at his beddes heed
Twenty bokes, clad in blak or reed,
Of Aristotle and his philosophye,
Than robes riche, or fithele, or gay sautrye.
(psaltery, kind of harp)
But al be that he was a philosophre,
Yet hadde he but litel gold in cofre;
But al that he mighte of his freendes hente,
On bokes and on lerninge he it spent,
And bisily gan for the soules preye
Of hem that yaf him wher-with to scoleye.
Of studie took he most cure and most hede.
Noght o word spak he more than was nede,
And that was seyd in forme and reverence,
And short and quik, and full of hy sentence,
Souninge in moral vertu was his speche,
And gladly wolde he lerne, and gladly teche.

CHAUCER *Canterbury Tales: Prologue*

PROHIBITION OF UNDESIRABLE BOOKS, OXFORD, C. 1340

This extract provides an interesting comparison with twentieth century thought and practice on the subject of university authority over students.

The Lord Chancellor desiring, as he is bound, that each and all of the scholars of the university and those set under them should be adorned with morals, desiring this has decreed and ordained that each regent master in grammar and any other public teacher of grammar should read his scholars only the book or books which treat of grammatical rules or science, or otherwise treating of ethics or metaphors or respectable poetry. To which Masters and other teachers the same Lord Chancellor forbids them to lecture on or expound the book of Ovid *De arte amandi* (*On the Art of Love*) and Pamphilius, and any other book which might entice or provoke his scholars to what is not allowed.

H. ANSTEY (ed.) *Munimenta Academica*, Vol. II, p. 441
(Rolls Series, 1868)

STATUTE FOR KEEPING THE PEACE, OXFORD, 1432

This extract illustrates the violence of university town life and the reference to differences between 'countries' refers to the feud in the university between the nations of North and South, divided roughly by the River Trent.

Since the unrestrained continuance in this University of execrable dissensions, which increase vices and idleness, has almost blackened its charming manners, its famous learning and its sweet reputation; and since there is no better punishment than a fine which in these days is more dreaded than anything, it is thought that imposing such a fine on the disturbers will be the quickest way to curb them, the Masters of the University unanimously order and decree that whoever is lawfully convicted of disturbing the peace, shall be fined according to the quantity and quality of his crime, over and above the usual penalties, viz: for threats of personal violence, twelvepence; for carrying of weapons against the statute, two shillings; for drawing weapons of violence, or pushing with the shoulder or striking with the fist, four shillings; for striking with a stone or club, six shillings and eight-pence; for striking with a knife, dagger, sword, axe, or other weapon of war, ten shillings; for carrying a bow and arrows with intent to harm, twenty shillings; for gathering armed men or other persons and conspiring to hinder the execution of justice or to inflict bodily harm on anyone, thirty shillings; for resisting the execution of justice, or going about by night, forty shillings as well as satisfaction to the injured party. And if any Master or Scholar should favour any person's cause because he is from his own country, or contend against another because he is from a different country, or do make any manifest occasion whereby any quarrel between country and country might arise, or if he being convicted of inciting such a quarrel he shall pay to the University over and above the accustomed penalties for disturbers of the peace.

H. ANSTEY (ed.) *Munimenta Academica*, Vol. I, pp. 304–5 (Rolls Series, 1868)

Legal Education in the Fifteenth Century

Sir John Fortescue's *De Laudibus Legum Angliae* was written between 1468 and 1471. Fortescue had an extensive experience of the workings of English law over some forty years, holding the Chief Justiceship from 1442 to 1461, and in this book he includes chapters which provide a first-hand account of the system of legal education of his day.

In the sixteenth century the Inns of Court became increasingly popular as places of higher education for the sons of the gentry.*

Herein the Chancellor shows why the laws of England are not taught in the Universities

The chancellor: 'In the Universities of England the sciences are not taught unless in the Latin language. But the laws of that land are learned in three languages, namely, English, French, and Latin; in English, because among the English the law is deeply rooted; in French, because after the French had, by duke William the Conqueror of England, obtained the land, they would not permit the advocates to plead their causes unless in the language that they themselves knew, which all advocates do in France, even in the court of parliament there. Similarly, after their arrival in England, the French did not accept accounts of their revenues, unless in their own idiom, lest they should be deceived thereby. They took no pleasure in hunting, nor in other recreations, such as games of dice or ball, unless carried on in their own language. So the English contracted the same habit from frequenting such company, so that they do to this day speak the French language in such games and accounting, and were used to pleading in that tongue, until the custom was much restricted by force of a certain statute; even so, it has been impossible hitherto to abolish this custom in its entirety, partly because of certain terms which pleaders express more accurately in French than in English, partly because declarations upon original writs cannot be stated too closely to the form of these writs as they can in French, in which tongue the formulas of such declarations are learned. Again, what is pleaded, disputed, and decided in the royal courts is reported and put into book form, for future reference, always in the French speech. Also, very many statutes of the realm are written

**Further reading:*

K. CHARLTON *Education in Renaissance England*, Chapter VI (London: Routledge and Kegan Paul, 1965)

in French. Hence it happens that the language of the people in France now current does not accord with and is not the same as the French used among the experts in the law of England, but is commonly corrupted by a certain rudeness. That cannot happen with the French speech used in England, since that language is there more often written than spoken. In the third language above mentioned, in Latin, are written all original and judicial writs, and likewise all records of pleas in the king's courts, and also certain statutes. Thus, since the laws of England are learned in these three languages, they could not be conveniently learned or studied in the Universities, where the Latin language alone is used. But those laws are taught and learned in a certain public academy, more convenient and suitable for their apprehension than any University. For this academy is situated near the king's courts, where these laws are pleaded and disputed from day to day, and judgements are rendered in accordance with them by the judges, who are grave men, mature, expert and trained in these laws. So those laws are read and taught in these courts as if in public schools, to which students of the law flock every day in term-time. That academy, also is situated between the site of those courts and the City of London, which is the richest of all the cities and towns of that realm in all the necessaries of life. And that academy is not situated in the city, where the tumult of the crowd could disturb the students' quiet, but is a little isolated in a suburb of the city, and nearer to the aforesaid courts, so that the students are able to attend them daily at pleasure without the inconvenience of fatigue.'

Here he shows the general organization of the academy of the laws of England

'But, prince, in order that the form and arrangement of this academy may be clear to you, I will now describe it as far as I can. For there are in this academy ten lesser inns, and sometimes more, which are called inns of Chancery. To each of them at least a hundred students belong, and to some of them a much greater number, though they do not always gather in them all at the same time. These students are, indeed, for the most part, young men, learning the originals and something of the elements of law, who, becoming proficient therein as they mature, are absorbed into the greater inns of the academy, which are called the Inns of Court. Of these greater inns there are four in number, and some two hundred students belong in the aforementioned form to the least of them. In these greater inns, no student could be maintained on less expense than £13. 6s. 8d. a year, and if he had servants to himself alone, as the majority have, then he will by so much the more bear expenses. Because of this costliness, there are not many who learn the laws in the inns except the sons of nobles. For poor and common people cannot bear so much cost for the maintenance of their sons. And merchants rarely desire to reduce their stock by such annual burdens. Hence it comes about that there is scarcely a man learned in the laws to be found in the realm, who is not noble or sprung of noble lineage. So they care more for their nobility and for the preservation of their honour and reputation than others of like estate. In these greater inns, indeed, and also in the lesser, there is, besides a school of law, a kind of academy of all the manners that the nobles learn. There they learn to sing and to exercise themselves in every kind of harmonics. They are also taught there to practise dancing and all games proper for nobles, as those brought up in the king's household are accustomed to practise. In the vacations most of them apply themselves to the study of legal science, and at festivals to the reading, after the divine services, of Holy Scriptures and of chronicles. This is indeed a cultivation of virtues and a banishment of all vice. So for the sake of the acquisition of virtue and the discouragement of vice, knights, barons, and also other magnates, and the nobles of the realm place their sons in these inns, although they do not desire them to be trained in the science of the laws, nor to live by its practice, but only by their patrimonies. Scarcely any turbulence, quarrels, or disturbance ever occur there, but delinquents are punished with no other punishment than expulsion from communion with their society, which is a penalty they fear more than criminals elsewhere fear imprisonment and fetters. For a man once expelled from one of these societies is never received into the fellowship of any other of those societies. Hence the peace is unbroken and the conversation of all of them is as the friendship of united folk. It is not, forsooth, necessary to relate here the manner in which the laws are learned in these inns, for, prince, you are not to experience it. But be assured that it is pleasant, and in every way suited to the study of that law, and also worthy of every regard. But I want you to know one point – that in neither Orleans, where the canon as well as the civil laws are studied, and whither students resort from all parts, nor Angers, nor Caen, nor any other University of France except only Paris, are so many students of mature age to be found as in this academy, though all the students there are of English birth alone.'

SIR JOHN FORTESCUE *De Laudibus Legum Angliae.*
Edited and translated by S. B. CHRIMES, pp. 115–21
(Cambridge Univ. Press, 1942)

The Petty School

The petty school in the sixteenth century was primarily a place for religious training. It always aimed to teach pupils to read and write, often teaching elementary accounting as well, but the religious aim was all pervasive. Its main reading texts were the A B C, the Catechism and Primer and perhaps the Psalter.

Sometimes the Usher at a grammar school would teach this elementary work but otherwise it would be provided by parish clerks, or 'such men and women of Trade, as Taylors, Weavers, Shop Keepers, Seamsters, and such others, as have undertaken the charge of teaching others', as Edmund Coote describes them in his *English Schoolmaster* (1596).

PROVISION OF PETTY SCHOOLS

Children (as we see) almost everie where at first taught either in private by men or women altogeather rude, and utterly ignoraunt of the due composing and just spelling of wordes: or else in common schooles most commonlie by boyes, verie seeldome or never by anie of sufficient skill, howsoever yet right spelling is but the least parte, or rather no part counted of learning. So that of all other little children chaunce into the worst handes: which thing also the pitiefull evente thereof sheweth over well. For how fewe be there under the age of seaven or eight yeares, that are towardly abled, and praysablie furnished for reading? And as manie there be above those yeares, that can neither readilie spell nor rightly write even the common wordes of our Englishe.

To the lit[l]e Children

Come, litle childe, let toyes alone,
  and trifles in the streete:
Come, get thee to the parish Clarke.
  H'is made a Teacher meete.
Frequent ye now the Taylers shop,
  and eeke the Weavers lombe:
Ther's neither these, but can with skill
  Them teach that thither come.

The Semstresse she (a Mistresse now)
  hath lore as much to reade,

As erst she had in many yeares
compast by silke and threede.
I can not all by name rehearse,
For many moe you see:
Come make your choyce, let toies alone,
and trifles: Learne A, B.

F. CLEMENT *The Petie Schole* (1587). Quoted in T. W. BALDWIN *William Shakspere's Petty School*, pp. 77–8, 138–9 (Univ. Illinois Press, 1943

AN ABC PRIMER IN ENGLISH AND LATIN c. 1538

These primers were elementary reading books but their purpose was more than the teaching of literacy, for they were also a first book of religious instruction for children. A child would probably master the ABC itself from a horn-book – a sheet of paper containing the alphabet and perhaps the ten digits and the Lord's Prayer, which was protected by a layer of translucent horn and mounted on a wooden frame with a handle so that it would survive the rough handling of children. Then the child would go on to a primer similar to the one from which an extract in facsimile is printed overleaf. There were numerous versions of these primers and in 1545 Henry VIII tried to standardize the position with the issue of an authorized Primer. The following extract from the Royal Injunction attached to this official primer gives a clear account of their purposes and also indicates the existence of various unauthorized primers, such as the one from which an extract is reproduced.

Among the manifolde business and most weightie affaires appertaining to our regal authoritie and office, we much tenderyng the youthe of our realmes (whose good education and vertuous bringing up redouneth most highly to ye honoure and prayse of almightie God) for divers good considerations, and specially for that the youth by divers personnes are taught the Pater Noster, Ave Maria, Crede, and X Comandementes, al in Latin, and not in English, by meanes whereof the same are not brought up in ye knowledg of ther faith, duties and obedience, wherein no Christen person ought to be ignoraunt. And for that oure people and subjectes whych have no understanding in the Latin tong and yet have the knowledge of readyng, may praye in theyr vulgar tong, which is to them best knowne: that by the meane thereof thei shuld be the more provoked to true devotion, and the better set their hartes upon those thinges that they pray for. And finally, for the avoyding of the diversitie of primer books that ar now abrod, wherof ar almost innumerable sortes, which mynister occasion of contentions and vain disputations, rather than to edify, and to have one uniforme ordre of al such bookes throughout al our dominions, both to be taught unto

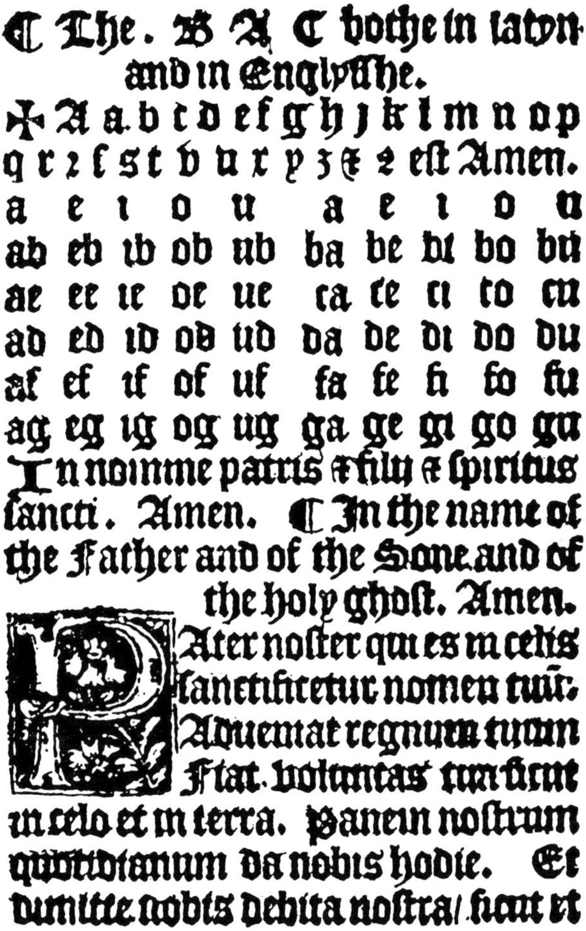
¶ The. B A C bothe in latyn
and in Englysshe.
✠ A a b c d e f g h i k l m n o p
q r ꝛ ſ s t v u x y z & ꝯ est Amen.
a e i o u a e i o u
ab eb ib ob ub ba be bi bo bu
ac ec ic oc uc ca ce ci co cu
ad ed id od ud da de di do du
af ef if of uf fa fe fi fo fu
ag eg ig og ug ga ge gi go gu
In nomine patris & filij & spiritus
sancti. Amen. ¶ In the name of
the Father and of the Sone and of
the holy ghost. Amen.
Pater noster qui es in celis
sanctificetur nomen tuũ.
Adveniat regnum tuum
Fiat. voluntas tua sicut
in celo et in terra. Panem nostrum
quotidianum da nobis hodie. Et
dimitte nobis debita nostra/ sicut et

The two pages reproduced here are from an ABC primer printed about 1538. These books were intended to give children the rudiments of the Christian religion and introduce them to the church services. This primer begins with the alphabet, the first sentence pronounced by the priest – in Latin and English – and then the Pater Noster and the Hail Mary, also in both languages.

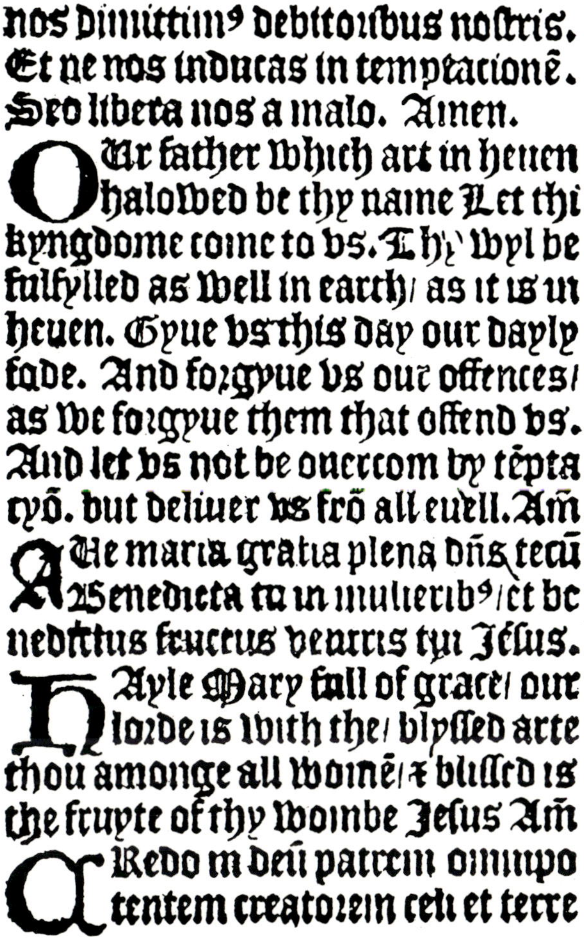
nos dimittim⁹ debitoribus nostris.
Et ne nos inducas in temptacionē.
Sed libera nos a malo. Amen.
OUr father which art in heuen
halowed be thy name Let thi
kyngdome come to vs. Thy wyl be
fulfylled as well in earth/ as it is in
heuen. Gyue vs this day our dayly
fode. And forgyue vs our offences/
as we forgyue them that offend vs.
And let vs not be ouercom by tēpta
cyō. but deliuer vs frō all euyll. Am
AUe maria gratia plena dn̄s tecū
Benedicta tu in mulierib⁹/ et be
nedictus fructus ventris tui Jesus.
HAyle Mary full of grace/ our
lorde is with the/ blyssed arte
thou amonge all womē/ & blissed is
the fruyte of thy wombe Jesus Am
CRedo in deū patrem omnipo
tentem creatorem celi et terre

It continues with the Creed and concludes with various prayers and graces to be used at meals. It is notable in the first line that the B and A are in reverse order, presumably by printer's error, and the cross at the beginning of the third line was a reminder to the child to make the sign of the cross before he began his lesson.

children and also to be used for ordinary prayers of all our people not learned in the latyn tong: have set furth thys Primer or boke of prayers in Englysh to be frequented and used in and throughout all places of oure said realmes and dominions, as well of the elder people, as also of the youth, for their common and ordinary prayers, willing, commaundyng and streghtly chargyng that for the better bringing up of youth in the knowledge of theyr duty towardes God, their prince, and all others in their degre, every Scholemaster and bringer-up of yong beginners in lernyng nexte after their A B C now by us also set furthe, do teache this primer or boke of ordinary prayers unto them in Englyshe, and that the youth customably and ordinarily use the same until they be of competent understanding and knowledge to perceive it in Latyn. At which time they may at their libertie ether use this primer in Englishe, or that whiche is by oure authoritie likewyse made in the Latyn tong, in all poinctes correspondent unto this in Englishe.

Quoted in E. S. SHUCKBURGH (ed.) *The ABC Both in Latyn & Englyshe*, pp. ix–xi (London, 1889)

The Dissolution of the Chantries

In 1547 an Act granted the property of the chantries and gilds to Edward VI. Where a school existed as part of any chantry foundation, it was to be allowed to continue, otherwise the property was to be confiscated and the money used to endow education. In July 1548 two commissioners were appointed to survey the endowments and to recommend which schools should be continued. The example of a Chantry Certificate and a School Continuance Warrant which follow illustrate the working of the Act.

The extent to which schools were harmed by this legislation is in dispute. The Chantry Certificates provide evidence of the existence of schools, but they must be treated with caution, since not every school mentioned could claim a continued existence and similarly the mention of grammar schooling did not necessarily imply that Latin had continued to be taught since the school's original foundation.*

ACT DISSOLVING THE CHANTRIES 1547

The king's most loving subjects, the Lords spiritual and temporal, and the Commons, in this present Parliament assembled, considering that a great part of superstition and errors in Christian religion has been brought into the minds and estimations of men, by reason of the ignorance of their very true and perfect salvation, through the death of Jesus Christ, and by devising and phantasing vain opinions of purgatory and masses satisfactory, to be done for them which be departed, the which doctrine and vain opinion by nothing more is maintained and upholden, than by the abuse of trentals, chantries, and other provisions made for the continuance of the said blindness and ignorance; and further considering and understanding, that the alteration, change, and amendment of the same, and converting to good and godly uses, as in erecting of grammar schools to the education of youth in virtue and godliness, the further augmenting of the Universities, and better provision for the poor and needy, cannot, in this present Parliament, be provided and conveniently done, nor cannot nor ought to have any other manner person to be committed, than to the king's highness, whose majesty, with and by the advice of his highness's most prudent

**The controversy and discussion on this matter may be seen in the following books:*

A. F. LEACH *English Schools at the Reformation* (London: Constable, 1896)

JOAN SIMON *Education and Society in Tudor England* (Cambridge Univ. Press 1966)

J. LAWSON *Medieval Education and the Reformation* (London: Routledge and Kegan Paul, 1967) council, can and will most wisely and beneficially, both for the honour of God and the weal of this his majesty's realm, order, alter, convert, and dispose the same.

And calling further to their remembrance, that in the Parliament holden at Westminster the seven-and-thirtieth year of the reign of our late sovereign lord King Henry VIII, farther to our most dread and natural sovereign lord the king that now is, it was ordained, enacted, and established amongst other things, that all and singular colleges, free chapels, chantries, hospitals, fraternities, brotherhoods, guilds, and other promotions mentioned in the said former Act . . . should from thenceforth, by authority of the same former Act, be adjudged and deemed, and also be in the very actual and real possession and seisin of the said late king, and of his heirs and successors for ever.

It is now ordained and enacted by the king our sovereign lord, with the assent of the Lords and Commons in this present Parliament assembled, and by the authority of the same, that all manner of colleges, free chapels, and chantries, shall, by the authority of this present Parliament, immediately after the feast of Easter next coming, adjudged and deemed, and also be, in the very actual and real possession and seisin of the king our sovereign lord, and his heirs and successors for ever . . .

And also that the same commissioners, or two of them at the least, by virtue of this Act and of the commission to them directed, shall have full power and authority to assign, and shall appoint (in every such place where guild, fraternity, [or] the priest or incumbent of any chantry *in esse*, the first day of this present Parliament, by the foundation ordinance or the first institution thereof, should or ought to have kept a grammar school or a preacher, and so has done since the feast of St. Michael the Archangel last past) lands, tenements, and other hereditaments of every such chantry, guild, and fraternity to remain and continue in succession to a schoolmaster or preacher for ever, for and toward the keeping of a grammar school or preaching, and for such godly intents and purposes, and in such manner and form, as the same commissioners, or two of them at the least, shall assign or appoint.

Provided always, and be it ordained and enacted by the authority aforesaid, that this Act, or any article, clause, or matter contained in the same, shall not in any wise extend to any college, hostel, or hall being within either of the Universities of Cambridge and Oxford; nor to any chantry founded in any of the colleges, hostels, or halls being in the same Universities; nor to the free chapel of St. George the Martyr, situate in the castle of Windsor; nor to the college called St. Mary's College of Winchester beside Winchester, of the foundation of Bishop Wykeham; nor to the college of Eton; nor to the parish church commonly called the Chapel in the Sea in Newton, within the isle of Ely, in the county of Cambridge; nor to any manors, lands, tenements, or hereditaments to them or any of them pertaining or belonging; nor to any chapel made or ordained for the ease of the people dwelling distant from the parish church, or such like chapel whereunto no more lands or tenements than the churchyard or a little house or close does belong or pertain; nor to any cathedral church or college where a bishop's see is, within this realm of England or Wales, nor to the manors, lands, tenements, or other hereditaments of any of them.

GEE and HARDY (eds.) *Documents Illustrative of the History of the English Church*, pp. 328–44 (London: Macmillan, 1914)

CHANTRY CERTIFICATE FOR WEST RIDING OF YORKSHIRE

Robert, Archbyshop of Yorke, Robert Chaloner, Thomas Gargrave, and Henrye Savyll, Commissioners.

7 Styllingflete Parish

The Colleage of Saynt Andrew, in Nether Acaster, within the sayd parishe of Styllingflete.

There ys a provost and three fellowes, being all preistes, wherof one doth kepe a free schole of grammer, according to the foundacion, and the sayd colledge ys distaunt from the parishe churche one myle.

The necessitie thereof ys for the inhabitaunts of Acaster aforesayd, being in nomber 200, the ryver of Owse, which is a great streame, runnyng betwixte the said colledge and the parishe churche, and in that place without a bridge.

Goods, 17s. 4d.; Plate, six ounces, parcell gylte.

The yerely value of the freehold landes and tenementes, belonging to the sayd colledge, £37. 15s. 0½d.

Whereof Resolutes and deductions, £2. 10s. 8d.

And so remayneth clere to the Kinges Majestie by yere, £35. 4s. 4½d.

Whereof The Provostes stypend of the sayd Colledge, William Alcocke, provost of the sayd colledge, of th'age of 67 yeres, indifferently learned, hath and receyved yerely for his stypend, £10, and hath none other lyvyng.

The stypend of 2 fellowes of the sayd colledge:

William Barton, of th'age of 63 yeres, and John Rawdon, of th'age of 49 yeres, 2 of the fellowes of the sayd colledge, have and receyve yerely for theyre stypendes, every of theyse, after the rate of £6 by yere, and have none other lyvings.

The scholemasters stypend of the sayd colledge:

William Gegoltson, schole master, of the sayd colledge, indifferently learned in grammar, of th'age of 38 yeres, hath and receyveth yerely for his stypend out of the revenue of the sayd colledge, £5, and hath none other lyving.

8 and 9 Rotherham Parish

The Colledge of Jesu in Rotherham aforesaid.

In the sayd towne and paryshe of Rotherham, being great and wide, there ys no preist found to serve the cure besydes the vicar and paryshe preist, which hertofore have ben accustomed to have helpe of the chauntrie preists aforeseyd, as nede hath requyred. The number of houslyng people ys 2,000.

The sayd colledge was founded for a preacher to preach 12 sermons every yere, three scholemasters of free scholes, viz.: grammer, song, and wyrtyng; 6 pore children, a butler, and a coke.

Goods, £32. 10s. Plate, gylte, 517½ ounces; parcell gylte, 520½ ounces. Plate, white, 24¼ ounces.

The yerely value of the freehold land belonging to the seyd colledge, £130. 16s. 1¼d.

Whereof Resolutes and deductions by yere, £7. 19s. 7¾d.

And so remayneth clere to the Kinges Majestie yerely, £122. 16s. 5½d.

The stipend of the preacher in the seyd colledge:

Robert, Bushop of Hull, provost of the sayd colledge, and founded for a preacher, as ys aforesaid, of th' age of 44 yeres, hath yerely for his salarie or stypende out of the revenue of the sayd colledge, £13. 6s. 8d.; with a gowne clothe, price 18s.; wood and coles sufficient for his chamber; and the yerely allowance for the fynding of 3 horses. Also he hath in other promocions and lyuings, viz.: of the Kinges Majestie one yerely pencion of 250 markes, and a prebend in the churche of Yorke of £58 by yere.

The grammer scole in the seid colledge:

Thomas Snell, scholemaster there, 36 yeres of age, bacheler of arte, of honest conversacion, qualities, and learnyng, hath and receyveth yerely for his stipend, £10; for his gowne clothe 12s.; for fyre to his chamber, 3s. 4d.; his barber and launder free; which amounteth yerely to £10. 15s. 4d.; and hath none other lyving.

The songe scole in the seyd colledge:

Robert Cade, scholemaster there, 38 years of age, hath and receyveth yerely out of the revenue of the sayd colledge, £6. 3. 4d. for his salarie; 12s. for his gowne clothe; 3s. 4d. for fyre to his chamber; his barber and launder free. In all, £7. 8s. 8d.; and hath none other lyving.

The wryting scole in the seid colledge:

John Addy, scholemaster there, 61 yeres of age, hath and receyveth yerely out of the sayd revenue, viz.: for his salarie, £5. 6s. 8d.; for a gowne clothe, 16s.; for fyre to his chamber, 3s. 4d.; his barber and launder free. In all, £6. 6s.; and hath none other lyving.

The 6 choristers, or pore children, in the seyd colledge:

The sayd children have yerely meat, drinck, and clothe, out of the revenue of the seyd colledge, which is worth to every of theym after the rate of £3. 6s. 8d. by yere; And hath none other lyving.

The butlers and the cokes stipends there:

John Pakyn, butler, of th'age of 40 yeres, and Robert Parkyn, coke, 45 yeres of age, hath every of theym yerely for his wages, £1. 6s. 8d., with meate, drincke, and lyvery.

Pore people:

There hath ben yerely distributed in almes to pore people, 6s., according to the ordinaunce and will of the founder.

41 and 42 Skipton in Craven

The Chauntry of Saynt Nicholas, used as a Free Grammer Schole, in the Paryshe Churche there.

The sayd parryshe of Skipton is great and wyde, wherein there is a vicar and a parysh preist only to serve the cure. The nomber of housling people is 1,300.

Stephane Ellis, incombent and scholemaster, 42 yeres of age, a good grammaryan (having scollers to the nomber of 120, and hath kept scole there theis fyves yere past), hath, over and besydes the proffits of this chauntry, one other chauntrie in Kyldwike, to the value of £4 by yere, for the better maynteynance of his lyving, unto hym gyven by the right honorable Henry, now the' erle of Cumberland, to th' entent to kepe a schole as is aforesaid, as by his deade apperith, dated the 35th yere of the late King of famous memorye, Henry th' eight.

The yerely value of the freehold land, £4. 16s. 4d.

Whereof Resolutes and deductions, by yere, 3s. 4d.

And so remaneth clere over and above the deductions, £4. 13s.

A. F. LEACH *English Schools at the Reformation*, pp. 298–301 (London: Constable, 1896)

SCHOOL CONTINUANCE WARRANT FOR LANCASHIRE 1548

Wee, Sir Walter Mildemay, Kt., and Robert Kelway, Esquier. Commissioners appointed by the King's Majesty's Commission to us directed touching order to be taken for the mayntenaunce and contynuance of Scoles and preachers, and of preestes and curates of necessitie for servynge of cures and mynistracion of sacramentes, and for money and other thinges to be contynewed and paide to the poore, and for dyuerse other thinges appoyneted to be done and executed by vertue of the same commyssion. To the Right Honorable Sir William Pagett, Knight of the Order, Chancellour of the Duchy of Lancaster, and to the chancellor of the same for, the time being greeting.

Forasmuch as it appeareth by the certificates of certaine of the particular surveyors of the kings majesties lands that the church of the late colledge of Manchester, in Manchester, in the countye of Lancaster, is a parish church, and that there is greate necessity to have a Vicar to be endowed there.

And that a Grammer scole hath beene heretofore continually kept in the said parish of Walton, with the revenues of the chauntry of St. Katherine, founded in the said chaple of Liverpoole, and that the Scole Master there had for his wages £5. 13s. 3¾d. yearly of the revenues of the same chauntry, which Scole is very meete and necessary to continue.

And that a Grammer Scole hathe likewise beene continually kept in the parish of Midleton, in the said countye, with the revenues of the chauntry, founded in the parish church there, And that the Scolemaster there had for his wages yearly £5. 10s. 8d., which scole [&c.]

And that a Grammer Scole hath been heretofore continually kept in the parish of Blackborne, in the said countie, with the revenues of the chauntrey founded at the alter of Our Lady in the church there, And that the Scolemaster there had for his wages yearly £4. 7s. 4d., which scole [&c.].

And that a Grammer Scole hath been heretofore continually kept in the parish of Leylaunde, in the said countie, with the revenues of the chauntry founded in the church there, And that the Scolemaster [&c.], £3. 17s 10d., which Scole [&c.].

And that a Grammer Scole [&c.] in the parish of Preston, in the said countie, with the revenues of the chauntrey of Our Lady founded in the church there, and that the Scholemaster [&c.], £2. 16s. 2¼d., which Scole [&c.].

And that a Grammer Scole [&c.], St. Michaell upon Wyer, in [&c.], with the revenues of the Chauntry of St. Katherine, founded in the parish church there, And that the Scolemaster [&c.], £5. 10s., which Scole [&c.]

And that a free scole hath beene heretofore continually kept in the parish of Manchester, in [&c.], with the revenues of the chauntry founded in the church there, And the Scolemaster [&c.], £4. 1s. 9d., which scole [&c.]. . . .

Wee, therefore, the said Commissioners, doe signyfye to you, the said chancellor of the said Duchy of Lancaster, that by virtue of the said commicion to us directed in fourme aforesaid [we have assigned and] appointed . . .

And that the said Grammer Scole, in the said parish of Walton, shall continue as heretofore hathe beene used, And that Humfrey Crosse, Scolemaster there, shall bee and remayne in the same rome, and shall have for his stipend and wages yerely, £5. 13s. 3d.

And that the said Grammer Scole in Midleton aforesaid shall continue still, And that Thomas Mawdesley, scolemaster there, shall bee and remayne in the same rowme there, and shall have for his wages yerely, £5. 10s. 8d.

And that the said Grammer Scole in Blackborne aforesaid shall continue, And that Thomas Burges, scolemaster ther [&c.], £4. 7s. 4d.

And that the said Grammar Scole in Leyland aforesaid shall continue, And that Tristram Taylor, Scolemaster there, shall bee and remayne still in the same roome [&c.] £3. 17s. 10d. . . . [MS. torn] Preston aforesaid shall continue, And that Nicholas Banister, Scolemaster there, shall bee and remayne in the same rowme, And that he shall have for his stipend and wages fifty-six shillings and two pence yearly.

And that the Grammer Scole in the said parish of St. Michaell upon Wyre shall continue, And that William Harrison Scolemaster there, shall continue in the same rowme, and shall have for his wages yearly, £5. 10s.

And that the said free scole in Manchester aforesaid shall continue. And that [*blank*] Pendilton, Scolemaster there, shall continue in the same roome of Scolemaster [&c.], £4. 1s. 9d.

And that the severall wages, stipends, and sumes of money appointed to bee continued in forme aforesaid, and every of them shall be paid from Easter last past forthward of the rents and revenues of the said [Duch]y of Lancaster, by the hand of such of the receyvours thereof for the tyme being as shall bee thought most meete and conveynient for the payment of the same, to the personnes above rehersed, and to such other persons as shall be in their rowmes and places for the tyme being, untill fur[ther or] other order or direction shall bee had or taken [in the] premisses.

Wherefore wee the said commissioners doe require you the said chancellor of the said Duchie of Lancaster to make out severall warrants accordingly for the payment of the said severall wages, stipends, and sums of money appointed to bee continued and paid in fourme aforesaid, and every part [and parc]ell thereof, to such the receyvours, and other officers of the revenues of the same Duchy, as you shall thinke most meete and conveynient for the ease, quietness, and commoditye of the same persons.

And this warrant shall bee as well to you the said chancellor of the said Duchy of Lancaster, as to all auditors, receyvours, and other officers and [ministers] of the same Duchy for the [time] being, sufficient discharge for the payment and allowance of the said severall stipends, wages, and somes of money to be continued and paid in fourme aforesaid.

Writtne the eleaventh day of August, in the second yeare of the reigne of Our Soveragne Lord Edward the 6th, by the grace of God King of England, France and Ireland, Defender of the fayth, and in earth of Church of England and alsoe of Ireland supreme head [1548].

ibid., pp. 123–6

Tudor and Stuart Grammar Schools

The grammar schools of England during the sixteenth and seventeenth centuries were notable for the unchanging continuity with which they pursued their aims and practices. The main reason for this lack of change was the control exerted upon them by various authorities, such as the Statutes of their founders, the powers which Bishops held in the licensing and examination of schoolmasters, and the prescription of textbooks by the King and Privy Council. The effect of this control was to make the schools agents for the inculcation of religion as practised in the Established Church, and also to establish Latin and Greek as the subjects of the curriculum. Thus the grammar schools did nothing to forward the study of 'modern subjects', such as mathematics, the natural sciences, English language and foreign languages. Modern subjects were advocated and pursued in the sixteenth century but mainly by writers and teachers of the nobility, who had more freedom to recommend a curriculum change and who were more open to the need to teach subjects which would provide utilitarian and prestige value for their pupils. The grammar schools remained purveyors of the classical curriculum.*

EARLY TUDOR *VULGARIA*

Tudor grammar school teachers recognized that if textbooks were to appeal to schoolboys they should have some topical interest, so various books called *Vulgaria* were compiled to supply pupils with the vocabulary of every-day life. John Stanbridge, Master at Magdalen School, Oxford, from 1488 to 1494 produced a notable *Vulgaria* which contained vocabulary lists arranged in hexameters so that they could be more easily committed to memory, as well as short sentences incorporating common phrases. Then as now there was controversy as to the best way to teach Latin expression. Some as William Horman who produced a *Vulgaria* in 1519, Lily, Colet and Erasmus favoured the imitation of good Latin authors: others as Robert Whittington, whose *Vulgaria* was printed in 1520, argued that a grounding in grammatical rules was the prime necessity. Whittington's viewpoint is made clear below in the extracts from his *Vulgaria* where each statement is introduced by a grammatical rule or 'precept'. Another *Vulgaria* written around 1500 by an author whose name is unknown but who seems to have been connected with

**Further reading:*

FOSTER WATSON *The English Grammar Schools to 1660: their curriculum and practice* (Cambridge Univ. Press, 1908)

FOSTER WATSON *The Old Grammar Schools* (Cambridge Univ. Press, 1916)

J. HOWARD BROWN *Elizabethan Schooldays* (Oxford: Blackwells, 1933)

Magdalen School, Oxford, consists mainly of pieces of English with Latin translations for use in the teaching of a grammar school. These various *Vulgaria* provide not only examples of school textbooks but also evidence about the school and social life of the early sixteenth century.

The following is from Stanbridge's *Vulgaria.*

Os facies oculus acies albugo/pupilla

hoc os/is	for a mouth
hec facies/ei	for a face
hic oculus/i	for an eye
hec acies/ei	for the syght of the eye
hec albugo/is	for the whyte of the eye
hec pupilla/e	for the apple of the eye

. . . . . .

e/matche	i/flynt stone	e/boxe	candell	e/idem
Sulphurata	silex	pixis	candela	lucerna
o/a candelstyck	i/torche	i/taper	e/lanterne	o/talowe.
Candelabrum	lichinus	cereus	lanterna	sepumque.

. . . . . .

The auctour

All lytell chyldren besely your style ye dresse.
Unto this treatyse with goodly advertence
These latyn wordes in your herte to impresse
To hende that ye may with all your intelligence
Serve god your maker holy unto his reverence
And yf ye do not the rodde must not spare
You for to lerne with his sharpe morall sence
Take now good hede and herken your vulgare.

. . . . . .

I wyll wrastle with the. Luctabor tecum.
If thou wrastle with me I shall laye the on thy backe.
Si mecum luctatus eris humi te prosternam.
What hast thou done. Quid fecisti.
I have dronke a ferthynge worthe of ale.
Exhausi ceruisiam quadrantis.
Leve thy chattynge. Desiste a tuis superbis gressibus.
I perceyve by many tokens thou ate not my frende.
Multis argumentis comperio te non meum amicum fore.
I was beten this mornynge. Dedi penas aurora.
The mayster hath bete me. Preceptor a me sumpsit penas.
Wype thy nose. Munge nasum.
It longeth to a scollar to speke latyn.
Attenit ad discipulum loqui latine.

Thou stynkest. Male oles.
I trow I shall be a good grammarian within a shorte whyle.
Puto me fore preceptum grammaticum brevi spacio.

BEATRICE WHITE (ed.) *The Vulgaria of John Stanbridge and the Vulgaria of Robert Whittington*, pp. 1, 9, 13–17 (Early English Text Society, 1932)

The following is from Whittington's *Vulgaria.*

Precept.

The verbe shall accorde with his nominatyfe or vocatyve case in persone and nombre as appereth here folowynge by rule and example.
Verbum cum recto casu quinto ve coheret
Persona et numero. docet ut Maro marce doceto.

Example.

My chylde gyf dylygent hede to his instruccyons.
Mi puer diligenter invigilato his preceptunculis.
Imitacyon of autours without precepts and rules is but a longe betynge about the busshe & losse of tyme to a yonge begynner.
Imitatio authorum sine preceptis est nisi temporis procrastinatio & iactura grammaticulo.

Precept.

The relatyve of substance shall accorde with his antecedent in gendre nombre & persone as appereth here folowynge by rule. &c.
Antea cedenti debet quadrare relatum
Substantis genere sic persona numeroque.

Example.

That teycher setteth the cart before the horse that preferreth imitacyon before preceptes.
Preposterus est ille preceptor qui imitationem preceptis anteponit.

ibid., pp. 35–6

The following is from the *Vulgaria* (author unknown). These extracts, for translation into Latin, give interesting glimpses of fifteenth-century school life: the learning of Latin as a spoken language, the schoolmaster's use of corporal punishment, school equipment such as pen, ink and books, the pupil's delight when the master is off sick, and the master's views of his pupils.

— why comyst thou hither?
— to se youe.
— whom, me?

— yee, the.
— and wyll thou do nothynge ellys?
— yes, I cum also to lurne.
— what wylt thou lurne?
— to speke latyn, to wryte right, and understonde all such thynges as be written allredy.
— ye say well.
— but I say?
— what?
— lurne thei with youe withoute betynge or nay?
— sum on ways, sum another; sum with betynge, sum with fairnesse.
— but what meanys shall I use to lurne withoute betynge? for I fere the rodde as the swerde.
— Gentle maister, I wolde desire iii thynges of you: onn that I myght not wake over longe of nyghtes, another that I be not bett when I com to schole, the thirde that I myght ever emong* go play me.
— Gentle scholar, I wolde that ye shulde do iii other thynges: onn that ye ryse betwyme off mornynges, another that ye go to your booke delygently, the thirde that ye behave yourselff agaynst gode devoutely, all menn honestly, and then ye shall have youre askynge.

Felows, what is youre mynde? are ye glade that the maister is recoverde of totheache? whatsumever ye thynke in youre mynde, I knowe my mynde, without doubte, and I were a riche mann I wolde spende a noble** worth of ale emonge goode gosseps so that he hade be vexede a fortnyght longer.

Methinkith thou lackest many thynges that is nede for a goode scolar to have: first, a pennar and an ynke-horne, and then bookes, and yet furthermore, the which is first and cheff and passeth all preceptes of maisters and all other doctrine, as exercise of latyn tongue and diligence.

As sone as I am cum into the scole this felow goith to make water and he goyth oute to the comyn drafte (privy). Sone after another askith licence that he may go drynke. another callith upon me that he may have licence to go home. Thies and such other leyth my scholars for excuse oftyntyms that they may be oute off the waye.

WILLIAM NELSON (ed.) *A Fifteenth Century School Book*, pp. 22, 28–9, 39 (Oxford: The Clarendon Press, 1956)

LILY'S GRAMMAR

In 1540 Henry VIII by Royal Proclamation prescribed the use of one particular Latin Grammar, namely Lily's Grammar, though it was in fact a com-

* emong = from time to time
**noble = gold coin worth about 10s.

pilation by Colet, Lily and Erasmus. It remained the standard grammar until its transformation into the *Eton Latin Grammar* of 1758, and consequently played an important role in the intellectual history of England, being the introduction to the classics for all who received a grammar school education from Shakespeare's time to that of Samuel Johnson. The following extract is from the edition of 1567 and gives the Proclamation of Queen Elizabeth I which repeats the authorization that her father Henry VIII had made and which Edward VI and Mary had confirmed.

Elizabeth by the Grace of God Queene of England, France and Ireland, defender of the faithe &c. to all and singular Scholemaisters and teachers of Grammar within this oure realme of England, and other Dominions, greeting. Whereas oure moste deere Father of famous memory, King Henrye the eight, among sundry and manifolde his greate and waighty affairs, appertaining to his Regall authority and Office, did not forget, ne neglect, the good and vertuous education of the tender youth of this saide Realme, but having a fervent zeale, bothe towards the Godly bringing up of the saide youth, and also a speciall regarde that they might attaine the Rudiments of the Latine tongue, with more facilitye then aforetime. And for avoyding of diversitie and tediousness of teaching, did cause one uniforme Grammar to be set forth, commaunding all Scholemaisters and teachers within this saide Realme, to teache, use and exercise the same. We setting before our eies this Godlye acte and example of this oure deere Father in this behalfe, not unconfirmed by oure deere Brother and Sister, Kynge Edwarde and Queene Mary: and also consideringe that by the learned youth of this saide Realme, infinite and singular commodities tendeth towards the commonwealth of the same, have thought good, by oure speciall authoritie to approve and ratifie that worthy acte of oure saide deere Father, concerning the premisses. Willing therefore and streyghtlye charginge and commaundinge all and singular Scholemaisters, to whome the charge and teaching of Grammar within this oure Realme and Dominions dothe appertaine, not to teache your youthe and Schollers with any other Grammar, then with this English Introductio hereafter ensuing, and the Latine Grammar anexed to the same, being of the onely printing of our welbeloved subjecte Reginalde Wolfe, appoynted by us to this same Office, upon pain of our Indignation, and as you wil aunswere to the contrary. And thus endevouring yourselves towardes the frutefull bringing up of your saide Schollers in good literature and vertuous conditions, you shall deserve of almightye God condigne rewarde, and of us worthy commendations for the same.

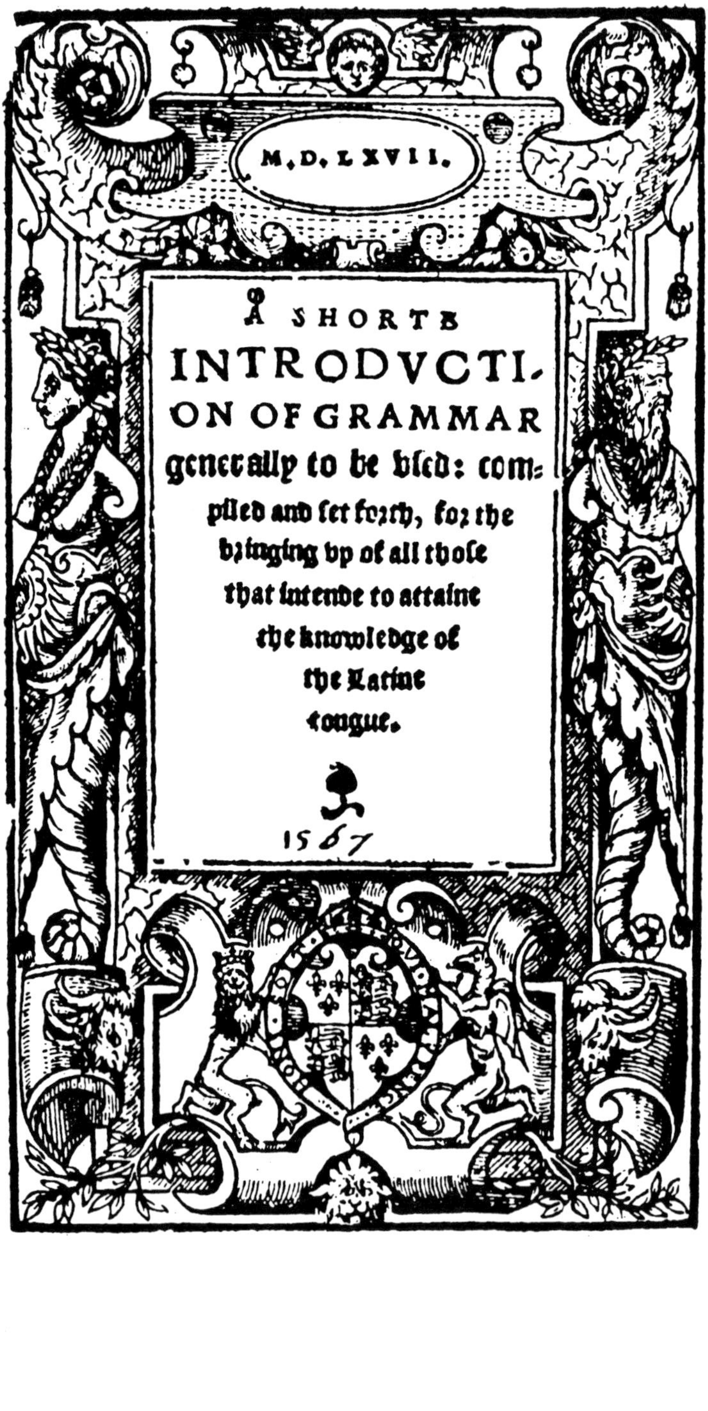

M.D.LXVII.

A SHORTE
INTRODVCTI-
ON OF GRAMMAR
generally to be vsed: com-
piled and set forth, for the
bringing vp of all those
that intende to attaine
the knowledge of
the Latine
tongue.

1567

AN INTRODVCTION
OF THE EYGHT PARTES OF
Latine Speache.

IN Speache be these eight partes folowinge:

Noune, Pronoune, Verbe, Participle,	declined.	Aduerbe, Coniunction, Preposition, Interiection,	vndeclined.

Of the Noune.

A Noune is the name of a thinge, that may be seene, felte, hearde, or vnderstande: As the name of my hande in Latine is Manus: the name of an house is Domus: the name of goodnes is Bonitas.

Of Nounes, some be Substantiues, and some be Adiectiues.

A Noune Substantiue is that standeth by him selfe, & requireth not an other worde to be ioyned with him: as Homo, *a man*. And it is declined with one article: as Hic magister, *a maister*. Or else with two at the moste: as Hic & hæc Parens, *a father or mother*.

A Noune Adiectiue is that can not stand by himselfe, but requireth to be ioyned with an other word: as Bonus, *Good*. Pulcher, *Faire*. And it is declined either with three Terminations: as Bonus, Bona, Bonum: or else with three Articles: as Hic, Hæc, & Hoc fœlix, *Happy*. Hic & hæc leuis, & hoc leue, *Light*.

A Noune Substantiue either is proper to the thinge that it betokeneth: as Eduardus, is my proper name, or else is common to mo: as Homo, is a common name to all men.

Numbres of Nounes.

IN Nounes be two numbres, the Singular, & the Plurall. The Singular numbre speaketh of one: as Lapis, *a stone*. The plu-

A.ii. rall

THE DIALOGUES OF JUAN LUIS VIVES

Vives was born in 1492 at Valencia in Spain, and after studying in Paris settled in Flanders from about 1512 until his death in 1540. He visited England frequently, taught for a while in 1522 at Oxford and was tutor to Princess Mary (afterwards Queen Mary I). However, in the divorce proceedings between Henry VIII and Catherine of Aragon, Vives supported the Queen, and Henry VIII only released him from prison on condition that he left England. Vives returned to Belgium but his educational influence continued notably in his *Linguae Latinae Exercitatio* or Dialogues written in 1539. They were composed to give pupils practice in the speaking of Latin, but Vives ensured that the subject matter consisted of topics which would interest boys by their relevance to daily life. There are references to the Dialogues as required reading at Eton College in 1561, at Westminster School in 1621, at Shrewbury School in 1562 and Hertford Grammar School in 1614, and it is likely that these are merely a few instances of the wide use of the Dialogues in school. The Dialogues give us a full picture of the life of a Tudor School boy, from his rising in the morning, through school including a school journey (not a twentieth century discovery!) school meals and school chatter. Banquets, the value of school-games, nature study and the purposes of education are also discussed.

Dedication of the School Dialogues to Philip (afterwards Philip II of Spain):

Vives to Philip, son and heir to the august Emperor Charles, with all good will.

Very great are the uses of the Latin language both for speaking and thinking rightly. For that language is as it were the treasure-house of all erudition, since men of great and outstanding minds have written on every branch of knowledge in the Latin speech. Nor can any one attain to the knowledge of these subjects except by first learning Latin. For which reason I shall not grudge, though engaged in the pursuit of higher researches, to set myself to help forward to some degree the elementary studies of youth. I have, in these Dialogues, written a first book of practice in speaking the Latin language as suitable as possible, I trust, to boys. It has seemed well to dedicate it to thee, Boy-Prince, both because of thy father's good-will to me, in the highest degree, and also because I shall deserve well of my country, that is, Spain, if I should help in the forming of sound morals in thy mind. For our country's health is centred in thy soundness and wisdom. But thou wilt hear more fully and often enough on these matters from John Martinius Siliceus, thy teacher.

FOSTER WATSON (ed.) *Tudor School Boy Life*, pp. xxi–xxii
(London: Dent, 1908)

This dialogue contains a division of the letters into vowels and consonants.

Praeceptor, Lusius, Aeschines, Pueri – teacher, Lusius, Aeschines, Boys

LUSIUS, so called from playing (ludendo).

AESCHINES, proper name of the Greek orator, who shamelessly declaimed against Demosthenes.

COTTA, proper name of a Roman citizen, so called from his anger.

PRAEC. Take the A B C tablet in your left hand, and this pointer in the right hand, so that you can point out the letters one by one. Stand upright; put your cap under your arm-pit. Listen most attentively how I shall name these letters. Look diligently how I move my mouth. See that you return what I say immediately in the same manner, when I ask for it again. Attention! Now you have heard it. Follow me now as I say it before you, letter by letter. Do you clearly understand?

LUS. It seems to me I do, fairly well.

Letters – Syllables – Vowel – Speech

PRAEC. Every one of these signs is called a letter. Of these, five are vowels, A, E, I, O, U. They are in the Spanish *oveia*, which signifies *sheep*. Remember that word! These with any letter you like, or more than one, make up syllables. Without a vowel there is no syllable and sometimes the vowel itself is a syllable. Therefore all the other letters are called consonants, because they don't constitute sounds by themselves unless a vowel is joined to them. They have some imperfect, maimed sound, e.g., *b*, *c*, *d*, *g*, which without *e* cannot be sounded. Out of syllables we get words, and from words connected speech, which all beasts lack. And you would not be different from the beasts, if you could not converse properly. Be watchful and perform your work diligently. Go out with your fellow-pupils and learn what I have set.

LUS. We are not playing today.

AESCH. No, for it is a work-day. What, do you think you have come here to play? This is not the place for playing, but for study.

LUS. Why, then, is a school called *ludus*?

AESCH. It is indeed called *ludus*, but it is *ludus literarius*, because here we must play with letters as elsewhere with the ball, hoop, and dice. And I have heard that in Greek it is called *schola*, as it were a place of leisure, because it is true ease and quiet of mind, when we spend our life in studies. But we will learn thoroughly what the teacher has bidden us, quite in soft murmur, so that we don't become a hindrance to one another.

LUS. My uncle, who studied letters some time in Bologna, has taught me that you better fix anything you wish in the memory if you pronounce it aloud. This is also confirmed by the authority of one called Pliny – I don't know who he was.

AESCH. If, then, any one should wish to learn his *formulae*, he should go off into the garden or into the churchyard. There he can shout aloud as if he would rouse the dead.

COTTA. You boys, do you call this learning thoroughly? I call it prattling and disputing! Up, now go all of you to the teacher, as he commanded.

ibid., pp. 18–20

In the following dialogue the school is described in six parts: teachers, honours, hours of learning and repetition, books, library, and the disputation. The name TYRO is that of the crude novice, a metaphor taken from military affairs of those as yet unskilled in war, to whom are opposed the *veterani*. SPUDAEUS is in Greek the diligent and industrious person, a name worthy of one who is studious.

I. *The Teachers*

TYRO. What a delightful and magnificent school! I suppose there is not in the whole academy any part more excellent.

SPUD. You judge rightly; add, also, what is of more importance, that elsewhere there are no more cultured and prudent teachers, who with such dexterity pass on their learning.

TYRO. It behoves us then to repay their trouble by attaining great knowledge.

SPUD. And this indeed by great shortening of the labour of learning!

TYRO. What does the schooling cost?

SPUD. You can at once give up so base and unreasonable a question. Can one in a matter of so great moment inquire as to payment? The very teachers themselves do not bargain for reward, nor is it suitable for their pupils to even think about it. For what reward could be adequate? Have you never heard the declaration of Aristotle that gods, parents, and masters can never be sufficiently recompensed? God created the whole man, the parents gave the body birth, the masters form the mind.

TYRO. What do those masters teach, and for how long?

SPUD. Each one has his separate class-room and the masters are for various subjects. Some impart with labour and drudgery the whole day long the elements of the art of grammar; others take more advanced work in the same subject; others propound rhetoric, dialectic, and the remaining branches of knowledge, which are called liberal or noble arts.

TYRO. Why are they so-called?

SPUD. Because every noble-minded person must be instructed in them. They are in contrast to the illiberal subjects of the market-place which are practised by the labour of the body or hands, which pertain to slaves and men who have but little wit. Amongst scholars some are 'tyrones' and others 'batalarii'.

II. *Grades or Honours of Scholars – Tyro – Batalarius – Licentiates – Doctors*

TYRO. What do these names signify?

SPUD. Both these names are taken from the art of warfare. 'Tyro' is an old word used with regard to the one who is beginning the practice of war. 'Batalarius' is the French name of the soldier who has already once been in a fight (which they call a battle) and has engaged in a close fight and has raised his hand against the foe, and so in the literary contests at Paris, 'batalarius' has begun to signify the man who has disputed publicly in any art. Teachers are chosen from them, and are called 'licentiates', because it is permitted them to teach, or, better still, they might be termed 'designate', i.e., the men marked out. At least they have taken the doctorate. Before the whole university, a hat is placed on their head as a sign that they have had their freedom conferred on them, and become *emeriti*. This is the supreme honour and the highest grade of dignity.

ibid., pp. 101–3

THE TEACHING OF LATIN

It is possible to find out a good deal about the mechanics of Latin teaching in the sixteenth and seventeenth centuries because, apart from the survival of textbooks, three authors in particular have left us accounts of school practice. These are Roger Ascham's *The Scolemaster* 1570, John Brinsley's *Ludus Literarius or the Grammar Schoole* 1612, and Charles Hoole's *A New Discovery of the Old Art of Teaching Schoole* 1660. All three were practising teachers. Ascham had been tutor to Queen Elizabeth I, Brinsley had kept a school at Ashby-de-la-Zouch and Hoole had been a schoolmaster at Rotherham and in London.

After learning the rules of Latin grammar pupils went on to 'make Latins' either by using vulgaria and vocabularies, or by the 'double' translation of classical Latin pieces, first into English and later back into Latin, a method recommended by Ascham and developed by Brinsley in what he called 'grammatical translation'. The next stage was for a pupil to attempt imitation of classical writers. Then came theme-writing, or the composition of formal argumentative essays on matters taken from the commonplace books which pupils were accustomed to keep. Another written exercise was verse composition. However, the main aim of the Grammar school curriculum was to teach Latin as a spoken language and the boys were encouraged to speak Latin, some schools appointing boy 'custodes' to report on those who spoke overmuch in English. Latin speaking was taught by means of Colloquies, as those of Vives, school plays, and the exercises of delivering orations and engaging in disputations.

Gradually, however, the teaching of Latin as a spoken language gave way under the pressure from the growth of the vernacular, and with the greater availability of textbooks, schools began to teach Latin as a written language and the oral element diminished.

The following extract from Ascham illustrates the 'making of Latins'. It criticizes the method recommended by Horman and Whittington, the authors of two notable Vulgaria, and instead suggests a method based upon the work of Johann Sturm of Strasburg, with whom Ascham had a long correspondence.

After the childe hath learned perfitlie the eight partes of speach, let him then learne the right joyning togither of substantives with adjectives, the nowne with the verbe, the relative with the antecedent. And in learninge farther hys Syntaxis, by mine advice, he shall not use the common order in common scholes, for making of latines: wherby, the childe commonlie learneth, first, an evill choice of wordes, (and right choice of wordes, saith *Cæsar*, is the foundation of eloquence) than, a wrong placing of wordes: and lastlie, an ill framing of the sentence, with a perverse judgement, both of wordes and sentences. These faultes, taking once roote in yougthe, be never, or hardlie, pluckt away in age. Moreover, there is no one thing, that hath more, either dulled the wittes, or taken awaye the will of children from learning, then the care they have, to satisfie their masters, in making of latines.

For, the scholer, is commonlie beat for the making, when the master were more worthie to be beat for the mending, or rather, marring of the same: The master many times, being as ignorant as the childe, what to saie properlie and fitlie to the matter.

Two scholemasters have set forth in print, either of them a booke, of soch kinde of latines, *Horman* and *Whittington*.

A childe shall learne of the better of them, that, which an other daie, if he be wise, and cum to judgement, he must be faine to unlearne againe.

There is a waie, touched in the first booke of *Cicero De Oratore*, which, wiselie brought into scholes, truely taught, and constantly used, would not onely take wholly away this butcherlie feare in making of latines, but would also, with ease and pleasure, and in short time, as I know by good experience, worke a true choice and placing of wordes, a right ordering of sentences, an easie understandyng of the tonge, a readines to speake, a facultie to write, a true judgement, both of his owne, and other mens doinges, what tonge so ever he doth use.

The waie is this. After the three Concordances learned, as I touched before, let the master read unto hym the Epistles of *Cicero*, gathered togither and chosen out by *Sturmius*, for the capacitie of children.

First, let him teach the childe, cherefullie and plainlie, the cause, and matter of the letter: then, let him construe it into Englishe, so oft, as the childe may easilie carie awaie the understanding of it: Lastlie, parse it over perfitlie. This done thus, let the childe, by and by, both construe and parse it over againe: so, that it may appeare, that the childe douteth in nothing, that his master taught him before. After this, the childe must take a paper booke, and sitting in some place, where no man shall prompe him, by him self, let him translate into Englishe his former lesson. Then shewing it to his master, let the master take from him his latin booke, and pausing an houre, at the least, than let the childe translate his owne Englishe into latin againe, in an other paper booke. When the childe bringeth it, turned into latin, the master must compare it with *Tullies* booke, and laie them both togither: and where the childe doth well, either in chosing, or true placing of *Tullies* wordes, let the master praise him, and saie here ye do well. For I assure you, there is no such whetstone, to sharpen a good witte and encourage a will to learninge, as is praise.

ROGER ASCHAM *The Scholemaster* (1570). Edited by W. A. WRIGHT, pp. 182–3 (Cambridge Univ. Press, 1904)

John Brinsley in his *Ludus Literarius*, first published in 1612, follows Ascham. This extract shows the example he gives of 'grammatical translation'.

In their little paper-bookes they may write the English on the first side, with the hard Latine words in the Margent, the Latine on the other over against it, in two columns; the first plaine after the Grammar order, the latter placed after the order of the Author: your selfe may make the words or phrases plaine to them, as they are set in the Margent.

In these examples all is very plaine; except that in the first sentence we say, and so translate in our English tongue, some divine inspiration; according as it is more elegantly in Latine, the Adjectives usually before the Substantives; and not inspiration some divine, which would be very harsh; and so likewise after [without any labour] although in the Grammaticall order in the Latine, the Substantive is to be set before the Adjective; as the child is to begin to make Substantive in Latine before the Adjective, and to make the Adjectives to agree unto, or to be framed according to the Substantives; as we have shewed in the rules observed in the Grammaticall translations.

If you thinke this course overtedious to write both wayes in Latine; then let them turn it only into the naturall order, thus *verbatim* by pen: and afterwards in the repeating that which they have made, aske of

An example of Dictating in English, and setting downe both English and Latine; and the Latine both plainly and elegantly.

Dictating according to the naturall order.	*Ordo Grammaticus.*	*Ordo Ciceronianus.*
No man *a* hath been *b* ever great without (*verb*) some divine *c* inspiration.	*Nemo fuit unquam magnus sine afflatu aliquo Divino.*	*Nemo magnus; sine aliquo afflatu divino umquam fuit.* 2. *de Natura Deor.*
There is nothing which God cannot *d* effect, and truely without any labour.	*Est nihil quod Deus non possit efficere, & quidem sine labore ullo.*	*Nihil est quod Deus efficere non possit, & quidem sine labore ullo.* 3. *de Nat. Deor.*
God cannot *e* be ignorant *f* of what minde every one is.	*Deus non potest ignorare, qua mente quisque, sit.*	*Ignorare Deus non potest, qua quisque mente sit.* 2. *de Divinatione.*

a *Hath ever bin*
b *At any time* (verb) *inspiration some divine*
c à flatus, *breathing into.*
d *Bring to passe.*
e Ignoro.
f *In what mind, or with what minde.*

them how *Tully* would place each word, and to give you reasons thereof: and then to reade the sentence in the booke unto them; so by the booke and some rules to direct them how to proceede.

For further practice in translating amongst all the higher, after they grow in some good sort to write true Latine *verbatim*, according to the former kinde of translating; let them still write downe the English as you dictate it, or out of a translation; & try who can come neerest unto *Tully* of themselves, composing at the first; and then after examine their exercises, bringing them to the Author.

For preventing of stealing, or any helpe by the Latine book, if you doubt thereof, you may both cause them to write in your presence, and also make choice of such places which they know not where to finde.

If you catch any one writing after another, and so deceiving both himselfe and you, correct him surely who suffereth him to steale.

For going on faster, and dispatching more in translating; beside their writing so, you may onely aske them the words or phrases in English, how they can utter them in Latine; and then let them give them in Latine every one his piece: first naturally, after, placing each sentence. Thus to goe thorow daily a side, or a leafe at a time, or as leisure will serve.

JOHN BRINSLEY *Ludus Literarius or The Grammar Schoole* (1612).
Edited by E. T. CAMPAGNAC, pp. 154–5
(Liverpool Univ. Press, 1917)

In the following extract Brinsley gives advice on the writing of letters, urging pupils to try and copy Cicero.

2. As they reade every Epistle, or before they are to imitate any one, make them as perfect in it as you can, and as time will permit: not onely in construing, parsing, reading out of the Grammaticall translation into the Latine; but also to be able to give every phrase, both Latine to English, and English to Latine.

Also cause them to make you a report what the summe of the Epistle is; and this if you will, both in English and Latine also, as was said of the Fables.

3. Cause them for their exercise to make another Epistle in imitation of *Tullies* Epistles, using all the phrases and matter of that Epistle; onely applying and turning it to some friend, as if they had the very same occasion then presently: and also changing numbers, tenses, persons, places, times: yet so, as thereby to make all the matter and phrases, each way most familiar to them, and fully their owne.

And first let them do this in a good English stile, as was said; I meane, in making an English Letter first: setting it after the manner, as they did their English Translation; of that page of their booke towards the left hand, or on the first columne, the Latine on the other over against it, sentence for sentence.

Herein they are onely to differ from the Translations, that they do not in these Letters sticke so much to words, to answer word for word both English and Latine; as to write purely and sweetly, as well in English as in Latine; and to expresse their mindes most fully in both, and in most familiar manner.

4. The next day to make another Epistle, as being sent from their friend to whom they writ, in answer to that which they writ the former day: and in that to answer every sentence from point to point, in as short manner as the former Epistle was, still retaining the same phrases as much as they can. I will take for example the first Epistle of *Sturmius*. The more easie it is for the children, the better it is.

M.C. Terentiæ *salutem plurimam dicit.*

Si vales, benè est: ego valeo. Nos quotidiè tabellarios vestros expectamus: qui si venerint, fortasse erimus certiores quid nobis faciendum sit: faciemusque te statim certiorem, valetudinem tuam cura diligenter. Vale. Calendis Septembris.

The summe of the Letter is; That *Tully* writes to his wife *Terentia:* signifying unto her, that he was in health: that he waited for the Letter-carriers daily: how by them he should know what to do; and that he would then certifie her of all things. And so concludeth, wishing her to looke well to her health. The Letter bare date the Calends of September.

An English Letter in imitation of Tully.

If you be in health, it is well: I am in health. I have long looked for your* Messengers. When they shall come, I shal be more certaine what I am to do; and then I will forthwith certifie you of all things. See that you look very carefully to your health.

The answer.

I rejoyce greatly of your health. I am sorry that you have looked for the Carriers so long. They will be with you very shortly, and then indeed you shal be more certain what to do.

An Epistle in imitation of Tully.

EPISTOLA.

Si vales benè est: ego quidē valeo: diu tabellarios vestros expectani. Gūvenerint certior ero quid mihi faciendum sit. Tum autē te omnib de rebus certiorem faciam. Tuam diligentissimè valetudinem fac ut cures.

**Letter carriers*

Responsio.

Te valere maximè lætor. Doleo quod tabellarios tam diu expectasti. Statim vobiscum erunt, & tum re vera certior eris quid tibi agendum sit.

ibid., pp. 168–9

The next extract is from Charles Hoole's treatise on the art of teaching and deals with the teaching of letter-writing.

To encourage them to begin to write of themselves, and to help their invention somewhat for inditing Epistles, you may take this course at once with a whole form together, which I have experienced to be very easie, and generally pleasing to young Scholars.

1. Ask one of your boyes, to whom, and for what, he is minded to write a letter; and, according as he shall return you an answer, give him some general instructions how to do it.

2. Then bid him and all his fellows let you see which of them can best indite an English letter upon that occasion, and in how short a time.

3. Let them every one bring his own letter fairly written, that you may shew them how to amend the imperfections you finde in it.

4. Take his, that hath done the best, and let every one give you an expression of his own gathering, for every word and phrase that is in it, and let it be different (if it may be) from that which another hath given already before him.

5. As they give in their expressions, do you, or an able Scholar for you, write them all down in a paper, making a note that directeth to the place to which they belong.

6. Then deliver them the paper, and let every one take such words or phrase, as is most agreeable to the composition of an Epistolary style (so that he take not the same that another useth) and bring the letter writ fair, and turned out of English into Latine. And thus you shall finde the same Epistle varied so many several wayes, that every boy will seem to have an Epistle of his own, and quite differing in words from all those of his fellowes, though the matter be one and the same.

CHARLES HOOLE *A New Discovery of the Old Art of Teaching Schoole.* Edited by E. T. CAMPAGNAC, pp. 152–4 (London: Constable, 1913)

Brinsley was concerned that Latin should be taught as a spoken language, and offers advice as to how this may be done, though he is critical of the use of 'custodes'. Brinsley's book is in the form of a dialogue, as this extract shows. The characters are Spoudeus and Philoponus, two men who had been contemporaries at college some twenty years previously and who now meet to discuss the problems they have met in their teaching careers.

14. Lastly, when you have laid a sound foundation, that they may be sure to have warrantable and pure phrase, by these meanes or the best of them, and all other their schoole exercises; then continuall practice of speaking shall undoubtedly accomplish your desire, to cause them to speake truely, purely, properly, and readily; Practice in a good way being here, as in all the rest, that which doth all.

Spoud. These things, or but the best of them, being constantly practised, cannot but effect marvellous much, and very surely; chiefly, if we could bring them to speake Latine continually, from that time that they begin to parse in Latine: but this I have had too much experience of, that without great severity they will not be brought unto: but they will speake English, and one will winke at another, if they be out of the Master's hearing.

Phil. It is indeed exceeding hard, to cause this to be practised constantly amongst schollers. That is a usuall custome in Schooles to appoint *Custodes*, or *Asini* (as they are tearmed in some places) to observe and catch them who speake English in each fourme, or whom they see idle, to give them the Ferula, and to make them *Custodes*, if they cannot answer a question which they aske.

But I have observed so much inconvenience in it, as I cannot tell what to say in this case: for oft-times, he who is the *Custos*, will hardly attend his owne worke for harkening to heare others to speake English.

Also there falleth out amongst them oft-times so much wrangling about the questions, or defending themselves, that they did not speak English, or were not idle, that all the whole fourme is troubled. So likewise when the *Custodes* are called for, before breaking up at dinner and at night, there will be so much contention amongst them, as is a disquieting and trouble to the Master. Moreover, this I have observed, that ever if there be any one simple in a fourme, or harder of learning then the rest, they will make him a right *Asinus*, causing such to be the *Custodes* continually, or for the most part, if they cannot answer: and to this end will be alwayes watching them; whereby many such are not only notably abused, but very much discouraged for being schollers, when they see themselves so baited at by all: some others are made over malapert thereby.

Besides all these, I doe not see any great fitnesse, that one scholler should smite another with the Ferula; because much malicing one another, with grudges and quarrels doe arise thereupon. So that the discommodities that follow the *Custodes* seeme to me to be many moe then the benefits can be; chiefly in losse of time, and hindering more in other learning, then can be gotten in that.

Spoud. I my selfe have had experience of most of these inconveniences: but what way will ye take then, to cause your schollers to speake Latine continually?

Phil. This is the best way that yet I can find, and to avoid the former inconveniences; First, to appoint the two Seniors in each fourme (of whom we shall speake after) as to looke to all other matters in the fourme, so to this more specially, that none speake English nor barbarous Latine: and if they be found partiall or negligent, then to preferre others into their places; besides the other censures to be inflicted upon them which I shall mention to you, when we shall come to speake of punishments; and so to have their due rewards, being found carefull. Secondly, the Master's owne eye and eare in the Schoole, to be continuall *Custodes* so much as may be, both for Monitors and others. Thirdly, if they do use to parse in Latine (and therefore must needs exercise themselves in that against that time that their Master doth come to heare them) and secondly, if they be kept in their places, and strictly looked unto for performing all exercises; I doe not see but they may be made to speake Latine in the schoole at schoole-times; neither that they shal have any great occasions of the contrary. Fourthly, for speaking Latine in all other places, it must only be by Monitors appointed weekely, as we shall have occasion to speak more after, and some severely corrected who are found most carelesse herein.

JOHN BRINSLEY *Ludus Literarius or The Grammar Schoole* (1612).
Edited by E. T. CAMPAGNAC, pp. 219–21
(Liverpool Univ. Press, 1917)

Brinsley was also concerned about the lack of English teaching, as this next extract shows. However his answer was to introduce English into the teaching of Latin rather than establish it as a separate subject of the curriculum.

But to tell you what I thinke, wherein there seemes unto mee, to bee a verie maine want in all our Grammar schooles generally, or in the most of them; whereof I have heard some great learned men to complaine; That there is no care had in respect, to traine up schollers so, as they may be able to expresse their minds purely and readily in our owne tongue, and to increase in the practice of it, as well as in the Latine or Greeke; whereas our chiefe indevour should be for it, and that for these reasons. 1. Because that language which all sorts and conditions of men amongst us are to have most use of, both in speech and writing, is our owne native tongue. 2. The puritie and elegancie of our owne language, is to be esteemed a chiefe part of the honour of our Nation: which we all ought to advance as much as in us lieth . . . 3. Because of those which are for a time trained up in schooles, there are very few which proceed in learning, in comparison of them that follow other callings.

Spoud. This complaint is not without just cause: for I doe not know any schoole, wherein there is regard had hereof to any purpose; notwithstanding the generall necessitie and use of it, and also the great commendation which it brings to them who have attained it: but I thinke every minute an houre, untill I heare this of you, how my trouble and shame may be avoided, and how I may obtaine this facultie to direct my children, how they may goe thus forward, not only in reading English perfitly, but also in the proprietie, puritie and copie of our English tongue, so as they may utter their mindes commendably of any matter which may concerne them, according to their age and place.

Phil. I will but name the meanes unto you now: for I shall have occasion to shew them all more particularly hereafter.

Besides the daily use of distinct reading over their English parts to get them perfectly, and of right reading all other things which they learne in Latine, as your selfe doe know; these meanes following, by the blessing of God will accomplish your desire.

1. The continuall use of the bookes of construing of *Lillies* Rules, by causing them to learne to construe, and to keepe their Grammar rules, onely by the helpe of those translations. This I finde one very good use of these books, besides some other which I shall mention after.

2. The daily use, and practice of Grammaticall translation in English, of all the Schoole Authours, which the yonger sort doe learne; causing them each day out of those to construe, and repeate, whatsoever they learne. This I also have prooved by happie experience, to be a rare helpe to make young Schollers to grow very much, both in English and

Latine. But of all these, for the manner, benefits, and use of them, I shall have occasion to speake at large.

3. Besides these, they would have every day some practice of writing English heedily, in true Orthographie; as also of translating into English; or, of writing Epistles, or familiar Letters to their friends, as well in English as in Latine. Amongst some of them, the reporting of a Fable in English, or the like matter, trying who can make the best report, doth much further them in this. And generally, amongst all those that can write, the taking of notes of Sermons, and delivering them againe, or making repetitions, is a speciall meanes. Also striving to expresse whatsoever they construe, not onely in proprietie, but in varietie of the finest phrase, who can give the best. This chiefly in the higher fourmes: So reading forth of Latine into English; first in proprietie, then in puritie. By these, and some use of the Historie of the Bible, and the like, which I shall be occasioned to mention after; you may finde their growth, according to your desire, and much above your expectation.

ibid., pp. 22–3

STATUTES OF RUTHIN GRAMMAR SCHOOL, FOUNDED 1574

School Statutes are a major source of information about schooling in this period. While it is true that the intentions of founders were not always adhered to in practice, nevertheless statutes provide evidence of the conditions in the schools, at least in the years immediately following their foundation.

This set of statutes illustrates various points: the qualifications of masters, the conditions of entry for pupils, the curriculum, including the emphasis on the speaking of Latin, the time-table, pupil pastimes and the provision for prayers and worship.

The school was founded by Gabriel Goodman, a native of Ruthin, and Dean of Westminster. As Dean he had drawn up the new statutes for Westminster School in 1560 and the statutes he compiled for Ruthin are similar, laying down even the same number of pupils as at Westminster, namely, one hundred and twenty.

Of the Pensions which the Master and usher shall exact or demand of Boys at their first Admission into School and of quarterly payments afterwards due to the Master and Usher

1. I ordain that the eldest son of a gentleman that hath thirty pounds a year or more at his admission into School shall pay the master 2s. 6d. and afterwards 2s. for every Quarter's Stipend.
2. I ordain that every younger or youngest son of a Gentleman at his admission into School shall pay ye Master 2s. and afterwards 1s. 6d. for every Quarter's Stipend.
3. I ordain that the eldest son of a Gentleman that hath twenty pounds

a year or more shall pay to the master at his Admission into the School 2s. and afterwards 1s. 4d. for every Quarter's Stipend.

4. I ordain that the younger or youngest son of the aforesaid Gentleman at his Admission to School shall pay the master 1s. 6d. for every Quarter afterwards 1s. 0½d.
5. I ordain that every Gentleman's Son who is possessed of Lands of ten pounds a year or more shall pay at his Admission 12d. to the master and for Quarterly Stipend shall pay him 8d.
6. I ordain that every Gentleman's Son or any one else possessed of Land of the value of 40s. yearly shall at their Admission to School pay the Master 8d. and for Quarterly Stipend shall pay him 6d.
7. I ordain that the sons of them that are not possessed of Land of the value of 40s. yearly shall at their Admission to School pay the Master 6d. and for Quarterly Stipend shall pay him 4d.
8. I ordain that every clergyman's son shall at his Admission to School pay the Master 6d. and for Quarterly stipend 4d.
9. I ordain that every clergyman's son whose Father is possessed of two Benefices or of one valued at twenty pounds a year or more shall at his Admission pay the Master 12d. and for Quarterly Stipend shall pay him 6d.
10. I ordain that all who were born in the Parish of Llanelidan or Borough of Ruthin shall at their Admission pay the Master 4d. and from hence shall be Freeboys for ever.
11. I ordain that the Master shall faithfully pay the usher one third part of these Stipends or pensions.
12. I ordain that the Boys at every Quarter's end shall pay the Master his Stipend according to the aforesaid Pensions, viz. on Monday preceeding Xmas day, the Feast of the Annunciation of the Blessed Virgin Mary or Lady Day, the Feast of St. John the Baptist or midsummer, The Feast of St. Michael or Michaelmas day, else they should be put out of school.

Of the Qualifications Required in the Master and Usher

I will and ordain that the Master be a man of good Credit and Report above twenty-five years of age a Master of Arts or Doctor of Grammar shall be wholly employed in educating and instructing of Boys where by he may teach his Scholars sound Learning and good Manners.

The Undermaster or Usher shall likewise be a learned man and of Good Credit a Bachelor of Arts and (because of his Station and Offices) skilful in teaching Boys shall not be under twenty years of Age and shall use constant Diligence and Industry in instructing his Scholars and both Masters shall be an example to tender youth in every virtue. They shall be single and unmarried.

Of the Master's and Usher's Office

The Master and usher shall take care as much as in them lyeth that their scholars not only attain to the manner of apprehending speaking and writing but also that they religiously worship God humbly obey their Parents and show due Deference to all by Prudence age and Fortune may require it of them. Let them be clean decent and modest in Body clothes and all things wherein they are concerned. Let them take Care to observe a Decorum in School, Street, and also at their Diversions. And that these Rules may be better observed the Master shall appoint some of the Senior Boys Monitors or Moderators who shall carry the names of Delinquents or faulty to the Master. In every Class he shall appoint a monitor. Of every other Class or Form he shall appoint a Moderator and they shall be subordinate to the Moderators of the upper Class. There shall be two Monitors in school two in Church and three in the Street and Feilds. The Master if he is in School shall correct and punish those whom he shall find guilty of a Fault or Negle-gence by Complaint of the Monitor; in the Masters Absence the Undermaster or Usher shall in this as well as in every other instance supply the place of the Master. And that the Boys may show greater esteem for his Office. I will and ordain that Monday at 9 o'clock in the morning every week (unless it be a holiday) an account to be taken in order to examine into Boys faults unless the Master should see occasion to omit or overlook it. But I think it expedient that some Crimes be immediately punished according to the Discretion of the Master and not delayed until Monday. I ordain that when Complaints or Accusations are heard in that solemn-like Judgement and Corrections made (unless pardon is sometimes granted) the Master shall make a speech to the Scholars upon the Occasion and shall earnestly exhort them to virtuous Actions or by sharp Reproof endeavour to dissuade and recall them from disgraceful ones and roughly reprehend them of Sloth or eloquently and smoothly persuade them to Diligence and Industry. And as to Indulgence and Severity my Will is that Moderation be observed. Boys shall not be struck on the Ears, Noses, Eyes or Faces. That the Worship of God may be chiefly observed, I ordain that every day in the morning at 6 of the clock at the ring of the Bell, the Master (unless lawfully hindered) and Scholars residing in the Town shall meet together in Church and shall then publicly offer Prayers to God.

In the Method of correcting Boys Morals the Undermaster shall be guided by the authority and Judgement of the Master.

Of School Exercises and Method of Teaching

Those who resort to this School for Instruction shall be divided into six

Classes; the three Senior Classes shall be under the Care of the Master; the other three under the Care of the Usher. The Usher shall go early after Prayers from Church to school for to teach. The Master shall go to School within half an hour after him; and at noon the Usher shall return to school within half an hour, the Master shall return within an Hour. The Usher going early to School shall begin at the first Class that is the lowest and there hear rehearsed to him one of the parts of speech and some Verb conjugated in the manner used at most schools, and shall clearly and plainly explain to his Scholars what may appear difficult and shall use the same kind of exercise with the Second and Third Class until 7 of the clock. The Master going early to School shall exercise the Senior Classes namely the 4th 5th and 6th in Latin and Greek rules of Grammar. Then all the Classes a short time before 7 o'clock shall recite by heart those Lessons which they read the day before. The Master shall give his scholars of the 4th Class a short time before 8 o'clock some sentence to be rendered from the english into latin. The Usher shall likewise propose or set forth some sentence to the 3rd and 2nd Class and also to the 1st but let it be the shortest. The Masters shall order them to write those sentences by them rendered into latin clearly and correctly, and next day to recite them by Heart before 9 o'clock. The exercises as prescribed above are to be expedited in such manner that all the Boys may go to breakfast half an hour before 8. A Theme shall be set forth or proposed to the three upper Classes on Saturday at noon, on which subject they shall write in Prose, which they shall deliver to their Master on Monday, then they shall write Verses which they shall deliver to the Master Tuesday following. A Theme shall be appointed to the same Classes Tuesday Evening which they shall show to the Master Wednesday and Thursday. The lower Classes shall translate something out of english into latin on the same days, which the Usher shall carefully examine. The Master shall read Monday and Wednesday at 9 o'clock in the morning to the 4th class Salust, to the 5th Justin and Ciceros Orations, to the 6th Isocrates Xenophen and Livy. On the same days and hour the Usher shall read to the third Class Terence, to the Second Æsope's Fabels, to the 1st Corderius's Dialogues. Tuesdays and Thursdays the Master at 9 o'clock in the Morning shall read to the 4th Class Ovid de tristibus, to the 5th Class Virgil to the 6th Seneca's Tragedies and Homer. The same days and hour the Usher shall read to the 3rd Class Cicero's Epistles selected by Sturmius, to the 2nd Class Erasmus his Colloquies and to the 1st Cato. From which Lectures the boys shall select phrases or forms of speech, Proverbs Adages Descriptions of Time, Place, Persons, Apothegms, and such like which the Boys shall write down.

In reading poetical Authors and others such places may be overlooked that may savour of what is contrary to Piety and good Moral. At 11 o'clock the boys may go to dinner.

At noon when the Usher is come to school he may require again of his Scholars what he read before Dinner to them and shall discuss every part of Speech and let him show whereby or by what manner forms of speech may be applyd and accomodated to use and examine what his Boys can do in that instance.

The Master is to ask or demand again from everyone of the Senior Classes what he had read to them before Dinner and taking occasion from those Authors which they read, he shall teach them how latin is translated into Greek or English rendered into Latin. Then let him take the Themes in hand treated on by his Scholars and pass an Hour in examining them. About half an Hour after three o'clock (if he pleases) he may go out of School and return within Half an Hour. The Master when returned to School at 4 o'clock shall read to the Fourth Class a Treatise of Figures of Prosody, to the 5th Susenbrotus of Tropes and Figures to the 6th Greek Grammar.

The Usher shall read to the 3rd Class Syntax of the Latin Grammar to the 2nd and 1st Grammar Etymology. Let them be dismissed at 5 o'clock. Thursday noon when the Usher is come to School he shall hear his scholars disputing for half an Hour on Grammar Rules and when that Exercise is ended they shall be employed in writing Examples. When the Master is come to School he shall hear his Scholars rehearse an Act out of Terence's Comedies or Plautus whom I require to be instructed by the Master. Both in the manner of Speaking and Gesture. The lower Class under the Master shall be employed in discussing Greek Problems.

Friday everyone shall translate first what was read to them the day before. Then they shall rehearse after Dinner until three o'clock what they had learnt in that Week and after three o'clock they shall repeat what they had learned the same Week between the Hours of 4 and 5 o'clock. Before 5 o'clock the Master shall read to the 4th Class Apothegms or Martials Epigrams, to the 5th Horace to the 6th Lucan. Before 5 o'clock the Usher is to read to the 3rd class Æsopes's Fables, to the 2nd Æsop's Fables, to the 1st Lewis's Introduction to Wisdom.

Saturday. The lower Classes shall first translate to the Usher what they read the Day before then shall repeat to him what was said or read by them in that Week. The senior or upper Classes shall translate to their Master what was read by them the day preceeding, then the Master shall appoint them some subject or Theme to write upon either in Prose or Verse. At ten of the clock in the Morning two or three of the Boys being thereunto appointed 8 days before by the Master shale with great Silence be heard declaiming on some subject. Saturday noon the Boys or Scholars shall meet at School at one o'clock and read or learn a Catechism until 2 o'clock then may they have leave unless the Master disapproves of it.

Of Some Things relating to School Discipline and Order

The Scholars residing in the Town or Borough of Ruthin shall in the Morning go directly from Church decently and in order by two and two into School on Comon Week Days.

The Boys shall meet at School on Sundays and Holidays as soon as the Bell Toles for Prayers, and from thence they shall two and two go orderly to Church the Master or Usher following them.

The boys of the senior or upper class shall speak Latin or Greek in School. The lower class Boys shall speak English and who ever does otherwise shall be deemed a Delinquent or faulty. Those whom the Master after one years Trial shall find to be of slow Parts and Unapt to learn shall be excluded from coming to school, provided their parents do not take them away after they are twice gently told of the Incapacity of their Children to learn. If anyone of the Boys cannot perfectly recite by heart one whole Rule of those he had learned (three words in a Rule excepted) or writes not according to the Rules of Orthography (trial thereof being made by the Master) or if in one of the upper classes he speaks English and if in one of the lower Classes he speaks Welsh he shall be deemed faulty and an Imposition given him. No Boys shall be admitted into this school if he exceeds sixteen years of Age, nor hath anyone a Right to continue in this School when he hath exceeded nineteen years of Age.

No boys shall be admitted into this school but for Instruction in the Modern Grammar Syntax.

If anyone withdraws himself from school or be absent from it longer than with the Masters Leave, he shall have no Right of returning thither again, unless by the consent of the Master. If a Boy buying not pens paper Books and other necessaries used by scholars at School, he shall within eight Days afterwards be excluded from coming to school unless the Master find its owing to Neglegence of Parents.

I will and ordain that the Master shall make Trial twice in a month at least what proficiency and progress the Boys of the lower Class Make, who are under the care of the usher, and he shall admonish the usher, if in any Instance found faulty in teaching, and that the Boys may be alured to use greater Diligence in minding their Studies.

The Boys shall once a year hold public Disputations, and particularly prizes shall be appropriated to every class to wit.

Books according to the Discretion and Will of the Master so that the Prizes be given to the boys who shall excel in their Exercises as Tokens of their better Performances, and moreover they shall at that time be Captains or Head Boys or their own proper Classes.

These Exercises or Disputation shall begin on the Noon of the day of the Queen's Accession to the Throne.

For the buying of the said Books or Prizes each of the Boys shall pay the Master a penny.

Moreover I ordain that a silver Pen be given to him that excels others in writing well, in token of Victory, whereby the boys may be the more excited to emulation in writing well.

The walls of the School or of any other contiguous building and glass windows shall not be damaged or defaced by the scholars by playing at ball or any like Diversion.

The Doors of the school shall be shut with as much silence as possible. Lest too great number Should cause such fatigue to the Master and Usher and incumber them too much in teaching the Boys well, I ordain that the number of scholars shall not exceed 120.

Of the Use of the Bedchamber adjoining to the School and of not Altering the Buildings

I ordain that the Bedchamber and study in the lower part of the School be for the use of the Master.

I forbid the Buildings of the School and Bedchamber adjoining, and the form of them to be altered by new windows or Doors or by any other Fashion.

Of the Salary of the Master and Usher

I ordain that the Tithes and Profits of one of the Portions of the Rectory of Llan Elidan shall be applied to these Uses. First I ordain that the Master shall pay forty shillings yearly to the Poor of the Parish of Llan-elidan, 20 shillings on Good Friday and the other 20 shillings the Day preceding Mid-Summer day.

Moreover I ordain that the Master shall Every Year reserve 40 shillings for and toward Repairing the School or shall imploy it to some other pious uses as thought proper by the warden and Master. I also ordain that the Master shall bestow 40 shillings for 4 sermons to be preached quarterly in the Parish of Llan-Elidan and shall pay 10 shillings every Quarter to a faithful and conscientious preacher. These 6 pounds deducted from the Tithes and Profits of one Portion of the Rectory of Llan-Elidan, the Remainder I ordain to be applied to the use of the Master and Usher; of which tithes and profits I ordain that a third part shall be the Ushers Divident or share, the other two parts I assign to the Master.

L. STANLEY KNIGHT *Welsh Independent Grammar Schools to 1660*, pp. 113–21. (Newtown Welsh Outlook Press, 1926)

PUNISHMENT IN SCHOOLS

This account by John Brinsley makes it clear that even if corporal punishment was not the only means of ensuring that pupils did their work and behaved properly, nevertheless it was the ultimate sanction. The 'Black Bill', it will be noted, survives today in many schools though under another name.

Of execution of justice in Schooles, by punishments

Phil.

For inflicting punishments, we ought to come there-unto unwillingly, and even inforced; and therefore to proceed by degrees: that who cannot be moved by any of the former meanes of preferments, nor incouragements, nor any gentle exhortation nor admonition, may be brought into order and obedience by punishment.

And therefore, first to begin with the lesser kindes of punishments; and also by degrees to the highest and severest, after this manner observing carefully the natures of every one, as was said.

1 To use reproofes; and those sometimes more sharpe according to the nature of the offender, and his fault.

2 To punish by losse of place to him who doth better according to our discretion.

3 To punish by a note, which may be called, the blacke Bill. This I would have the principal punishment, I meane most of use: for you shall finde by experience, that it being rightly used, it is more availeable then all other, to keepe all in obedience; and specially for any notoriously idle or stubborne, or which are of evill behaviour any way.

The manner of it may be thus:

To keepe a note in writing: or which may more easily be done; to keepe a remembrance of all whom you observe very negligent, stubborne, lewd, or any way disobedient, to restraine them from all liberty of play.

And therefore, to give them all to know so much beforehand, that whosoever asketh leave to play, or upon what occasion soever, yet we intend alwaies to except all such; and that the liberty is granted onely for the painfull and obedient, which are worthy to have the priviledges of schollers, and of the schoole, because they are such, and are an ornament to the schoole: not for them who are a disgrace unto it.

So alwayes at such playing times, before the *Exeatis*, the Master and Ushers to view every fourme thorow; and then to cause all them to sit still, whom they remember to have been negligent, or faulty in any special sort worthy that punishment, and to doe some exercises in writing besides; either those which they have omitted before, or such as wherein they cannot be idle.

But herein there must be a speciall care, when they are thus restrained from play, that either Master or Usher, if it can be conveniently, have an eye to them, that they cannot loyter; or some one specially appointed to see that they do their taskes.

Also that they be called to an account the next morning, whether they have done the taskes injoyned, under paine of sixe jerkes to be surely paid.

Moreover, for all those who are notoriously stubborne, or negligent, or have done any grosse fault, or cause them to sit thus, not onely one day, but every play-day continually until they shew themselves truely sorry for their faults, and doe amend; becomming as dutiful, and submisse as any other, and until they do declare by good signes, their desire and purpose to please and obey their Master; unlesse they be released at very great suite, or upon sufficient sureties of their fellowes, to incurre otherwise their penalty if they amend not.

This course straightly observed, partly through the shame of being noted in the rank of disordered fellowes, and also lest their Parents should know it; and partly through depriving them of play, and more also through this strict account to be given of their taskes, and severity of correction otherwise, will more tame the stubbornest and proudest, through God's blessing, then any correction by rod: and this without danger to the scholler, or offence to their friends.

And therefore, when rod and all other meanes faile, let us looke carefully to this, not to leave one stubborne boy untill he be brought as submisse and dutifull as any of the rest. For, those being brought into obedience, the rest may easily be kept in order, with very little correction, whereas one stubborne boy suffered, will spoile, or at leastwise indanger all the rest.

Sometimes in greater faults, to give three or foure jerkes with a birch, or with a small red willow where birch cannot be had. Or for terror in some notorious fault, halfe a doozen stripes or moe, soundly laid on, according to the discretion of the Master.

Some do only keep a bill, and more carefully their severall principall disorders; and now and then, shew them their names and faults mildly, how oft they have been admonished; and when they take them in hand, pay them soundly, and by this policy keepe them in great obedience.

In this correction with the rod, speciall provision must be had for sundry things.

1 That when you are to correct any stubborne or unbroken boy, you make sure with him to hold him fast; as they are inforced to do, who are to shoo or to tame an unbroken colt.

To this end to appoint 3 or 4 of your Schollers, whom you know to be honest, and strong inough, or moe if neede be, to lay hands upon him together, to hold him fast, over some fourme, so that he cannot stirre hand nor foot; or else if no other remedy will serve, to hold him to some post (which is farre the safest and free from inconvenience) so as he cannot any way hurt himselfe or others, be he never so peevish. Neither that he can have hope by any device or turning, or by his apparell, or any other meanes to escape. Nor yet that any one be left in his stubbornnesse to go away murmuring, powting, or blowing and puffing untill he shew as much submission as any, & that he will lie stil of himselfe without any holding; yet so as ever a wise moderation be kept. Although this must of necessitie be looked into; because besides the evill ensample to others, there is no hope to do any good to count of, with any untill their stomacks be first broken: and then they once thorowly brought under, you may have great hope to worke all good according to their capacity; so that it may be, you shall have little occasion to correct them after.

Moreover, a very child suffered in his stubbornnesse, to scape for his struggling, will in a short time come to trouble two or three men to take him up, and to correct him without danger of hurting himselfe or others.

2. To be very wary for smiting them over the backes, in any case, or in such sort as in any way to hurt or indanger them: To the end to prevent all mischiefes, for our owne comfort; and to cut off all occasions from quarrelling parents or evill reports of the Schoole. And withall, to avoid for these causes, smiting them upon the head, with hand, rod, or ferula. Also to the end that we may avoid all danger and feare for desperate boyes hurting themselves, not to use to threaten them afore, and when they have done any notorious fault, nor to let them know when they shall be beaten; but when they commit a new fault, or that we see the Schoole most full, or opportunity most fit, to take them of a sodaine.

JOHN BRINSLEY *Ludus Literarius or The Grammar Schoole* (1612).
Edited by E. T. CAMPAGNAC, pp. 286–9
(Liverpool Univ. Press, 1917)

QUALIFICATIONS NECESSARY FOR A SCHOOLMASTER

The founder of Chigwell School, Samuel Harsnet, Archbishop of York, made the following stipulations in the Statutes for Chigwell School.

Item, I constitute and appoint that the Latin schoolmaster be a Graduate of one of the Universities, not under Seven-and-twenty Years of Age, a Man skilful in the Greek and Latin Tongues, a good Poet, of a sound Religion, neither *Papist* nor *Puritan*, of a grave Behaviour, of a sober and honest Conversation, no Tipler nor Haunter of Alehouses, no *Puffer* of *Tobacco;* and above all, that he be apt to teach and severe in his Government. And all Election or Elections otherwise made I declare them to be void *ipso facto;* and that as soon as the Schoolmaster do enter into Holy Orders, either Deacon or Priest, his place to become void ipso facto, as if he were dead.

Item, I ordain that the Second Schoolmaster, touching his Years and Conversation, be in all points endowed and qualified as is above expressed touching the Latin Schoolmaster; that he write fair Secretary and Roman Hands; that he be skilful in Cyphering and Casting of Accounts, and teach his Scholars the same Faculty . . .

Quoted in N. CARLISLE *A Concise Description of the Endowed Grammar Schools in England and Wales*, Vol. I, pp. 417–18 (London, 1818)

ORBIS SENSUALIUM PICTUS OF COMENIUS

The educational ideas of the Moravian born Comenius (1592–1670) were given concrete and effective form in what still remains today the most effective means of initiating educational change – namely a school textbook. In 1658 he published at Nuremberg his *Orbis Sensualium Pictus* and so spread his pedagogical ideas of learning through the senses, of learning by doing and more particularly of learning a language by beginning with the concrete objects and experiences of life and relating the words of language to these.

Orbis Pictus was immediately successful, going through numerous editions published throughout Europe in Latin, French, German, Italian and Polish. In England its success was made certain by Charles Hoole, who in 1659 produced an English version of the book which continued in various re-editions throughout the eighteenth century. Hoole, as he had shown in his *New Discovery of the Old Art of Teaching School,* was concerned primarily to teach the 'old art' of Latin and Greek. Nevertheless he wanted to teach it in as liberal and effective way as possible and he quickly saw the value of the visual approach of Comenius. In the Preface to his translation he had this to say.

For to pack up many words in memory, of things not conceived in the mind, is to fill the head with empty imaginations, and to make the learner more to admire their multitude, and variety (and thereby to become discouraged) than to care to treasure them up, in hopes to gain more knowledge of what they mean.

He (Comenius) hath therefore in some of his later works seemed to move retrograde, and striven to come nearer to the reach of tender wits; and in this present Book, he hath (according to my judgment) descended to the very Bottom of what is to be taught, and proceeded (as Nature itself doth) in an orderly way; first to exercise the Senses well, by presenting their objects to them, and then to fasten upon the intellect by impressing the first motions of things upon it, and linking them one to another by a rational discourse. Whereas indeed, we generally missing this way, do teach children as we do Parrots, to speak they know not what, nay, which is worse, we, taking the Way of teaching little ones by Grammar only at the first, do pusle their imaginations with abstractive terms and secundary intentions, which, till they become somewhat acquainted with things, and the words belonging to them, in the language which they learn they cannot apprehend what they mean . . .

And because any good thing is the better, being the more communicated: I have herein imitated a child who is forward to impart to other what himself hath well liked. You then who have the care of little children, do not too much trouble their thoughts and clog their memories with bare Grammar Rudiments, which to them are harsh in getting, and fluid in retaining (because indeed to them they signifie nothing, but a mere swimming notion of a general term, which they know not what it meaneth till they comprehend also particulars but by this or the like Subsidiarie, inform them, first with some knowledge of things, and words wherewith to express them, and then their Rules of speaking will be better understood and more firmly kept in mind. Else how should a child conceive what a Rule meaneth when he neither knoweth what the Latine word importeth, nor what manner of thing it is which is signified to him in his own native Language which is given him thereby to understand the Rule).

JAMES BOWEN (ed.) *Joannes Amos Comenius: Orbis Sensualium Pictus*. Facsimile of 3rd London edition, 1672 (Sydney Univ. Press, 1967)

Cornix cornicatur. *á á* A a
The Crow cryeth.
Agnus balat. *be e e* B b
The Lamb blaiteth.
Cicáda ſtridet. *ci ci* C c
The Graſhopper chirpeth.
Vpupa dicit. *du du* D d
The Whooppoo ſaith.
Infans ějulat. *é é é* E e
The Infant cryeth.
Ventus flat. *fi fi* F f
The Wind bloweth.
Anſer gingrit. *ga ga* G g
The Gooſe gaggleth.
Os halat. *háh háh* H h
The Mouth breatheth out.
Mus mintrit. *i i i* I i
The Mouſe chirpeth.
Anas tetrinnit. *kha kha* K k
The Duck quacketh.
Lupus ululat. *lu ulu* L l
The Woolf howleth.
Vrſus murmurat. *mum mum* M m
The Bear grumbleth.

Orbis Pictus began what has increasingly become the main aid for teachers and parents in their teaching of the young – the illustrated text book. These pages from the facsimile of the 3rd London Edition, 1672, give some indication of the quality of what is perhaps the most influential school book ever produced.

Natatus.

Swimming.

Men are wont alſo to ſwim over waters upon a bundle of flags, 1 & beſides upon blown Beaſt-bladders; 2. and after, by throwing their Hands & Feet 3. abroad.	Solent etiam tranare aquas, ſuper *ſcirpeum faſcem*, 1. porrò ſuper inflatas *boum Veſicas*; 2. deinde, liberè *jactatu* *manuum pedumque*. 3.
At laſt they learned to tread the water, 4. being plunged up to the girdle-ſtead, and carrying their Cloathes upon their Head.	Tandem didicerunt *calcare aquam*, 4. cingulo tenus immerſi, & veſtes ſupra caput geſtando.
A Diver, 5. can ſwim alſo under the water, like a Fiſh.	*Urinator*, 5. etiam natare poteſt ſub aquâ, ut Piſcis.

The Elizabethan Church and Education

Under Elizabeth I the State, through the Established Church, insisted that schoolmasters should teach the practices of the Church of England and uncompromising puritans or Roman Catholics were not allowed to teach. The Church and the State were one and to express religious dissent was to lay oneself open to a charge of political treason.

The following extracts illustrate the ways in which control over education could be exerted either through Royal Injunctions, Ecclesiastical Canons, or Act of Parliament.*

THE INJUNCTIONS OF ELIZABETH 1559

These extracts from the Injunctions show the concern of the State through the Church to regulate education. Note the provision of the Royal Grammar.

The queen's most royal majesty, by the advice of her most honourable council, intending the advancement of the true honour of Almighty God, the suppression of superstition throughout all her highness's realms and dominions, and to plant true religion to the extirpation of all hypocrisy, enormities, and abuses (as to her duty appertaineth), doth minister unto her loving subjects these godly Injunctions hereafter following.

XII. And, to the intent that learned men may hereafter spring the more, for the execution of the premises, every parson, vicar, clerk, or beneficed man within this deanery, having yearly to dispend in benefices and other promotions of the Church 100*l*., shall give [3*l*. 6s. 8d. in] exhibition to one scholar [in any of the universities] and for as many hundred pounds more as he may dispend, to so many scholars more shall give like exhibition in the University of Oxford or Cambridge, or some grammar school, which, after they have profited in good learning, may be partners of their patron's cure and charge, as well in preaching, as otherwise in executing of their offices, or may, when need shall be, otherwise profit the commonwealth with their counsel and wisdom.

XXXIX. Item, that every schoolmaster and teacher shall teach the Grammar set forth by King Henry VIII of noble memory, and continued in the time of King Edward VI, and none other.

**Further reading:*

A. C. F. BEALES *Education Under Penalty: English Catholic Education from the Reformation to the Fall of James II: 1547–1689* (University of London, The Athlone Press, 1963)

XL. Item, that no man shall take upon him to teach, but such as shall be allowed by the ordinary, and found meet as well for his learning and dexterity in teaching, as for sober and honest conversation, and also for right understanding of God's true religion.

XLI. Item, that all teachers of children shall stir and move them to the love and due reverence of God's true religion now truly set forth by public authority.

XLII. Item, that they shall accustom their scholars reverently to learn such sentences of Scriptures as shall be most expedient to induce them to all godliness.

XLIII. Item, forasmuch as in these latter days many have been made priests, being children, and otherwise utterly unlearned, so that they could read to say Matins or Mass, the ordinaries shall not admit any such to any cure or spiritual function.

GEE and HARDY (eds.) *Documents Illustrative of the History of the English Church*, pp. 424, 433–4 (London: Macmillan, 1914)

RELIGIOUS DUTIES OF SCHOOLMASTERS 1571

It was the primary duty of teachers to train their pupils to take part in church services as the following instructions make clear. Teachers were also ordered to use the Catechism, which Alexander Nowell, Dean of St Paul's, had written and which came into print in 1570.

Of Scholemasters

It shall not be lawfull for any to teach the Latine tongue, or to instructe children, neyther openly in the scholes, neyther privately in any mans house, but whome the Byshop of that dioces hath alowed, and to whom he hath geven licence to teach under that seale of hys office. And here we except (for honours sake) the Lordes of the Parliament: but the Bishop shall allow no Scholemaister, nor accompt him worthy of yt office, but whom he shal finde in his judgement to be learned, and worthy of that place, and whome he shall see commended by the testimonie of godly men, touching hys life and manners, and especially hys religion.

Scholemaisters shall teach no Grammer, but onely that, which the Queenes Majestie hath commaunded to be read in all Scholes, through the whole Realme, neyther any other Latine Catachisme, then that which was sette forth, in the yeare, 1570. The whiche also, that is translated into English, we wil have taught unto children that are ignorant of the Latine tongue.

All other bookes they shall teach, whereby the fulnes and finenes of the Latine & Greeke toung may be learned, & those especially, which profits to the knowledge of Christ and godlynes. And once every yeare they shall signifie to the Byshop, what chosen scholers they have of all their number, which are of that aptnes, and so forward in learning, that there may be good hope they will become fitte, either for the common wealth, or for the holy ministerie. By this hope the parents beying allured, will more willingly keepe them at schole.

But chiefly they shal so order and frame the tongues of children, that they may pronounce openly, plainly, and distinctly. And as often as any sermon shalbe, they shall either send them, or bring them to church, that from their childhode, they may be brought up in godliness: & lest they should heare it negligently: at their return to schole, they shall call and examine every one, what they have learned out of that sermon: and that the myndes of children, may be the more styrred up to vertue and diligence: they shall rebuke the idle and sluggish, and shall prayse the attentive and diligent.

Ecclesiastical Canons of 1571. Quoted in T. W. BALDWIN
William Shakspere's Petty School, p. 86
(Univ. Illinois Press, 1943)

ACT AGAINST JESUITS 1585

Although the Jesuits came under the penalties of the Elizabethan Supremacy Act, this was the first act passed specifically against Jesuits and later re-enforced under James I. It is noteworthy that the Act included penalties for sending children abroad for education.

Whereas divers persons called or professed Jesuits, seminary priests, and other priests, which have been, and from time to time are made in the parts beyond the seas, by or according to the order and rites of the Romish Church, have of late years come and been sent, and daily do come and are sent, into this realm of England . . . not only to withdraw her highness's subjects from their due obedience to her majesty, but also to stir up and move sedition, rebellion, and open hostility within the same her highness's realms and dominions, to the great endangering of the safety of her most royal person, and to the utter ruin, desolation, and overthrow of the whole realm, if the same be not the sooner by some good means foreseen and prevented:

For reformation whereof be it ordained, established, and enacted by the queen's most excellent majesty, and the Lords spiritual and temporal, and the Commons, in this present Parliament assembled, and by the authority of the same Parliament, that all and every Jesuits, seminary priests, and other priests whatsoever made or ordained out of the realm of England or other her highness's dominions, or within any of her majesty's realms or dominions, by any authority, power, or jurisdiction derived, challenged, or pretended from the see of Rome, since the feast of the Nativity of St John Baptist in the first year of her highness's reign, shall within forty days next after the end of this present session of Parliament depart out of this realm of England, and out of all other her highness's realms and dominions, if the wind, weather, and passage shall serve for the same, or else so soon after the end of the said forty days as the wind, weather, and passage shall so serve . . .

And every person which after the end of the same forty days, and after such time of departure as is before limited and appointed, shall wittingly and willingly receive, relieve, comfort, aid, or maintain any such Jesuit, seminary priest, or other priest, deacon, or religious or ecclesiastical person, as is aforesaid, being at liberty, or out of hold knowing him to be a Jesuit, seminary priest, or other such priest, deacon, or religious or ecclesiastical person, as is aforesaid, shall also for such offence be adjudged a felon, without benefit of clergy, and suffer death, lose, and forfeit, as in case of one attained of felony.

And be it further enacted by the authority aforesaid, if any of her majesty's subjects (not being a Jesuit, seminary priest, or other such priest, deacon, or religious or ecclesiastical person, as is before mentioned) now being, or which hereafter shall be of, or brought up in, any college of Jesuits, or seminary already erected or ordained, or hereafter to be erected or ordained, in the parts beyond the seas, or out of this realm in any foreign parts, shall not within six months next after proclamation in that behalf to be made in the city of London, under the great seal of England, return into this realm, and thereupon within two days next after such return, before the bishop of the diocese, or two justices of peace of the county where he shall arrive, submit himself to her majesty and her laws, and take the oath set forth by Act in the first year of her reign; that then every such person which shall otherwise return, come into, or be in this realm or any other her highness's dominions, for such offence of returning or being in this realm or any other her highness's dominions, without submission, as aforesaid, shall also be adjudged a traitor, and suffer, lose and forfeit, as in case of high treason . . .

And be it further enacted by the authority aforesaid, that it shall not be lawful for any person of or under her highness's obedience, at any time after the said forty days, during her majesty's life (which God long preserve) to send his or her child, or other person, being under his or her government, into any the parts beyond the seas out of her highness's obedience, without the special licence of her majesty, or of four of her highness's privy council, under their hands in that behalf first had or obtained (except merchants, for such only as they or any of them shall send over the seas only for or about his, her, or their trade of merchandise, or to serve as mariners, and not otherwise) upon pain to forfeit and lose for every such their offence the sum of one hundred pounds.

GEE and HARDY (eds.) *Documents Illustrative of the History of the English Church*, pp. 485–8 (London: Macmillan, 1914)

The Education of the Gentry

Under the influence of Renaissance thought the concept of the education fit for a gentleman was broadened. The medieval concern to educate a man in knightly skills – such as running, riding, jousting, and dancing – continued, but the need for a literary education was now realized to be equally important if a man was to serve his monarch in some administrative or diplomatic office. To this was also added an education in courtly manners in imitation of the court life of some Italian principalities, an education which implied new behaviour patterns and social attitudes.

The gentry gained this education in various ways. The employment of private tutors was the most common means but in addition young men would attend academies abroad and the universities and Inns of Court at home, while self-help also played an important part in that the gentry educated themselves from the numerous manuals which now, with the development of printing, became available.*

DIFFERING ATTITUDES TO LEARNING AMONG THE GENTRY

The following extract illustrates the differing attitudes to learning held amongst the gentry in the early years of the sixteenth century. Some still hold that the knightly pursuits best become a gentleman, while others under the influence of the Renaissance wish for a more literate and educated gentry. The extract is from a letter to John Colet written by Richard Pace, then the King's Secretary, in 1517 as a preface to his book *De Fructu qui ex Doctrinae percipitur.*

It remains that I now explain to you what moves me to compile and publish a treatise with this title. When, two years ago, more or less, I had returned to my native land from the city of Rome, I was present at a certain feast, a stranger to many; where, when enough had been drunk, one or other of the guests – no fool, as one might infer from his words and countenance – began to talk of educating his children well. And, first of all, he thought that he must search out a good teacher for them, and that they should at any rate attend school. There happened

**Further reading:*

L. STONE 'The Educational Revolution in England 1560–1640' *Past and Present*, Vol. 28, July 1964

L. STONE *The Crisis of the Aristocracy 1558–1641* (Oxford: Clarendon Press, 1965)

J. SIMON *Education and Society in Tudor England* (Cambridge Univ. Press, 1966)

K. CHARLTON *Education in Renaissance England* (London: Routledge and Kegan Paul, 1965) to be present one of those whom we call gentle-men, and who always carry some horn hanging at their backs, as though they would hunt during dinner. He, hearing letters praised, roused with sudden anger, burst out furiously with these words. 'Why do you talk nonsense, friend?' he said, 'A curse on those stupid letters! all learned men are beggars: even Erasmus, the most learned of all, is a beggar (as I hear), and in a certain letter of his calls *τήν κατάρατον πενιαν* (that is, execrable poverty) his wife, and vehemently complains that he cannot shake her off his shoulders right into *βαθυκήτεα πόντον*, that is, into the deep sea. I swear by God's body I'd rather that my son should hang than study letters. For it becomes the sons of gentlemen to blow the horn nicely, to hunt skilfully, and elegantly carry and train a hawk. But the study of letters should be left to the sons of rustics.' At this point I could not restrain myself from answering something to this most talkative man, in defence of good letters. 'You do not seem to me, good man,' I said, 'to think rightly. For if any foreigner were to come to the king, such as the ambassadors of princes are, and an answer had to be given to him, your son, if he were educated as you wish, could only blow his horn, and the learned sons of rustics would be called to answer, and would be far preferred to your hunter or fowler son; and they, enjoying their learned liberty, would say to your face, "We prefer to be learned, and, thanks to our learning, no fools, than boast of our fool-like nobility." ' Then he upon this, looking round, said, 'Who is this person that is talking like this? I don't know the fellow.' And when some one whispered in his ear who I was, he muttered something or other in a low voice to himself; and finding a fool to listen to him, he then caught hold of a cup of wine. And when he could get nothing to answer, he began to drink, and change the conversation to other things.

F. J. FURNIVALL (ed.) *The Babees Book*, pp. xiii–xiv (Early English Text Society, 1868)

CASTIGLIONE'S *IL CORTEGIANO (THE COURTIER)* 1528

Under the influence of Humanist ideas the education of a 'gentleman' in the sixteenth century came to comprise three parts; namely knightly exercises. literary studies, and courtly manners.

Baldassare Castiglione's *Il Cortegiano* became the classic text for the last of these three, the courtly manners. It described life at the Court of the Montefeltre Dukes of Urbino, and soon after it was published in 1528 there were copies of it in England. In 1561 Sir Thomas Hoby translated it into English and by 1603 this had gone through three more editions. In addition there were several reprintings of a Latin translation of the work by Bartholomew Clerke, first published in 1571. Roger Ascham in *The Scholemaster* recommended

Castiglione's book and it became the accepted standard of behaviour for English gentlemen.

The book is in the form of conversations which took place in the Palace of Urbino in 1507, and various topics are discussed including the characteristics of a gentleman, behaviour towards a prince and inevitably perhaps the nature of love.

This extract shows the emphasis placed on physical skills as one of the attributes of a perfect gentleman.

Weapons are also often used in various sports during peace-time, and gentlemen often perform in public spectacles before the people and before ladies and great lords. So I wish our courtier to be an accomplished and versatile horseman and, as well as having a knowledge of horses and all the matters to do with riding, he should put every effort and diligence into surpassing the rest just a little in everything, so that he may always be recognized as superior. And as we read of Alcibiades, that he surpassed all those peoples among whom he lived, and each time in regard to what they claimed to be best at, so this courtier of ours should outstrip all others, and in regard to the things they know well. Thus it is the peculiar excellence of the Italians to ride well with the rein, to handle spirited horses very skilfully, and to tilt and joust; so in all this the courtier should compare with the best of them. In tourneys, in holding his ground, in forcing his way forward, he should compare with the best of the French; in volleying, in running bulls, in casting spears and darts, he should be outstanding among the Spaniards. But, above all, he should accompany his every act with a certain grace and fine judgement if he wishes to earn that universal regard which everyone covets.

There are also many other sports which, although they do not directly require the use of weapons, are closely related to arms and demand a great deal of manly exertion. Among these it seems to me that hunting is the most important, since in many ways it resembles warfare; moreover, it is the true pastime of great lords, it is a suitable pursuit for a courtier, and we know that it was very popular in the ancient world. It is also fitting that the courtier should know how to swim, jump, run and cast the stone, for, apart from the usefulness of these accomplishments in war, one is often required to display one's skills and such sports can help to build up a good reputation, especially with the crowd which the courtier always has to humour. Another noble sport which is very suitable for the courtier to play is tennis, for this shows how well he is built physically, how quick and agile he is in every member, and whether he has all the qualities demonstrated in most other games. I think no less highly of performing on horseback, which is certainly very exhausting and difficult but more than anything else serves to make a man wonderfully agile and dextrous; and apart from its usefulness, if agility on horseback is accompanied by gracefulness, in my opinion it makes a finer spectacle than any other sport. Then if our courtier possesses more than average skill in all these sports, I think he should ignore the others, such as vaulting on the ground, tight-rope walking and that kind of thing, since these are more like acrobatics and hardly suitable for a gentleman.

CASTIGLIONE *The Book of the Courtier*. Translated by GEORGE BULL, pp. 62–4 (Harmondsworth: Penguin Books 1967)

This next extract suggests that a gentleman should be modest, and while seeking honour take care to make it appear that his superiority is effortless.

In the same way, gentleness is most impressive in a man who is a capable and courageous warrior; and just as his boldness is magnified by his modesty, so his modesty is enhanced and more apparent on account of his boldness. Hence to talk little and to do much, and not to praise oneself for praiseworthy deeds but to dissimulate them politely, serve to enhance both these virtues in anyone who knows how to employ this method discreetly; and the same holds true for all the other good qualities. Then in everything he does or says I should like our courtier to follow certain general rules which, I think, contain the essence of all I have to tell you. And first and most important, he should (as the Count so rightly advised yesterday evening) above all avoid affectation. Next let him consider well whatever he does or says, the place where he does it, in whose presence, its timing, why he is doing it, his own age, his profession, the end he is aiming at, and the means that are suitable; and so, bearing all these points in mind, let him prepare himself discreetly for all he wishes to do or say . . . If you remember, yesterday evening the Count said he wished the courtier's chief profession to be that of arms, and he spoke at length about the way he should pursue it. So we shall not repeat this. All the same, it should also be understood from the rule I gave that when the courtier finds himself involved in a skirmish or pitched battle, or something of that nature, he should arrange to withdraw discreetly from the main body and accomplish the bold and notable exploits he has to perform in as small a company as possible and in view of all the noblest and most eminent men of the army, and, above all, in the presence, or if possible under the very eyes, of the prince he is serving. For it is certainly right to exploit the things one does well. And I believe that just as it is wrong to seek false glory or what is not deserved, so also it is wrong to cheat oneself of due honour and not to seek that praise which is the only true reward of prowess. And I recall in the past having known men who, though very able, were extremely stupid in this regard and would as soon risk their lives to capture a flock of sheep as in being the first to scale the walls of a besieged town; but this is not how our courtier will behave if he bears in mind the motive that leads him to war, which ought to be honour pure and simple. But, then, if he happens to engage in arms in some public spectacle, such as jousting, tourneying or volleying, or other kind of physical recreation, mindful of where and in whose presence he is, he will make sure that he is as elegant and attractive in the exercise of arms as he is competent, and that he feeds the eyes of those who are looking on with everything that can give him added grace. He will ensure that the horse he has is beautifully caparisoned, that he himself is suitably attired, with appropriate mottoes and ingenious devices to attract the eyes of the onlookers in his direction as surely as the loadstone attracts iron. He will never be one of the last to show himself, knowing that the crowd, and especially the women, scrutinize the first far more than the last . . . if anyone is anxious to wrestle, to run or to jump with peasants, then he ought, in my opinion, to do it casually, out of *noblesse oblige*, so to say, and certainly not in competition with them; and he should be almost certain of winning, or else not take part at all, for it is too sad and shocking, and quite undignified, when a gentleman is seen to be beaten by a peasant, especially in a wrestling-match. Hence I think it would be as well to abstain at least when there are many onlookers, because the advantage in winning is very negligible and the disadvantages in being beaten very serious. The game of tennis is also nearly always played before an audience, and it is one of those spectacles which gains considerably from the presence of a crowd. So I would like our courtier to take part in this game and in all others, apart from those involving the use of arms, as an amateur, making it clear that he neither seeks nor expects any applause. Nor, even though his performance is outstanding, should he let it be thought that he has spent on it much time or trouble. Neither should he behave like those people who are fond of music and, whenever they are speaking with someone, if there is a lull in the conversation always start to sing *sotto voce*; or like others who, walking through the streets or in church, are for ever dancing; or like others who, when they meet a friend in the square or wherever it happens to be, immediately act as if about to fence or to wrestle, depending on their favourite sport . . .

ibid., pp. 114–18

SIR THOMAS ELYOT'S *GOVERNOUR* 1531

The effect of the educational ideals of Italian humanism is very clearly seen in Sir Thomas Elyot's *The Boke named the Governour*. Elyot insists that learning is essential for the gentry and, though there is a place in his curriculum for such courtly pursuits as dancing and such manly exercises as wrestling and in particular for archery, nevertheless the main theme of the book is to persuade the governing class to educate itself for the tasks of government with literary, historical and philosophical studies.

The Governour published in 1531, is significant as the first book on Education to be written and printed in English, but it has wider importance in that it became the standard work for the upper classes as an account of the studies suitable for potential servants of the ruling prince. If the traditions of medieval knightly education provided the sixteenth-century nobility with its curriculum for knightly exercises as horsemanship and the use of weapons, and Castiglione's *Courtier* gave them an account of manners and behaviour, Elyot's book furnished them with a textbook of studies. The extent of its influence may be judged from the fact that the book went through nine editions between 1531 and the end of the century.

Elyot recommends that at the age of seven a tutor should be employed to teach the child the parts of speech in his own langage and also some music or painting and carving so that the child is not fatigued 'with continuall studie or lernyng'. Then the child should begin Latin and Greek and read the works of the poets such as Homer and Virgil.

After that the childe hathe ben pleasantly trained, and induced to knowe the partes of speche, and can seperate one of them from an other, in his owne langage, it shall then be time that his tutor or governour do make diligent serche for suche a maister as is exellently lerned both in greke and latine, and therewithall is of sobre and vertuous disposition, specially chast of livyng, and of moche affabilite and patience: leste by any uncleane example the tender mynde of the childe may be infected, harde afterwarde to be recovered. For the natures of children be nat so moche or sone advanced by thinges well done or spoken, as they be hindred and corrupted by that whiche in actis or wordes is wantonly expressed. Also by a cruell and irous maister the wittes of children be dulled; and that thinge for the whiche children be often tymes beaten is to them ever after fastidious: whereof we nede no better autor for witnes than daily experience . . .

Nowe lette us retourne to the ordre of lernyng apt for a gentyll man. Wherein I am of the opinion of Quintilian that I wolde have hym lerne greke and latine autors both at one time: orels to begyn with greke, for as moche as that it is hardest to come by: by reason of the diversite of tonges, which by fyve in nombre: and all must be knowen, or elles uneth any poet can be well understande. And if a childe do begyn therin at seven yeres of age, he may continually lerne greke autours thre yeres, and in the meane tyme use the latin tonge as a familiar langage: whiche in a noble mannes sonne may well come to passe, havynge none other persons to serve him or kepyng hym company, but suche as can speak latine elegantly. And what doubt is there but so may he as sone speake good latin, as he maye do pure frenche, whiche nowe is broughte in to as many rules and figures, and as longe a grammer as is latine or greke . . .

Grammer beinge but an introduction to the understanding of autors, if it be made to longe or exquisite to the lerner, hit in a maner mortifieth his corage: And by that time he cometh to the most swete and pleasant redinge of olde autors, the sparkes of fervent desire of lernynge is extincte with the burdone of grammar, lyke as a lyttel fyre is sone quenched with a great heape of small stickes: so that it can never come to the principall logges where it shuld longe bourne in a great pleasaunt fire.

Nowe to folowe my purpose: after a few and quicke rules of grammer, immediately, or interlasynge hit therwith, wolde be redde to the childe Esopes fables in greke, in which argument children moche do delite . . .

I could reherce divers other poetis whiche for mater and eloquence be very necessary, but I feare me to be to longe from noble Homere: from whom as from a fountaine proceded all eloquence and lernyng . . .

Nat withstandinge, for as moche as the saide warkes be very longe, and do require therfore a great time to be all lerned and kanned some latine autour wolde be therwith myxte, and specially Virgile; whiche, in his warke called *Eneidos*, is most lyke to Homere, and all moste the same Homere in latine.

And here I conclude to speke any more of poetis, necessary for the childehode of a gentill man: for as moche as these, I doubt nat, will suffice untill he passe the age of xiii yeres. In which time childhode declineth, and reason waxeth rype, and deprehendeth thinges with a most constant jugement. Here I wolde shulde be remembred, that I require nat that all these warkes shud be throughly radde of a childe in this tyme, whiche were almost impossible. But I only desire that they have, in every of the saide bokes, so moche instruction that they may take therby some profite.

SIR THOMAS ELYOT, *The Governour*, pp. 32–40 (London: Dent, 1907)

Towards the age of fourteen Elyot recommends the beginning of more mature studies as logic and rhetoric but to these he adds more 'modern' subjects such as cosmography and history, culminating by the age of seventeen in the study of moral philosophy.

After that xiv yeres be passed of a childes age, his maister if he can, or some other, studiouslye exercised in the arte of an oratour, shall first rede to hym some what of that parte of logike that is called *Topica*, eyther of Cicero, or els of that noble clerke of Almaine, which late floured, called Agricola: whose warke prepareth invention, tellynge the places from whens an argument for the profe of any mater may be taken with litle studie: and that lesson, with moche and diligent lernyng, havyng mixte there with none other exercise, will in the space of halfe a yere be perfectly kanned. Immediately after that, the arte of Rhetorike wolde be semblably taught, either in greke, out of Hermogines, or of Quintilian in latine, begynnyng at the thirde boke, and instructyng diligently the childe in that part of rhethorike, principally, whiche concerneth persuation: for a moche as it is moste apte for consultations. There can be no shorter instruction of Rhetorike than the treatise that Tulli wrate unto his sonne, which boke is named the partition of rhetorike. And in good faythe, to speake boldly that I thinke: for him that nedeth nat, or doth nat desire, to be an exquisite oratour, the litle boke made by the famous Erasmus (whom all gentill wittis are bounden to thanke and supporte), whiche he calleth *Copiam Verborum et Rerum*, that is to say, plentie of wordes and maters, shall be sufficient . . .

. . . Demosthenes and Tulli, by the consent of all lerned men, have preeminence and soveraintie over all oratours: the one reignyng in wonderfull eloquence in the publike weale of the Romanes, who had the empire and dominion of all the worlde: the other, of no lasse estimation, in the citie of Athenes, whiche of longe tyme was accounted the mother of Sapience, and the palaice of musis and all liberall sciences . . . The utilitie that a noble man shall have by redyng these oratours, is, that, whan he shall happe to reason in counsaile, or shall speke in a great audience, or to strange ambassadours of great princes, he shall nat be constrayned to speake wordes sodayne and disordred, but shal bestowe them aptly and in their places . . .

. . . All be it there is none so good lernynge as the demonstration of cosmographie by materiall figures and instrumentes, havynge a good instructour. And surely this lesson is both pleasant and necessary. For what pleasure is it, in one houre, to beholde those realmes, cities, sees, ryvers, and mountaynes, that uneth in an olde mannes life can nat be journaide and pursued: what incredible delite is taken in beholding the diversities of people, beastis, foules, fisshes, tress, frutes, and herbes: to knowe the sondry maners and conditions of people, and the varietie of their natures, and that in a warme studie or perler, without perill of the see, or daunger of longe and paynfull journayes: I can nat tell what more pleasure shulde happen to a gentil witte, than to beholde in his owne house every thynge that with in all the worlde is contained . . .

. . . Wherefore it maye nat be of any wyse man denied, but that Cosmographie is to all noble men, nat only pleasant, but profitable also, and wonderfull necessary . . .

. . . Cosmographie beinge substancially perceived, it is than tyme to induce a childe to the redinge of histories: by fyrst to set hym in a fervent courage, the mayster in the mooste pleasant and elegant wise expressinge what incomparable delectation, utilitie, and commodite, shal happen to emperours, kinges, princis, and all other gentil men by reding of histories: shewinge to hym that Demetrius Phalareus, a man of excellent wisdome and lerninge, and which in Athenes had ben longe exercised in the publick weale, exhorted Ptholomee, kyng of Egipt, chiefly above all other studyes, to haunte and embrace histories, and suche other bokes, wherin were contayned preceptes made to kynges and princes: sayng that in them he shulde rede those thinges whiche no man durst reporte unto his persone. Also Cicero, father of the latin eloquence, calleth an historie the witnesse of tymes, maistres of life, the lyfe of remembrance, of trouthe the lyght, the messager of antiquite . . .

. . . In the lerning of these autors a yonge gentilman shal be taught to note and marke, nat only the ordre and elegancie in declaration of the historie, but also the occasion of the warres, the counsailes and preparations on either part, the estimation of the capitaines, the maner and fourme of theyr governance, the continuance of the bataile, the fortune and successe of the holle affaires. Semblably out of the warres in other dayly affaires, the astate of the publike weale, if hit be prosperous or in decaye, what is the very occasyon of the one or of the other, the forme and maner of the governance therof, the good and evyll qualities of them that be rulers, the commodities and good sequele of vertue, the discommodies and evyll conclusion of vicious licence.

Surely if a noble man do thus seriously and diligently rede histories, I dare affirme there is no studie or science for him of equal commoditie and pleasure, havynge regarde to every tyme and age.

By the time that the childe do com to xvii yeres of age, to the intent his courage be bridled with reason, hit were nedefull to rede unto hym some warkes of philosophie; specially that parte that may enforme him unto vertuous maners, whiche parte of philosophie is called morall Wherfore there wolde be radde to hym, for an introduction, two the fyrste bokes of the warke of Aristotell called *Ethicæ*, wherin is contained the definitions and propre significations of every vertue; and that to be lerned in greke; for the translations that we yet have be but a rude and grosse shadowe of the eloquence and wisedome of Aristotell. Forthewith wolde folowe the warke of Cicero, called in Latin *De officiis*, whereunto yet is no propre englisshe worde to be gyven; but to provide for it some maner of exposition, it may be sayde in this fourme: 'Of the dueties and maners appertaynynge to men.' But above all other, the warkes of Plato wolde be most studiously radd when the jugement of a man is come to perfection, and by the other studies is instructed in the fourme of speakynge that philosophers used. Lorde god, what incomparable swetnesse of wordes and mater shall he finde in the saide warkes of Plato and Cicero; wherin is joyned gravitie with dilectation, excellent wysedome with divine eloquence, absolute vertue with pleasure incredible, and every place is so infarced with profitable counsaile, joyned with honestie, that those thre bokes be almoste sufficient to make a perfecte and excellent governour . . . And here I make an ende of the lernynge and studie wherby noble men may attayne to be worthy to have autorite in a publike weale. Alway I shall exhorte tutours and governours of noble chyldren, that they suffre them nat to use ingourgitations of meate or drinke, ne to slepe moche, that is to saye, above viii houres at the moste. For undoubtedly bothe repletion and superfluous slepe be capitall enemies to studie, as they be semblably to helth of body and soule.

ibid., pp. 41–9

THE EDUCATION OF GREGORY CROMWELL

The following extracts from the letters of Henry Dowes, tutor to Thomas Cromwell's son, Gregory, provide illustrative detail of the studies a young man might pursue with a tutor. Education at home by a tutor rather than at a school was recommended by most Tudor theorists on the education of the gentry. It is notable that knightly pursuits as well as manners and learning figure in the daily timetable.

The order of his studie, as the houres lymyted for the Frenche tongue, writinge, plaienge att weapons, castinge of accomptes, pastimes of instruments, and suche others, hath been devised and directed by the prudent wisdome of Mr. Southwell . . .

. . . But forcause some was spente in the servyce of the wylde goddes, it is so moche to be regarded after what fashion yeouth is educate and browght upp, in whiche tyme that this is lerned (for the moste parte) will nott all holelie be forgotten in the older yeres, I thinke it my dutie to asserteyne your Maistershippe how he spendith his tyme . . . And firste, after he hath herde Masse he taketh a lecture of a Diologe of Erasmus Colloquium, called Pietas Puerilis, whereinne is described a veray picture of oone that sholde be vertuouselie brought upp; and forcause it is so necessary for hime, I do not onelie cause him to rede it over, but also to practise the preceptes of the same, and I have also translated it into Englishe, so that he may conferre theime both togithers, whereof (as lerned men affirme) cometh no smalle profecte . . . after that, he exerciseth his hande in writing one or two houres, and redith uppon Fabian's Chronicle as longe; the residue of the day he doth spende uppon the lute and virginalls. When he rideth (as he doth very ofte) I tell hime by the way some historie of the Romanes or the

Greekes, whiche I cause him to reherse agayn in a tale. For his recreation he useth to hawke and hunte, and shote in his long bowe, which frameth and succedeth so well with hime that he semeth to be therunto given by nature.

SIR HENRY ELLIS *Original Letters Illustrative of English History* (First Series, 1825), Vol. I, pp. 341–4

ASCHAM'S PLEA TO THE NOBILITY TO PURSUE LEARNING

Roger Ascham's *The Schoolmaster* published in 1570 exhorts the nobility to educate their sons in the new learning. If they neglect to do this, then they must expect to see 'meaner mens children' secure those positions in governmental offices which had customarily gone to the nobility.

There is an other discommoditie, besides crueltie in scholemasters in beating away the love of learning from children, which hindreth learning and vertue, and good bringing up of youth, and namelie yong jentlemen, verie moch in England. This fault is cleane contrary to the first. I wished before, to have love of learning bred up in children: I wishe as moch now, to have yong men brought up in good order of living, and in some more severe discipline, then commonlie they be. We have lacke in England of soch good order, as the old noble *Persians* so carefullie used: whose children, to the age of xxi. yeare, were brought up in learnyng, and exercises of labor, and that in soch place, where they should, neither see that was uncumlie, nor heare that was unhonest. Yea, a yong jentleman was never free, to go where he would, and do what he liste him self, but under the kepe, and by the counsell, of some grave governour, untill he was, either maryed, or cald to beare some office in the common wealth.

And see the great obedience, that was used in old tyme to father and governours. No sonne, were he never so old of yeares, never so great of birth, though he were a kynges sonne, might not mary, but by his father and mothers also consent . . . Our tyme is so farre from that old discipline and obedience, as now, not onelie young jentlemen, but even verie girles dare without all feare, though not without open shame, where they list, and how they list, marie themselves in spite of father, mother, God, good order, and all. The cause of this evill is, that youth is least looked unto, when they stand [in] most neede of good kepe and regard. It availeth not, to see them well taught in yong yeares, and after whan they cum to lust and youthfull dayes, to give them licence to live as they lust them selves. . . This evill, is not common to poore men, as God will have it, but proper to riche and great mens children, as they deserve it. In deede from seven, to seventene, yong jentlemen commlie be carefullie enough brought up: But from seventene to seven and twentie (the most dangerous tyme of all a mans life, and most slipperie to stay well in) they have commonlie the reigne of all licens in their owne hand, and speciallie soch as do live in the Court. And that which is most to be merveled at, commonlie, the wisest and also best men, be found the fondest fathers in this behalfe. And if som good father wold seick some remedie herein, yet the mother (if the house hold of our Lady) had rather, yea, & will to, have her sonne cunnyng & bold, in making him to lyve trimlie when he is yong, than by learning and travell, to be able to serve his Prince and his contrie, both wiselie in peace, and stoutelie in warre, whan he is old.

The fault is in your selves, ye noble mens sonnes, and therefore ye deserve the greater blame, that commonlie, the meaner mens children, cum to be, the wisest councellours, and greatest doers, in the weightie affaires of this Realme. And why? for God will have it so, of his providence: bicause ye will have it no otherwise, by your negligence.

And God is a good God, & wisest in all his doinges, that will place vertue, & displace vice, in those kingdomes, where he doth governe. For he knoweth, that Nobilitie, without vertue and wisedome, is bloud in deede, but bloud trewelie, without bones & sinewes: & so of it selfe, without the other, verie weeke to beare the burden of weightie affaires . . .

Therfore, ye great and noble mens children, if ye will have rightfullie that praise, and enjoie surelie that place, which your fathers have, and elders had, and left unto you, ye must kepe it, as they gat it, and that is, by the onelie waie, of vertue, wisedome, and worthinesse.

ROGER ASCHAM *The Scholemaster* (1570). Edited by W. A. WRIGHT, pp. 203–6 (Cambridge Univ. Press, 1904)

Ascham goes on to give an account of the curriculum he would have young noblemen follow. It is notable that it suggests a balance between knightly and courtly pursuits on the one hand and learning on the other. The extract ends with the recommendation that Castiglione's *Il Cortegiano* should be read widely.

And, I do not meene, by all this my taulke, that yong Jentlemen, should alwaies be poring on a booke, and by using good studies, shold lease honest pleasure, and haunt no good pastime. I meene nothing lesse: For it is well knowne, that I both like and love, and have alwaies, and do yet still use, all exercises and pastimes, that be fitte for my nature and habilitie. And beside naturall disposition, in judgement also, I was never, either Stoick in doctrine, or Anabaptist in Religion, to mislike a merie, pleasant, and plaifull nature, if no outrage be committed, against lawe, mesure, and good order.

Therefore, I wold wishe, that, beside some good time, fitlie appointed, and constantlie kepte, to encrease by readinge, the knowledge of the tonges and learning, yong jentlemen shold use, and delite in all Courtelie exercises, and Jentlemanlike pastimes. And good cause whie: For the self same noble Citie of Athenes, justlie commended of me before, did wiselie and upon great consideration, appoint, the Muses, *Apollo*, and *Pallas*, to be patrones of learninge to their yougthe. For the Muses, besides learning, were also Ladies of dauncinge, mirthe and ministrelsie: *Apollo*, was god of shooting, and Author of cunning playing upon Instrumentes: *Pallas* also was Laidie mistres in warres. Wherbie was nothing else ment, but that learninge shold be alwaise mingled, with honest mirthe, and cumlie exercises: and that warre also shold be governed by learning, and moderated by wisdom, as did well appeare in those Capitaines of *Athenes* named by me before, and also in *Scipio* & *Cæsar*, the two Diamondes of Rome.

Therefore, to ride cumlie: to run faire at the tilte or ring: to plaie at all weapones: to shote faire in bow, or surelie in gon: to vaut lustely: to runne: to leape: to wrestle: to swimme: To daunce cumlie: to sing, and playe of instrumentes cunnyngly: to Hawke: to hunte: to playe at tennes, & all pastimes generally, which be joyned with labor, used in open place, and on the day light, conteining either some fitte exercise for warre, or some pleasant pastime for peace, be not onelie cumlie and decent, but also verie necessarie, for a Courtlie Jentleman to use . . .

To joyne learnyng with cumlie exercises, *Conto Baldesær Castiglione* in his booke, *Cortegiano*, doth trimlie teache: which booke, advisedlie read, and diligentlie folowed, but one yeare at home in England, would do a yong jentleman more good, I wisse, then three yeares travell abrode spent in *Italie*. And I mervell this booke, is no more read in the Court, than it is, seyng it is so well translated into English by a worthie Jentleman Syr. *Th. Hobbie*, who was many wayes well furnished with learnyng, and very expert in knowledge of divers tonges.

And beside good preceptes in bookes, in all kinde of tonges, this Court also never lacked many faire examples, for yong jentlemen to folow: And surelie, one example, is more valiable both to good and ill, than 20 preceptes written in bookes: and so *Plato*, not in one or two, but diverse places, doth plainlie teach.

If kyng *Edward* had lived a litle longer, his onely example had breed soch a rase of worthie learned jentlemen, as this Realme never yet did affourde.

Present examples of this present tyme, I list not to touche: yet there is one example, for all the Jentlemen of this Court to folow, that may well satisfie them, or nothing will serve them, nor no example move them, to goodnes and learning.

It is your shame, (I speake to you all, you yong Jentlemen of England) that one mayd should go beyond you all, in excellencie of learnyng, and knowledge of divers tonges. Pointe forth six of the best given Jentlemen of this Court, and all they together, shew not so much good will, spend not so much tyme, bestow not so many houres, dayly orderly, & constantly, for the increase of learning & knowledge, as doth the Queenes Majestie her selfe. Yea I beleve, that beside her perfit readines, in *Latin*, *Italian*, *French*, & *Spanish*, she readeth here now at Windsore more Greeke every day, than some Prebendarie of this Chirch doth read *Latin* in a whole weeke. And that which is most praise worthie of all, within the walles of her privie chamber, she hath obteyned that excellencie of learnyng, to understand, speake, & write, both wittely with head, and faire with hand, as scarse one or two rare wittes in both the Universities have in many yeares reached unto. Amongest all the benefites yt God hath blessed me with all, next the knowledge of Christes true Religion, I counte this the greatest, that it pleased God to call me, to be one poore minister in settyng forward these excellent giftes of learnyng in this most excellent Prince. Whose onely example, if the rest of our nobilitie would folow, than might England be, for learnyng and wisedome in nobilitie, a spectacle to all the world beside. But see the mishap of men: The best examples have never such forse to move to any goodnes, as the bad vaine, light and fond, have to all ilnes.

ibid., pp. 216–20

A COUNTRYMAN'S VIEW OF LEARNING 1618

This extract, dating from the early part of the seventeenth century, provides an interesting comment on the spread of education among the gentry. It shows quite explicitly that not all were convinced of the necessity of learning or courtly manners, and this antagonism between Court and Country had wider political implications, contributing to the divisions which eventually culminated in the Civil War.

Now for learning, what your neede is thereof I know not, but with us, this is all we goe to schoole for; to read common Prayers at Church, and set downe common prises at Markets; write a Letter, and make a Bond; set downe the day of our Births, our Marriage Day, and make our Wills when we are sicke, for the disposing of our goods when we are dead: these are the chiefe matters that we meddle with, and we find enough to trouble our heads withall; for if the fathers knowe their owne children, wives their owne husbands from other men, maydens keep their by your leaves from subtle batchelors; Farmers know their cattle by the heads, and Sheepheards know their sheepe by the brand, What more learning have we need of, but that experience will teach us without booke? We can learne to plough and harrow, sow and reape, plant and prune, thrash and fanne, winnow and grinde, brue and bake, and all without booke; and these are our chiefe businesse in the Country, except we be Jury-men to hang a theefe, or speake truth in a mans right, which conscience & experience wil teach us with a little learning. Then what should we study for, except it were to talke with the man in the Moone about the course of the Starres? No, Astronomy is too high a reach for our reason: we will rather sit under a shady tree in the Sunne to take the benefit of the cold ayre, then lye and stare upon the Starres to mark their walke in the heavens, while wee loose our wits in the cloudes: and yet we reverence learning as well in the Parson of our parish, as our Schoolemaster, but chiefely, in our Justices of peace, for under God and the King they beare great sway in the Country. But for great learning, in great matters, and in great places, wee leave it to great men. If we live within the compasse of the Law, serve God and obey our King, and as good Subjects ought to doe, in our duties and our prayers dayly remember him, What neede we more of learning?

NICHOLAS BRETON *The Court and Country or A Briefe Discourse Dialogue-wise set downe betweene a Courtier and a Countryman* (1618). Edited by W. C. HAZLITT in *Inedited Tracts*, pp. 191–2 (New York: Burt Franklin, 1963)

Universities in the Sixteenth Century

The growth of the view that education was no longer a matter merely for clerks, but the proper attribute of a gentleman, led to an increased demand for places at the universities. The sons of the nobility and the gentry now flocked to Oxford and Cambridge, and though their purpose was often more social than academic, nevertheless they acquired an acquaintance with higher education which could not fail to have some impact on society.*

WILLIAM HARRISON'S DESCRIPTION OF THE UNIVERSITIES

William Harrison wrote his *Description of England* for Holinshed's *Chronicle* and it was first published in 1577 and then enlarged for a second edition of 1587. Harrison had studied at both Oxford and Cambridge before taking Holy Orders and becoming Chaplain to Sir William Brooke, Lord Cobham, and Rector of Radwinter in Essex. His account is comprehensive, dealing with the buildings, the students, including the difficulties of poor men's sons in gaining entrance, the studies and the degrees.

In my time there are three noble universities in England, to wit, one at Oxford, the second at Cambridge, and the third in London; of which, the first two are the most famous, I mean Cambridge and Oxford, for that in them the use of the tongues, philosophy, and the liberal sciences, besides the profound studies of the civil law, physic, and theology, are daily taught and had: whereas in the latter, the laws of the realm are only read and learned, by such as give their minds unto the knowledge of the same. In the first there are not only diverse goodly houses builded four square for the most part of hard freestone or brick, with great numbers of lodgings and chambers in the same for students, after a sumptuous sort, through the exceeding liberality of kings, queens, bishops, noblemen and ladies of the land: but also large livings and great revenues bestowed upon them (the like whereof is not to be seen in any other region, as Peter Martyr did oft affirm) to the maintenance only of such convenient numbers of poor mens sons as the several stipends bestowed upon the said houses are able to support . . .

**Further reading:*

M. H. CURTIS *Oxford and Cambridge in Transition* 1558–1642 (Oxford: Clarendon Press, 1959)

C. E. MALLET *A History of the University of Oxford*, 3 vols, especially Vol. 2 on 16th and 17th centuries (London: Methuen, 1924–7)

K. CHARLTON *Education in Renaissance England*, Chapter V (London: Routledge and Kegan Paul, 1965)

The colleges of Oxford, for curious workmanship and private commodities, are much more stately, magnificent, and commodious than those of Cambridge: and thereunto the streets of the town for the most part more large and comely. But for uniformity of building, orderly compaction and regiment, the town of Cambridge, as the newer workmanship, exceedeth that of Oxford which otherwise is, and hath been, the greater of the two by many a fold although I know diverse that are of the contrary opinion. This also is certain, that whatsoever the difference be in building of the town streets, the townsmen of both are glad when they match and annoy the students, by encroaching upon their liberties, and keep them bare by extreme sale of their wares, whereby many of them become rich for a time, but afterward fall again into poverty, because that goods evil gotten do seldom long endure . . .

In each of these universities also is likewise a church dedicated to the Virgin Mary, wherein once in the year, to wit, in July, the scholars are holden, and in which such as have been called to any degree in the year precedent, do there receive the accomplishment of the same, in solemn and sumptuous manner. In Oxford this solemnity is called an Act, but in Cambridge they use the French word Commencement; and such resort is made yearly unto the same from all parts of the land, by the friends of those which do proceed, that all the town is hardly able to receive and lodge those guests . . .

The common schools of Cambridge also are far more beautiful than those of Oxford, only the divinity school at Oxford excepted, which for fine and excellent workmanship, cometh next the mould of the king's chapel in Cambridge, than the which, two with the chapel that king Henry the seventh did build at Westminster, there are not (in mine opinion) made of lime and stone three more notable piles within the compass of Europe.

In all other things there is so great equality between these two universities, as no man can imagine how to set down any greater; so that they seem to be the body of one well ordered commonwealth, only divided by distance of place, and not in friendly consent. In speaking therefore of the one, I can not but describe the other; and in commendation of the first, I can not but extol the latter; and so much the rather, for that they are both so dear unto me, as that I can not readily tell unto whether of them I owe the most good will. Would to God my knowledge were such, as that neither of them might have cause to be ashamed of their pupil; or my power so great, that I might worthily requite them both for those manifold kindnesses that I have received of them. But to leave these things, and proceed with other more convenient for my purpose. The manner to live in these universities, is not as in some other of foreign countries we see daily to happen, where the students are enforced for want of such houses, to dwell in common inns and taverns, without all order or discipline. But in these our colleges we live in such exact order, and under so precise rules of government, as that the famous learned man Erasmus of Rotterdam being here among us fifty years passed, did not let to compare the trades in living of students in these two places, even with the very rules and orders of the ancient monks: affirming moreover in flat words, our orders to be such as not only came near unto, but rather far exceeded all the monastical institutions that ever were devised.

In most of our colleges there are also great numbers of students, of which many are found by the revenues of the houses, and other by the purveyances and help of their rich friends; whereby in some one college you shall have two hundred scholars, in others an hundred and fifty, in diverse a hundred and forty, and in the rest less numbers; as the capacitie of the said houses is able to receive: so that at this present, of one sort and other, there are about three thousand students nourished in them both . . . They were erected by their founders at the first, only for poor mens sons, whose parents were not able to bring them up unto learning: but now they have the least benefit of them, by reason the rich do so encroach upon them. And so far hath this inconvenience spread it self, that it is in my time an hard matter for a poor man's child to come by a fellowship (though he be never so good a scholar, and worthy of that room). Such packing also is used at elections, that not he which best deserveth, but he that hath most friends, though he be the worst scholar, is always surest to speed; which will turn in the end to the overthrow of learning. That some gentlemen also, whose friends have been in times past benefactors to certain of those houses, do intrude into the disposition of their estates, without all respect of order or statutes devised by the founders, only thereby to place whom they think good (and not without hope of some gain), the case is too too evident: and their attempt would soon take place, if their superiors did not provide to bridle their indevors. In some grammar schools likewise, which send scholars to these universities, it is lamentable to see what bribery is used; for yer the scholar can be preferred, such bribage is made, that poor mens children are commonly shut out, and the richer sort received (who in time past thought it dishonour to live as it were upon alms) and yet being placed, most of them study little other than histories, tables, dice, and trifles, as men that make not the living by their study the end of their purposes, which is a lamentable hearing. Beside this, being for the most part either gentlemen, or rich mens sons, they oft bring the universities into much slander. For, standing upon their reputation and liberty, they ruffle and roist it out, exceeding in apparel, and banting riotous company (which draweth them from their books unto another trade). And for excuse, when they are charged with breach of all good order, think it sufficient to say that they be gentlemen, which grieveth many not a little. But to proceed with the rest.

Every one of these colleges have in like manner their professors or readers of the tongues and several sciences, as they call them, which daily trade up the youth there abiding privately in their halls, to the end they may be able afterward (when their turn cometh about, which is after twelve terms) to shew themselves abroad, by going from thence into the common schools and public disputations . . . there to try their skills, and declare how they have profited since their coming thither.

Moreover in the public schools of both the universities, there are found at the princes charge (and that very largely) five professors and readers, that is to say, of divinity, of the civil law, physic, the Hebrew, and the Greek tongues. And for the other lectures, as of philosophy, logic, rhetoric, and the quadrivials, although the latter (I mean arithmetic, music, geometry, and astronomy, and with them all skill in the perspectives, are now smally regarded in either of them) the universities themselves do allow competent stipends to such as read the same, whereby they are sufficiently provided for, touching the maintenance of their estates, and no less encouraged to be diligent in their functions.

These professors in like sort have all the rule of disputations and other school exercises, which are daily used in common schools severally assigned to each of them, and such of their hearers, as by their skill shewed in the said disputations, are thought to have attained to any convenient ripeness of knowledge, according to the custom of other universities, although not in like order, are permitted solemnly to take their deferred degrees of school in the same science and faculty wherein they have spent their travel. From that time forward also, they use such difference in apparel as becometh their callings, tendeth unto gravity, and maketh them known to be called to some countenance.

The first degree, is that of the general sophisters, from whence, when they have learned more sufficiently, the rules of logic, rhetoric, and obtained thereto competent skill in philosophy, and in the mathematicals, they ascend higher unto the estate of bachelors of art, after four years, of their entrance into their sophistry. From thence also giving their minds to more perfect knowledge in some or all the other liberal sciences & the tongues, they rise at the last, (to wit, after other three or four years) to be called masters of art, each of them being at that time reputed for a doctor in his faculty, if he profess but one of the said sciences (beside philosophy) or for his general skill, if he be exercised in them all. After this they are permitted to choose what other of the higher studies them liketh to follow, whether it be divinity, law, or physic; so that being once masters of art, the next degree, if they follow physic, is the doctorship belonging to that profession; and likewise in the study of the law, if they bend their minds to the knowledge of the same. But if they mean to go forward with divinity, this is the order used in that profession. First, after they have necessarily proceeded masters of art, they preach one sermon to the people in English, and another to the university in Latin. They answer all comers also in their own persons unto several questions of divinity in the open schools, at one time, for the space of two hours; and afterward reply twice against some other man upon a like number, and on two several dates in the same place: which being done with commendation, he receiveth the fourth degree, that is, bachelor of divinity, but not before he hath been master of art by the space of seven years, according to their statutes.

The next and last degree of all, is the doctorship, after other three years, for the which he must once again perform all such exercises and acts as are afore remembered; and then is he reputed able to govern and teach others, & likewise taken for a doctor . . . Thus we see, that from our entrance into the university unto the last degree received, is commonly eighteen or peradventure twenty years, in which time if a student hath not obtained sufficient learning, thereby to serve his own turn, and benefit his commonwealth, let him never look, by tarrying longer, to come by any more. For after this time & 40 years of age, the most part of students do commonly give over their wonted diligence, & live like drone bees on the fat of colleges, witholding better wits from the possession of their places, & yet doing little good in their own vocation and calling. I could rehearse a number (if I listed) of this sort, as well in the one university as the other. But this shall suffice instead of a larger report, that long continuance in those places is either a sign of lack of friends, or of learning, or of good and upright life, as bishop Fox (founder of Corpus Christi College, Oxford) sometime noted, who thought it sacrilege for a man to tarry any longer at Oxford than he had a desire to profit.

A man may (if he will) begin his study with the law or physic (of which this giveth wealth, the other honour) so soon as he cometh to the university, if his knowledge in the tongues and ripeness of judgement serve therefore: which if he do, then his first degree is bachelor of law, or physic, and for the same he must perform such acts in his own science, as the bachelors or doctors of divinity, do for their parts, the only sermons except, which belong not to his calling. Finally, this will I say, that the professors of either of those faculties come to such perfection in both universities, as the best students beyond the sea do in their own or elsewhere. One thing only I mislike in them, and that is their usual going into Italy, from whence very few without special grace do return good men, whatsoever they pretend of conference or practice, chiefly the physicians, who under pretence of seeking of foreign samples, do oftentimes learn the framing of such compositions as were better unknown than practised, as I have heard oft alleged, and therefore it is most true that doctor Turner said; Italy is not to be seen without a guide, that is, without special grace given from God, because of the licentious and corrupt behaviour of the people.

There is moreover in every house a master (or provost) who hath under him a president, and certain censors or deans, appointed to look to the behaviour and manners of the students there, whom they punish very severely if they make any default, according to the quantity and quality of their trespasses. And these are the usual names of governors in Cambridge. Howbeit in Oxford the heads of houses are now and then called presidents in respect of such bishops as are their visitors and founders. In each of these also they have one or more treasurers whom they call Bursars beside other officers, whose charge is to see unto the welfare and maintenance of these houses. Over each university also there is a several chancellor, whose offices are perpetual, howbeit their substitutes, whom we call vicechancellors, are changed every year, as are also the proctors, taskers, masters of the streets and other officers for the better maintenance of their policy and estate . . .

To these two also we may in like sort add the third, which is at London (serving only for such as study the laws of the realm) where there are sundry famous houses, of which three are called by the name of Inns of Court, the rest of the chancery, and all builded before time for the furtherance and commodity of such as apply their minds to our common laws. Out of these also come many scholars of great fame, whereof the most part have heretofore been brought up in one of the aforesaid universities, and prove such commonly as in process of time, rise up (only through their profound skill) to great honour in the commonwealth of England. They have also degrees of learning among themselves, and rules of discipline, under which they live most civilly in their houses, albeit that the younger sort of them abroad in the streets are scarce able to be bridled by any good order at all. Certes this error was wont also greatly to reign in Cambridge and Oxford, between the students and the burgesses: but as it is well left in these two places, so in foreign countries it cannot yet be suppressed.

WILLIAM HARRISON *Description of England*, Bk. II, chap 3 (1587).
Edited by F. J. FURNIVALL, pp. 70–83 (London, 1877)

STATUTES REGARDING STUDENTS' DRESS, OXFORD, 1576

The concern to regulate student dress in the sixteenth century provides a notable contrast with conditions in twentieth century universities, and also indicates the differences in function which university authorities have seen as appropriate to themselves in the past.

Decrees and orders made by the Authoritye of the Convocation holden the xxiii and xxuii Iulii Anno Domini 1576 for the reformation of excesse and some disorders in aparell.

1. Inprimis it is ordered that all they that shale proceede this next Acte shall provide them Gownes and Hoodds against that time and then weare the same when they come abrode into the universitye uppon paine of forfeiting 6s. 8d.

2. Item that every one which by the Decree made for that purpose is bound to weare a Square Capp shale before the 6 of Julye next cominge provide him such a one and allwayes after weare the same or the like according to the meaning of the same decree under the Paine thereto annexed.

3. Item that the Statute of the Relme for Ruffs and hoes shall be observed and put in exequution at all times after the first day of October nexte followinge and that none of the Persons mencioned in the saide Statute shale weare any Scalions of Velvet, of Silke or of any other colour then black or any Gascons or Venetians at all ether within the universitye or without under paine of forfeyting 8s. 4d. for the first time, and for the second time 26s. 8d. and so toties quoties.

4. Item that after the sayde 6 Day of July no Maister of Art nor Bachiler nor Scholler of College nor Hall of what facultye somever he be shale weare any Dublet or Jerkin of Blew, greene, Redd, white, or other lite colour or layd with lace gard, welt or Cutt or Pincked except he weare a cote with the sleeves on uppon the same and that none of the Persons before saide shale make ether any such or any of Silcke or Velvett in Part or in all blackefacing only excepted after the saide Day. Provided neverthelesse that it shall be lawfull for Lords and knights Sones and the Heires of Esquires not being Graduats to weare Dublets or Jerkins of Silk so they be of decent colour and fascion to be allowed by the Vicechancelor the paine of thos that transgress this order is the first time 3s. 4d. and 2 time 6s. 4d. and so toties quoties.

5. Item that no Graduat or Scholler of any College shale weare when he is abroad out of the universitye any Hatt of any other colour then Blacke or having any other colour but one or therin but blacke or Fether Broch Aglet or Bugle and that no other Graduat or Scholler or Ecclesiasticall Person shale within the universitye weare any other Hatt then such except Lords and knights sones and the Heyres of Esquires under paine of forfeyting 2s. 6d. for the firste Time 5s. for the 2 and so toties quoties.

6. Item that the Statute allreadye made for wearing of Gownes and

Hoodds shall be observed and putt in exequution at all times after the first of October next insuing and that no Scholler other then such as are before excepted shale after that day weare any gowne of any light colour or of Tuft Mockadoe except it be Blacke or any Layd on with any Lace or Garde under the paine of forfeytinge 2s. 6d. for the first time, 5s. for the 2 time and so toties quoties . . .

9. Item that the Proctors for the time being shale levye thes paines uppon such as they shall see or ootherwise know to offend against any of the præmises and that if any taken in any the offenses aforsaide by the Proctors or otherwise prooved before them to have committed the same shale deny to pay any the saide Paines by them forfeited or being required to pay them doe not within 3 dayes after such request or demande made thereof pay the same: he shale then by the Proctors be accused to the Vicechanceller, by him to be judged to pay dubble that paine which he before had forfeyted, and if the Proctors shall not demande the Paines before mencioned of such as they shall know or see to offende against any of the orders or decrees aforsaide . . . then thei for every such default shale forfeyt the Triple value of the paine forfeyted by such persons.

STRICKLAND GIBSON (ed.) *Statuta Antiqua Universitatis Oxoniensis*, pp. 403–5 (Oxford: Clarendon Press, 1931)

STATUTE TO PREVENT DISORDER, OXFORD, 1584

This extract gives an interesting picture of student social life, including a ban on attendance at plays, together with the views of the Chancellor, the Earl of Leicester, on the value of drama.

Statuts provided for all such disorders as latly have bin complained of by her Majestie and so certified unto us by the Right honorable the Earele of Leycester our Chauncellor in his last letters concerninge the reformacion of abuses in this Universitye.

1. In Primis wheare as her highnesse is informed that all orderly procedinge unto our degrees by tolleracions and dispensacions is almost quite taken awaye. It is provided that all exercise and tearme of yeares shall be fullfilled be fore it shall be lawfull to propose any grace for any bachiler of devinitye lawe or phisicke and that no bachiler in anye of these faculties shall have his grace proposed to be doctor be fore he have reade his cursorye and those of devinitye have made theare sermons ad clerum except kinges sunns Earles sunns and all Lordes sonnes and all Lords of the parleament.

2. Item wheare as bye our olde statutes every bachiler must reade certaine bookes of aristotle for his forme which lectures for that they have bin divers times read very unprofitably it is decreed that in sted

of that every bachiler shall reade for his forme six sollemne lectures three in morrall and three in naturall Philosophy out of Aristotle betwene one and twoo of the Clocck in the tearme time the parvis bell knowlinge theare unto as unto other lecturs and so graces to be asked under that forme and that no grace be proposed ether for scholler to be bachiler or bachiler to be master be fore both tearme of years and all exercises theere unto belonginge be fulfilled.

3. Item it is decreed that everye student in devinitye beinge minister whether he be of Colledge or Hawle shall be comppelled to preach in his course accordinge to his senioritye in the universitye beinge warned theare unto by the bedle six weeks be fore his time or to provid sum sufficient person to supplye his place whome the vicechauncellor shall like of or to sustaine the penaltye which is appoynted for those that do not answeare in thear course and in that manner to be executid.

4. Item it beinge crediblie informed that diverse ministers abidinge in this universitye especially non residentes do use open plainge at foot ball and maintaininge of quarrelles to the great discredit of this universitye and the vocacion wheare unto they are called. It is theare fore provided that if any minister or deacon shall go in to the feelde to playe at football or beare any weapon to make any fray or mainetaine anye quarrell he shall forth with be banished the universitie and a speciall letter sent to the Boshopp of the dioces (if he be beneficed) to geve intelligence of his banishment and that he cannot under pretence of studie in the universitie be absent from his charge. It is furder provided that if any master Bachiler or scholler not beinge ministers beinge above the age of eightene shall offend in any of thease thinges in this statute specified he shall forfeite for the first time 20s. and suffer imprisonment as in case of perturbance of peace. The second time 40s. and to suffer as before the third time banishment of the universitye with owt restitution. And if it happen any person beinge under the age of eightene to offend against the meaninge of this statute he shall suffer open punnishment in St Maries Church accordinge to the discrecion of the vicechauncellor or Proctors.

Item uppon consideracion of sicknesse wheare with this universitye of late hath oftentimes been grevoslye visited by reson of the extraordenary concuorse of people at unsesonable times of the yeare to see stage playse and games it hath bin thought a matteir most convenient as well for the maintaninge of health amounge us as allso for the detaninge of the younger sort from extraordinary spendinge more then theire smale exhibicion will beare and most of all that they maye not be spectators of so manye lewde and evil sportes as in them are practised, that no commen stage players be permitted to use or do anye such thinge with in the precincte of the universitye. And if it happen by extraordinarye meanes that stage players shall gett or obtaine leave by the maior or other wayse yet it shall not be lawfull for any master bachiler or scholler above the age of eighteene to repaire or go to see anye such thinge under paine of imprisonment . . .

The confirmacion of thease statutes above specified by the right honorable the L. of Leycester our Chauncellor by his one hande.

As I like and alowe all thease statutes and articles above written and namelye in the fivth article do think the prohibicion of commen stage players very requisite so wolde I not have it meant theare bye theat the tragedies commodies and other shewes of exercises of learninge in that kinde usid to be sett fourth by universitye men should be forbedden but acceptinge them as commendable and greate furderances of learninge do wish them in anye wise to be continuid at fit times and incresed and the youth of the universitye by good meanes to be incurragid to the decent and frequent settinge fourth of them. R. Leycester.

STRICKLAND GIBSON (ed.) *Statuta Antiqua Universitatis Oxoniensis*, pp. 431–4 (Oxford: The Clarendon Press, 1931)

FOUNDATION OF LECTURESHIP IN ANATOMY, OXFORD, 1624

Universities were slow to develop scientific studies but this extract indicates their beginning in the seventeenth century on a new basis which was more experimental and less reliant upon the works of the classical authorities such as Aristotle, and in the case of medicine, Galen.

Statutes and ordinances made and established by the Chancelor Masters and Schollers of the Universitie of Oxon. by and with the consent of Richard Tomlins of the Citty of Westminster Esquier, touching and concerning a Lecture of Anatomy founded and constituted by the said Richard Tomlins in the said Universitie.

Forasmuch as the knowledge and true understanding of mans body and the partes and faculties of the same doth much conduce to the honor and glory of god our mightie and wonderfull creator And is also of great use to the Professors of Divinitie, Philosophy and all other good Literature and more particularly necessary for the faculties and Artes of Phisicke and Chirurgery, the perfection whereof doth much avayle to the safety health and comfort of the whole Common wealth in the conservation of theire persons: And that there is as yet in neither of the Universities of this Kingdome (thoughe otherwise the most florisshing of the whole Christian world) any such Anotomy Lecture founded or establisshed Therefore hee the said Richard Tomlins first and chiefly to the honor and glory of god, as also for the good and benefitt of this common wealth, and out of his Reverent respect and affection to the said famous Universitie of Oxon., doth by these presentes (with the consent and approbation of the said Universitie) found constitute and ordayne an Anatomye Lector to bee for ever read and performed in the said Universitie in manner and forme following.

1. First the said Richard Tomlins doth nominate and make speciall choyce of his worthy frend Thomas Clayton Doctor of Phisicke and his Majesties Professor thereof in the said Universitie to bee the first Reader of the said Lecture, whome hee doth request to undergoe the same, and to bee very carefull (nowe especially in the beginning thereof) in the performance of the same to the most advancing and furthering of the uses beefore specified, and for a perpetuall Succession and continuance of the said Office and place of Anatomy Reader after the death of the said Dr Clayton or other avoyding of the said place, the said Founder doth ordayne and appointe that the Kings Professor of Phisicke in the said Universitie for the time being shall ever heereafter bee the Reader of the said Anatomy Lecture.

2. The said Reader of Anatomy shall every Springe immediately after the Assisses commonly called the Lent Assisses for the County of Oxon., upon the procuring of a Sounde body of one of the Executed persons (if any such bee) or of some other body assoone as conveniently may bee, cause the said body to bee prepared and dissected by a skilfull Chirurgian: And hee the said Reader shall publiquely shewe, teach and deliver the Scituation, Nature, Use and office, of the partes of the body in ffoure distinct Lectures or publique meetings in forme following.

3. The next Morning or the second at the furthest after the death of the person to be dissected (in the publique Phisicke Schoole or other place appointed for the same) the body shall bee ready prepared beetwixt 8 and 9 of the Clocke in the forenone and the Reader with the Chirurgian standing by him (for the severing lyfting up and shewing of the parts) shall for two houres space shewe the Scituation, Nature and office of the partes commonly called Naturall videlicet Liver Spleene Stomake Guttes &c.

4. The same day in the afternoone the Reader beginning at two of the Clocke shall (in two houres) further deliver and teache the Scituation, Nature and use of the same Naturall partes.

5. The next morning immediately following The Reader shall deliver publiquely (in two houres as aforesaid), the Scituation Nature and office of the partes commonly called Vitall videlicet Hart Lunges &c.

6. The same day after noone (beginning at two of the Clocke) the Reader shall in two houres shew and teach the Scituation Nature and Office of the Animall partes and faculties videlicet the Brayne &c.

7. The said Reader shall also every Michelmas terme beginninge at the usuall houres of the Phisicke Lecture in three distinct Lectures

reade the Sceleton or History of the bones with theire Scituation Nature and office three severall dayes in one weeke publiquely in the Schooles.

13. The Auditors or Hearers necessarily bound to Attend the said Lectures shal bee all the Studentes of Phisicke and all the Chirurgions in the Universities and every one of the said Studentes (*not licentiate to practise phisicke*) and Chirurgians fayling to bee present, shall for every such absence (not allowed by the Reader) forfeyte the Summe of 2s. the one halfe thereof to bee devided amongst the Beedles of Artes the rest to the use of the said Lecture.

14. That every one admitted by the Universitie to Practise phisicke or Chirurgy shall before hee propose his grace for the said Licence bring Testimony or make faith that hee hath bin present at least at one whole Anatomicall dissection and at one whole reading of a sceleton. *Except hee bee dispenced with by congregation.*

STRICKLAND GIBSON (ed.) *Statuta Antiqua Universitatis Oxoniensis*, pp. 551–4 (Oxford: The Clarendon Press, 1931)

The Puritan Revolution and Education

Much of the educational legislation of the Long Parliament was abortive and the work of Cromwell and his Council during the Protectorate was limited in its effects. Nevertheless the ideas of Puritan reformers as Samuel Hartlib (1600–1662), John Dury (1596–1680) and the Moravian Comenius (1592–1670) had a delayed effect in influencing educational development in subsequent centuries and particularly in the Dissenting Academies which developed after the religious legislation of the Restoration had evicted many scholars from their existing teaching posts and livings.*

SAMUEL HARTLIB ON THE IMPORTANCE OF EDUCATION IN THE COMMONWEALTH

Samuel Hartlib who had encouraged John Dury to write *The Reformed School*, wrote a preface to it on its publication c. 1650. In this extract he makes clear his own and the Puritan view of the central importance of education, and in particular of school teachers, as a means of social betterment.

For it is not possible that the extraordinary strains and distempers whereinto we are fallen in these times, can be reformed without some extraordinary ability, either of outward authority and power to restrain exemplary disorderliness, or of inward conviction, to lead men captive under the yoke of Christ; which are things wholly decayed, nowadays, amongst the professions of men. Seeing, then, the corruptions of those that are of age are too strong and sturdy to be conquered by ordinary and weak means, and none extraordinary or strong enough are apparent, it followeth that there is none other way left but to deal with the young ones before any corrupt habits and perverse engagements be confirmed upon them; that they may be trained up from their infancy to a course of reformation, both of virtue and learning. But because the training up of scholars in one school or two, though very great and most exactly reformed, will be but an inconsiderable matter in respect of a whole nation and have no great influence upon the youth thereof, where so many schools remain unreformed and propagate corruptions, therefore the propagation of reformed schools is mainly aimed at; and to that

**Further reading:*

W. A. L. VINCENT *The State and School Education 1640–1660 in England and Wales* (Society for the Promotion of Christian Knowledge, 1950)

effect, the training up of reformed schoolmasters is one of the chief parts of this design.

Now to endeavour to make out this, that the readier way to reform both Church and Commonwealth is to reform the schools of education therein, and that the way to reform these is to send forth reformed schoolmasters amongst them, is, as I suppose, altogether superfluous; for it cannot be thought that any rational man should be such a stranger unto the affairs of human societies as not to see that from the ordinary schools all magistrates and ministers and officers of state are taken throughout the nations of the world to be set over others, and that the impressions both of vice and virtue which they have received in the schools, are exercised and become effectual for good or evil, afterward, in their places towards the Church and Commonwealth: so that the schools are to be looked upon as the ordinary and natural fountains of a settlement, as of our corruption so of our reformation, if God will bless us with any. And the schoolmaster in a well ordered Commonwealth is not less considerate than either the minister or the magistrate, because neither the one nor the other will prosper or subsist long without him. I shall not need to add anything further concerning this subject to make thee sensible either of the usefulness of the undertaking or of the scope of my negotiation in it.

JOHN DURY *The Reformed School.* Edited by H. M. KNOX, pp. 19–20 (Liverpool Univ. Press, 1958)

DURY'S VIEW OF THE PURPOSE OF EDUCATION

In this extract Dury presents the Puritan view of education, emphasizing its serious and social purposes. It is noteworthy that he suggests that girls should receive education as well as boys.

The rule, then, according to which their education is to be reformed fundamentally, is this.

That no time of the day is to be lost without some teaching exercise; and that nothing is to be taught but that which is useful in itself to the society of mankind, therein fitting them for employments approvable by the Gospel, and which will bring them to behave themselves so as it becometh those who are called to walk with the lamb upon Mount Sion in the presence of God, that is, as saints in his Church.

Upon this ground, all the matters of show and appearance which please the fancies of men in the world, whether they be in points of knowledge or practice (wherein all the time of the youth is most commonly spent in ordinary schools), are to be laid aside in the course of this education.

Therefore as to the girls, the ordinary vanity and curiosity of their dressing of hair and putting on of apparel, the customs and principles of wantonness and bold behaviours which in their dancings are taught them, and whatsoever else doth tend only to foment pride and satisfy curiosity and imaginary delights shall be changed, by this our course of education, into plain, decent cleanliness and healthful ways of apparelling themselves; and into such exercises of their hearts, heads and hands, which may habituate them through the fear of God to become good and careful housewives, loving towards their husbands and their children when God shall call them to be married, and understanding in all things belonging to the care of a family, according to the characters which Solomon doth give of a virtuous godly woman. And such as may be found capable of tongues and sciences (to perfect them in graces and the knowledge of Christ, for all is to be referred to him, above the ordinary sort) are not to be neglected, but assisted towards the improvement of their intellectual abilities.

As for the boys, the same rule is to be observed in the way of their education, both for tongues, sciences and employments. So that all the preposterous methods of teaching the same, by which not only their time is lost but their spirits and affections are inured to evil customs of disorderliness, of vanity, pride and self-conceitedness, which is the root of all our contentions about matters of learning and science falsely so called, and all the unprofitable exercises of their mind and body in things which take them off from the aim of Christianity unto the customs of the world shall be altered into profitable employments which may fit them to be good Commonwealthsmen, by the knowledge of all things which are fundamental for the settlement of a state in husbandry, in necessary trades, in navigation, in civil offices for the administration of justice, in peace and war, and in economical duties by which they may be serviceable to their own families and to their neighbours.

JOHN DURY *The Reformed School*. Edited by H. M. KNOX, pp. 25–6 (Liverpool Univ. Press, 1958)

DURY'S RULES OF TEACHING

Dury's views on teaching method were revolutionary in their time, but they have since become increasingly acceptable. They were similar to the views of other reformers as Comenius and this is shown in the following extract with its emphasis on the vernacular and the teaching of 'words' through 'things', for Comenius embodied these ideas in his textbook for children *Orbis Sensualium Pictus* (see pp. 120–3). Languages are seen as means to 'real truths in sciences' rather than ends in themselves. The final part of the extract provides a wise and succinct account of some general principles of pedagogy.

From these maxims we gather these following rules of teaching:

1. The teaching of arts and sciences ought not to be suspended upon the teaching of unknown tongues, but made familiar unto the children's capacity in their mother-tongue first and afterward enlarged by the use of other tongues.

2. The arts and sciences which lead us most directly unto the use of the creatures without any reflexion upon our own faculties are first to be taught, because they may be taken up by the simple acts of sense, imagination and memory without much reasoning.

3. The arts and sciences which lead us to reflect upon the use of our own faculties are not to be taught till we are fully acquainted with their proper objects and the direct acts of the faculties about them.

4. The knowledge of tongues is the proper effect of memory and not of any reasoning ability, because they depend upon the observation only of that which is the constant custom of people and not upon any rational inducement why they do so; whence followeth: (1) that those things which are most helpful and subservient unto memory are to be set awork in teaching languages rather than those that employ the judgment; (2) that the ways which fix and order the imagination most effectually towards the sound of the words and the thing signified thereby, are most advantageous to this way of teaching; (3) that the teaching of words is not further useful than the things signified thereby are familiar to the imagination; and that the teaching of rules before the material sense of the words is known or before the formal coherence of things which their construction is to represent in a sentence can be apprehended, is wholly preposterous and unprofitable to the memory.

5. So far as children are capable of traditional knowledge, so far in every degree of science they may be taught the tongues which serve for that use; but till they be fitted for the one, the other is useless to them.

6. Whatsoever in the teaching of tongues doth not tend to make them a help unto traditional knowledge by the manifestation of real truths in sciences is superfluous and not to be insisted upon, especially towards children; whence followeth that the curious study of criticisms and observations of styles in authors, and of strains of wit which speak nothing of reality in sciences, are to be left to such as delight in vanities more than in truths.

From these maxims and rules the rationality of the ensuing method may be made out to the full, if time did permit. But we shall not insist upon that now; only we shall show that by them we are led to teach and consider matters of learning in this order.

First, to consider the children that are to be taught; secondly, the things which are to be taught unto them; thirdly, the manner and way of teaching the same.

Concerning the children, we must reflect upon their ordinary capacities and distinguish the same into their natural degrees.

Concerning the things which are to be taught, we must reflect upon a twofold proportion therein: first, we must find out that which is proportionate to the degree of everyone's capacity; secondly, we must order everything which is suitable to each capacity proportionally to the end for which it is to be taught, as in its proper place it is subordinate unto other things which must follow in the course of education.

Concerning the way and manner of teaching and proposing the same, we must study by the properties of things to be taught to find all manner of advantages, and according to circumstances determine the way which will bring no loss of time nor be wearisome and tedious to the children, and which will make the matters taught most easy for their apprehension and delightful to their affections in apprehending the same.

For I suppose that this conclusion in this matter is as firm as any mathematical demonstration in other matters, viz., if all degrees of children's capacities be fitted with proper objects; if none of the things which any of the faculties can receive be left untaught; if no time be lost in teaching, nor any thing offered before it be seasonable; if that which is taught in the first place be not disjointed from that which followeth after but made a step thereunto; if all matters offered, by their conjunction, make him that receiveth them a perfect man, leading him without distraction to his true end; and if no servile constraint be laid upon the inclination of him that is taught, by forcible means to break his spirits, but his affections raised to a delightful willingness to receive that which is offered, by allurements and general insinuations readily: if (I say) all these things be observed in the course of teaching, then little or nothing will be wanting which can be wished for towards the advancement of learning in this way or can be prosecuted by rational endeavours and human industry.

JOHN DURY *The Reformed School*. Edited by H. M. KNOX, pp. 41–4 (Liverpool Univ. Press, 1958)

THE CURRICULUM OF THE REFORMED SCHOOL

Dury provides a detailed account of the curriculum suitable for the various ages and capacities of pupils, and this extract, covering the ages thirteen to twenty, is interesting in providing a model which was later put into effect in the Dissenting Academies of the late seventeenth and eighteenth centuries. Note the emphasis put on practice and 'ocular inspection'.

Thirdly, from thirteen or fourteen till nineteen or twenty the things which are to be taught them and wherein they shall be exercised, are all the useful arts and sciences which may fit them for any employment in Church and Commonwealth. Here then all the means of traditional and rational learning are to be set afoot; and to this effect they shall be taught their grammar rules more exactly and fully than formerly and brought to read authors in all the sciences whereof they have gained the foundations, with directions how to observe the marrow and method of them and out of them to gather to themselves an encyclopedia. To this effect:

1. The Latin authors of agriculture, Cato, Varro, Columella, may be put into their hands by parcels to be an enlargement unto that which they have already been taught concerning husbandry.

2. The natural history of Pliny and others by choice parcels are also to be perused by them and brought home to what they have formerly seen, together with the histories of meteors, minerals, etc.

3. In like manner some models and books of architecture, enginery, fortification, fireworks, weapons, military discipline, and navigation are to be looked upon.

4. The Greek authors of moral philosophy, Epictetus, Cebus, Arrianus, Plato, Xenophon, Plutarch, and some Latin tracts in this kind should be read by them and an account taken of their proficiency thereby.

5. The doctrine of economics, of civil government, and natural justice and equity in the laws of nations should be offered unto them as the grounds of that jurisprudentia whereof the sum is to be given out of the Institutions of Justinian and Regulae Juris.

6. The theory of all the mathematics, with the full practice of that which was deficient in their former institution; where the optics with the instruments belonging thereunto and the art of dialling is to be entertained, and in arithmetic the way of keeping accounts.

7. The principles of natural philosophy and the main grounds of medicine, with the instruments of distilling and other chemical operations, and the art of apothecaries are to be offered unto them partly in books, partly in the operations themselves, by an ocular inspection thereof and of their drugs.

8. The art of chirurgery described in books, with an ocular inspection of all their tools, and compositions of plaisters and ointment and the use thereof.

9. The rules of logic, rhetoric and poesy, showing them first how to analyse authors and observe their art of reason and utterance to persuade; and then how to order their own thoughts and expression to search out truths and to declare the same, historically, philosophically, oratorically, poetically.

10. Directions for the study of all human histories and what to observe in them for the attainment of wisdom and prudency in the government of a man's own life, wherewith the directions to observe the ways

of others, the rules of judgment, discretion, prudency and civil conversation to order their own ways aright towards all, are to be given unto them; which is to be concluded with a special recognition and insight into Solomon's Proverbs and Ecclesiastes. And so they are to be sent into the world to apply themselves to any employment or more particular study whereunto God shall call them. For now they will be fitted thereunto so far as human industry can advance them.

JOHN DURY *The Reformed School.* Edited by H. M. KNOX, pp. 47–9 (Liverpool Univ. Press, 1958)

The Clarendon Code

The Clarendon Code, so called after the leading minister of Charles II in the years immediately after his Restoration, re-imposed ecclesiastical control over schoolmasters. The Act of Uniformity and the Five Mile Act were aimed particularly at Protestant Dissenters, preventing them from continuing their occupations as schoolmasters. One long term result of this legislation was the growth of Dissenting Academies.

In 1700 the judgment in Cox's case relieved all but grammar schools from ecclesiastical control, when it decided that 'writing schools, reading schools, dancing schools, etc.' were exempt from previous legislation. Earlier in 1670, judgment had been given in Bate's case that the patron of a school had the right to present the master of his own choice, and though in theory such a master still had to have an episcopal licence to teach, in practice it was often possible to avoid this ruling. The enforcement of subscription by schoolteachers to the Thirty Nine Articles of the Church of England depended upon individual bishops and their officers, and not all were as zealous as they might have been in this duty. Consequently as the eighteenth century progressed, freedom to follow the occupation of schoolmaster increased, though grammar schools continued on the whole under ecclesiastical jurisdiction.*

THE UNIFORMITY ACT 1662 ENJOINS OATH ON ALL TEACHERS

Now in regard that nothing conduces more to the settling of the peace of this nation (which is desired of all good men), nor to the honour of our religion, and the propagation thereof, than an universal agreement in the public worship of Almighty God . . . be it enacted by the king's most excellent majesty, by the advice and with the consent of the Lords spiritual and temporal, and of the Commons, in this present Parliament assembled, and by the authority of the same, that all and singular ministers in any cathedral, collegiate, or parish church or chapel, or other place of public worship within this realm of England, dominion of Wales, and town of Berwick-upon-Tweed, shall be bound to say and use the Morning Prayer, Evening Prayer, celebration and administration of both the sacraments, and all other the public and common prayer, in such order and form as is mentioned in the said book annexed and joined to this present Act, and entitled, The Book of

**Further reading:*

W. A. L. VINCENT *The Grammar Schools 1660–1714* (London: John Murray, 1969)

Common Prayer and Administration of the Sacraments, and other Rites and Ceremonies of the Church, according to the Use of the Church of England . . .

And be it further enacted by the authority aforesaid, that every dean, canon, and prebendary of every cathedral or collegiate church, and all masters and other heads, fellows, chaplains, and tutors of or in any college elsewhere, and every parson, vicar, curate, lecturer, and every other person in Holy Orders, and every schoolmaster keeping any public or private school and every person instructing or teaching any youth in any house or private family as a tutor or schoolmaster, who upon the first day of May, which shall be in the year of our Lord God 1662, or at any time thereafter, shall be incumbent or have possession of any deanery, canonry, prebend, mastership, headship, fellowship, professor's place or reader's place, parsonage, vicarage, or any other ecclesiastical dignity or promotion, or of any curate's place, lecture, or school, or shall instruct or teach any youth as tutor or school-master, shall before the feast-day of St. Bartholomew which shall be in the year of our Lord 1662, or at or before his or their respective admission to be incumbent or have possession aforesaid, subscribe the declaration or acknowledgement following, *scilicet*:–

'I, *A.B.*, do declare that it is not lawful, upon any pretence whatsoever, to take arms against the king; and that I do abhor that traitorous position of taking arms by his authority against his person or against those that are commissionated by him; and that I will conform to the liturgy of the Church of England, as it is now by law established: and I do declare that I do hold there lies no obligation upon me, or on any other person, from the oath commonly called the Solemn League and Covenant, to endeavour any change or alteration of government either in Church or State; and that the same was in itself an unlawful oath, and imposed upon the subjects of this realm against the known laws and liberties of this kingdom.'

Which said declaration and acknowledgment shall be subscribed by every of the said masters and other heads, fellows, chaplains, and tutors of or in any college, hall, or house of learning, and by every public professor and reader in either of the Universities, before the vice-chancellor of the respective Universities for the time being or his deputy: and the said declaration or acknowledgment shall be subscribed before the respective archbishop, bishop, or ordinary of the diocese, by every other person hereby enjoined to subscribe the same; upon pain that all and every of the persons aforesaid failing in such subscription shall lose and forfeit such respective deanery, canonry, prebend, mastership, headship, fellowship, professor's place, reader's place, parsonage, vicarage, ecclesiastical dignity or promotion, curate's place, lecture, and school, and shall be utterly disabled and (*ipso facto*) deprived of the same . . .

And if any schoolmaster, or other person, instructing or teaching youth in any private house or family as a tutor or schoolmaster, shall instruct or teach any youth as a tutor or schoolmaster, before licence obtained from his respective archbishop, bishop, or ordinary of the diocese, according to the laws and statutes of this realm (for which he shall pay twelve pence only), and before such subscription and acknowledgment made as aforesaid; then every such schoolmaster and other, instructing and teaching as aforesaid, shall for the first offence suffer three months' imprisonment without bail or mainprize; and for every second, and other such offence, shall suffer three months' imprisonment without bail or mainprize, and also forfeit to his majesty the sum of five pounds: and after such subscription made, every such parson, vicar, curate and lecturer shall procure a certificate under the hand and seal of the respective archbishop, bishop, or ordinary of the diocese (who are hereby enjoined and required upon demand to make and delivery the same), and shall publicly and openly read the same, together with the declaration or acknowledgment aforesaid, upon some Lord's day within three months then next following, in his parish church where he is to officiate, in the presence of the congregation there assembled, in the time of divine service; upon pain that every person failing therein shall lose such parsonage, vicarage or benefice, curate's place, or lecturer's place respectively, and shall be utterly disabled and (*ipso facto*) deprived of the same; and that the said parsonage, vicarage or benefice, curate's place, or lecturer's place shall be void, as if he was naturally dead.

GEE and HARDY (eds.) *Documents Illustrative of the History of the English Church*, pp. 603–9 (London: Macmillan, 1914)

THE FIVE MILE ACT 1665 PREVENTS DISSENTERS HOLDING SCHOOLS

Whereas divers parsons, vicars, curates, lecturers, and other persons in Holy Orders, have not declared their unfeigned assent and consent to the use of all things contained and prescribed in the Book of Common Prayer and Administration of the Sacraments . . .

Be it therefore enacted by the king's most excellent majesty . . . that the said parsons, vicars, curates, lecturers, and other persons in Holy Orders, or pretended Holy Orders, or pretending to Holy Orders, and all stipendiaries and other persons who have been possessed of any ecclesiastical or spiritual promotion, and every of them, who have not declared their unfeigned assent and consent as aforesaid, and subscribed the declaration aforesaid, and shall not take and subscribe the oath following:

'I, *A.B.*, do swear that it is not lawful upon any pretence whatsoever to take arms against the king; and that I do abhor that traitorous position of taking arms by his authority against his person, or against those that are commissionated by him in pursuance of such commissions; and that I will not at any time endeavour any alteration of government, either in Church or State.'

And all such person and persons as shall take upon them to preach in any unlawful assembly, conventicle, or meeting, under colour or pretence of any exercise of religion, contrary to the laws and statutes of this kingdom, shall not at any time, from and after the four-and-twentieth day of March which shall be in this present year of our Lord God, 1665, unless only passing upon the road, come or be within five miles of any city or town corporate, or borough that sends burgesses to the Parliament, within his majesty's kingdom of England, principality of Wales, or of the town of Berwick-upon-Tweed, or within five miles of any parish, town, or place wherein he or they have since the Act of Oblivion been parson, vicar, curate, stipendiary, or lecturer, or taken upon them to preach in any unlawful assemble, conventicle, or meeting, under colour or pretence of any exercise of religion, contrary to the laws and statutes of this kingdom, before he or they have taken and subscribed the oath aforesaid, before the justices of peace at their quarter sessions to be holden for the county, riding, or division next unto the said corporation, city or borough, parish, place or town, in open court (which said oath the said justices are hereby empowered there to administer); upon forfeiture of (*sic*) every such offence the sum of forty pounds of lawful English money, the one third part thereof to his majesty and his successors, the other third part to the use of the poor of the parish where the offence shall be committed, and the one third part thereof to such person or persons as shall or will sue for the same by action of debt, plaint, bill, or information, in any court of record at Westminster, or before any justices of assize, *oyer* and *terminer*, or gaol delivery, or before any justices of the counties palatine of Chester, Lancaster, or Durham, or the justices of the great sessions in Wales, or before any justices of peace in their quarter sessions, wherein no essoin, protection, or wager of law shall be allowed.

Provided always, and be it further enacted by the authority aforesaid, that it shall not be lawful for any person or persons restrained from coming to any city, town corporate, borough, parish, town, or place as aforesaid, or for any other person or persons as shall not first take and subscribe the said oath, and as shall not frequent divine service established by the laws of this kingdom, and carry him or her self reverently, decently, and orderly there, to teach any public or private school, or take any boarders or tablers that are taught or instructed by him or her self, or any other, upon pain for every such offence to forfeit the sum of forty pounds, to be recovered and distributed as aforesaid. Provided also, and be it further enacted by the authority aforesaid, that it shall be lawful for any two justices of the peace of the respective county, upon oath to them of any offence against this Act, which oath they are hereby empowered to administer, to commit the offender for six months without bail or mainprize, unless upon or before such commitment he shall, before the said justices of the peace, swear and subscribe the aforesaid oath and declaration.

GEE and HARDY (eds.) *Documents Illustrative of the History of the English Church*, pp. 620–3 (London: Macmillan, 1914)

TESTIMONIES TO THE CONFORMITY OF SCHOOLMASTERS

These extracts illustrate the difficulties teachers might experience in securing a licence to teach in the decades following the Clarendon Code legislation against non-conformists.

1679

Wee whose names are heerunto subscribed beeing Inhabitants of the Towne and parish of Whitby doe humbly certifie That whereas wee are informed, some persons have cast an asperation upon Mr. Christopher Stephenson on whose behalf wee formerly Certified, desireing that hee might have a license to teach schoole in Whitby, that he is a nonconformist a Consorter with quakers and phanaticks, which was an obstruction to his proceedings in that good way of educating children, which wee know to be false and a scandall upon him, for that we have seen him a constant Church man both in Whitby and Fylingdales ever since his Coming to this parte of the Countrie, and noe consorter with phanaticks otherwise then all others doe in ordinary Communication and to this wee sett our hands this 4 Aug. 1679.
28 signatures

J. S. PURVIS (ed.) *Educational Records*, p. 63. Borthwick Inst. Historical Research document ref. No. R. IV. N. 65 (Univ. York, St Antony's Press, 1959)

1714

We John Killingbeck Clerke Vicar of the parish and parish Church of Leeds in the County of Yorke, and Mathew Towers one of the Churchwardens of the said parish Church of Leeds, do hereby Certifie that Christopher Jackson, John Lucas, Richard Bateson, William Walker, Jeremiah Mason, Lazarus Bott and Lawrence Moore Schoolmasters within the Town and Mainryding of Leeds afforesaid, upon the Lords day commonly called Sunday the first of August One Thousand Seven-hundred and fourteen immediately after divine Service and Sermon, did in the parish Church above written, receive the Sacrament of the Lords Supper according to the usage of the Church of England. In Witness whereof, we have hereunto Subscribed our hands, the day and year above written.

Signatures of the Vicar and The Churchwarden

Mr. Chancellor

The persons herein mencion'd being School-Masters in this Town who teach Grammar-Schools, apprehending themselves to be under the obligation of takeing Licences by vertue of the late Act of Parliament, for the preventing the Growth of Schism, do make their Application to you for the same, in obedience to the said Act. This certificate will shew that they all receiv'd the Holy Sacrament according to the Church of England in this parish Church on August the first. I do hereby testify that they all live in constant communion with the established Church; and do believe them all to be sufficiently qualifyd both as to Learning and sobriety for their Respective charges.

Witness my hand Aug. 1 1714 Jo. Killingbeck.

ibid., p. 57, document ref. No. R.IV.N.1367

FORM OF LICENCE TO TEACH

From 1581 subscription to the Thirty Nine Articles of the Established Church was compulsory for teachers before they were granted by the bishop a licence to teach. Not until 1869 with the Endowed Schools Act was this abolished though from 1700 onwards subscription in many areas was only partial. Diocesan Subscription Books are a source of much material for the history of education in the latter half of the seventeenth and the eighteenth century, giving information about the status of teachers and the existence of various types of schools.

The following extract shows the form of licence given in the Diocese of Norwich to a Grammar school teacher.

Charles, by divine permission Bishop of Norwich To our well beloved in Christ William Howarth of Ipswich in the County of Suffolk and within our Diocese of Norwich and jurisdiction, Clerk, Greeting. We do by these presents give and grant unto you (in whose literary abilities, morals, probity and ample learning we fully confide) our Licence and authority to perform the Office of master of the free Grammar School in Ipswich aforesaid, To which you were unanimously appointed at a great Court thereheld the 13 March 1800 as it is asserted, by publickly teaching and instructing youth there in grammar and such good authors whether in the Latin, Greek or English Tongue as are approved by the laws and statutes of this realm by observing the ordinances and statutes of the said school and by doing, performing and discharging all such other things belonging and appertaining to the office of Master of the said school as ought to be done, performed and discharged by the master thereof. Giving you hereby (as far as by Law we may) full power and authority to have, receive, take, and enjoy all the rights, dues, rents, profits and emoluments whatsoever of and belonging to the said office of master of the said free school. You having first in our presence subscribed and sworn to all things which the law in this case requires to be subscribed and sworn to And we will this our licence to endure during our pleasure and so long as you shall behave yourself worthily in your said office Given under our Episcopal Seal Dated, &c . . .

E. H. CARTER *The Norwich Subscription Books*, pp. 99–100 (London: Nelson, 1937)

Charity Schools

The term 'charity school' was used in the eighteenth century, and subsequently by historians, to cover schools of various types and origins. Too much reliance on the records of the Society for Promoting Christian Knowledge, founded in 1698, has suggested to some that there was an increase in the provision of elementary education solely due to the agency of the Church of England. Other sources make it clear that nonconformists and dissenters were also active in this field. Certainly there was an increase in schools for the poor, and these were often provided by the pooling of subscriptions from the rich in the manner of a joint-stock company. The aim was primarily social and religious – the reformation of the manners of the poorer classes, the reduction of crime through the teaching of religion and the teaching that the poor should accept their inferior position in life as part of the Divine plan. As means to these ends, reading and some writing were taught so that the Scriptures could be read; in some schools to these elementary literary skills were added some arithmetic and trade skills, such as knitting or spinning, so that the poor should be fitted for some employment and not relapse into idleness, becoming a burden on the parish ratepayers. Often the schools admitted girls as well as boys, which in itself was a notable innovation, and they usually provided a distinctive dress for their pupils in an attempt to clothe the poor decently, though an additional benefit of this was the constant reminder that it gave to the children themselves and to the rest of society, that they were indeed 'charity-children', provided for by others.*

AN ACCOUNT OF CHARITY SCHOOLS 1711

From 1704 to 1811 the Society for the Promotion of Christian Knowledge published an *Account of the Methods whereby the Charity-Schools have been Erected and Managed* (though the title differed in some editions). The editions from 1704 to 1732 are the most useful for the historian of education for, apart from the account they give of the purposes of charity schools, the qualifications of schoolmasters and the methods of management, they also give an alphabetical list of schools in the counties and often in addition the Society's annual Charity Sermon.

It is manifest, That a Christian and Useful Education of the Children

**Further reading:*

M. G. JONES *The Charity School Movement* (Cambridge Univ. Press, 1938)
JOAN SIMON 'Was there a Charity School Movement? The Leicestershire Evidence', in B. SIMON (ed.) *Education in Leicestershire 1540–1940*, pp. 55–100 (Leicester Univ. Press, 1968)

of the Poor, is very necessary to their Piety, Virtue, and honest Livelihood.

'Tis also as plain and evident, That Piety, Virtue, and an honest way of Living, are not only of absolute Necessity to their Happiness both *Here* and *Hereafter;* but are necessary also to the Ease and Security of all other People whatsoever: In as much as there is no Body but may stand in need of their Help, or be liable to receive Injuries from them.

But that which ought more especially to be the Beginning, and End of Christian Charity, is the glory of God, and the Good of Mankind. And these great and most desirable Ends cannot be by private Persons more universally and effectually secured, than by Contributing to the Christian Education and useful bringing up of the Poor.

Therefore there having of late been several Schools, called CHARITY SCHOOLS, Erected for that Purpose, namely, *For the Education of Poor Children in the Knowledge and Practice of the Christian Religion, as profess'd and Taught in the Church of England; and for Teaching them such other things as are most suitable to their Condition;* it may be of Use to give a short Account of them, and to shew how they have been Erected, and are Governed: That other People seeing the Practicableness, as well as *Charity* and *Usefulness* thereof, may be moved to encrease the Number of them.

These Schools have been sometimes propos'd by the Minister, to some of his Parish, and sometimes by two or three Persons of a Place, to the Minister of the Parish, and such others as they thought would join with them. And when four or five had agreed theron, their Way was to express in a few lines the Necessity and Usefulness of the Design on a Roll of Parchment, and subscribe thereto such sums as each of them thought fit to pay yearly (during Pleasure) towards the Charge: And generally the Minister subscribed first. And the Design thus set on Foot, they shew'd the Roll to others, and those to others, who subscribed also as they thought fit. So that when the Design became pretty well known, it commonly met with so good success, as the Subscribers have been able to set up a School in about seven or eight Months Time. After a competent Sum of Money subscribed, the next Thing the Subscribers did, was their agreeing upon, and settling certain Rules and Orders for the Governing these Schools; for the better effecting the End of the Charity, and easier Managing the same, to the Satisfaction of all concern'd, and without giving Offence. In many Schools in and about London, the Orders are to the Effect following:

I. The Master to be Elected for this School shall be

1. A Member of the Church of England, of a sober Life and Conversation, and not under the Age of 25 Years.
2. One that frequents the holy Communion.

3. One that hath a good Government of himself and Passions.
4. One of a Meek Temper and Humble Behaviour.
5. One of a good Genius for Teaching.
6. One who understands well the Grounds and Principles of the *Christian Religion*, and is able to give a good Account thereof to the Minister of the Parish, or Ordinary, on Examination.
7. One who can write a good Hand, and who understands the Grounds of Arithmetic.
8. One who keeps good Orders in his Family.
9. One who is approved by the Minister of the Parish (being a Subscriber) before he be presented to be Licensed by the Ordinary.

. . . . . .

II. The following Orders shall be observed by the Master and Scholars,

1. The Master shall constantly attend his proper Business in the School, during the Hours appointed for Teaching, viz. from 7 to 11 in the morning, and from 1 to 5 in the Evening, the *Summer* Half-Year: And from 8 to 11 in the Morning, and from 1 to 4 in the Evening, the *Winter* Half-Year; that he may improve the Children in good Learning to the utmost of his Power, and prevent the Disorders that frequently happen for want of the Master's Presence and Care.
2. To the End the *chief Design* of this School, which is for the *Education of Poor Children in the Knowledge and Practice of the Christian Religion, as Professed and Taught in the Church of England*, may be the better promoted: the Master shall make it his chief Business to Instruct the Children in the *Principles* thereof, as they are laid down in the *Church-Catechism;* which he shall first teach them to *pronounce* distinctly and plainly; and then, in order to practise, shall explain it to the meanest capacity by some good *Exposition* approved of by the Minister: And this shall be done constantly twice a week, that every thing in the Catechism may be the more perfectly repeated and understood; and afterwards shall more largely inform them of their Duty by the Help of the *Whole Duty of Man:* And the Master shall take particular Care of the Manners and Behaviour of the Poor Children; and by all proper Methods shall discourage and correct the Beginnings of Vice, and particularly *Lying*, *Swearing*, *Cursing*, *taking* God's Name in vain, and the Prophanation of the Lord's Day &c. at the same Time minding them of such Parts of the Holy Scriptures and of the Catechism, where those things are mentioned as forbidden by God, and the contrary things as commanded . . .
3. When any Number of the Children can say the Catechism, the Master shall give Notice thereof to the *Minister*, in order to their being Catechized in the Church.
4. The Master shall teach them the true Spelling of Words, and

Distinction of Syllables, with the Points and Stops, which is necessary to true and good Reading, and serves to make the Children more mindful of what they Read.

5. As soon as the Boys can Read competently well, the Master shall teach them to Write a fair legible Hand, with the Grounds of Arithmetick, to fit them for Services or Apprenticeships. Note the Girls learn to read, &c. and generally to knit their Stockings and Gloves; to Mark, Sew, Make and Mend their Cloaths: and several learn to Write, and some to Spin their Cloaths.

6. The Master shall bring the Children to Church twice every Lord's Day and Holy Day; and shall teach them to behave themselves with all Reverence while they are in the House of God, and to join in the publick Services of the Church. For which purpose they are always to have ready their Bibles bound up with the Common-Prayer.

   N.B. In many places the Masters and Mistresses bring the Children to Church every Day.

7. The Master shall use Prayers Morning and Evening in the School; and shall teach the Children to pray at Home when they rise and go to Bed, and to use Graces before and after Meat . . .

8. The Names of the Children shall be called over every Morning and Afternoon, to know whether they come constantly at School-Hours: And if any be missing, their names shall be put down with a Note for *Tardy*, and another for *Absent*. Great Faults, as Swearing, Stealing, &c. shall be noted down in Monthly or Weekly Bills, to be laid before the Subscribers or Trustees every Time they meet, in order to their Correction or Expulsion . . .

. . . . . .

IV. That the Children to be taken into this School, shall be real Objects of the Charity, and be living in (or near to) the said Parish of —— and be of the full Age of *Seven* Years, and not above the age of *Twelve* Years. And before any Child is admitted, the Subscriber presenting such Child, shall duly inform himself of the Condition of his Parents, and of his Age, &c. And moreover an Examination shall be made by the Treasurer and Trustees, or by the Subscribers, whether he be a real Object of the Charity, and also otherwise qualified to be admitted in respect of Age and Place of Habitation, &c.

An Account of Charity Schools in Great Britain and Ireland, pp. 3–7 (Society for the Promotion of Christian Knowledge, 1711)

The next extract is from that part of the *Account* which deals with 'The present State of the Charity Schools in England'. Other parts deal with charity schools in Wales, North-Britain and Ireland. The extract shows quite clearly the varied origin of schools which this *Account* lumps together as 'charity schools', and the mixed quality of the entries as sources for the educational historian.

Keinton, Somersetshire Several poor Children are here put to school at the charge of the Minister.
Kennet, Cambridgeshire A school maintained by the Offertory, and some Contributions.
Kettering, Northamptonshire 10*l. per Annum* for ever left towards the Support of a Sch. which is for 28 G. (girls) who are cloathed. The Subscriptions are about 40*l. per Annum.*
Kiderminster, Worcestershire A convenient House is fitted up for a Sch. for 40B. (boys) who are taught and clothed. There are also about 20 poor Ch. taught at 2 other Sch. The Sub. is 30*l. per Ann.* The rest has been made up providentially by other Benefactions.
Kilmersdon, Somersetshire A Sch. for 40 Ch. The Master's Salary is 20*l. per Ann.* Books for the Ch. are provided: All at the Expence of a private Person, who has endowed it with 20*l. Per Ann.* for ever after his Decease. A School-House lately built by the same Person with the Assistance of the Inhabitants and others.
Kingswood, Gloucestershire A Sch. founded and maintained by a Gentleman for all the poor Ch. its Management capable of great Improvements.
Kirk-Deighton, Yorkshire 7*l. per Annum* is given by 3 Persons for a School here.
Kirkby-Overblows, Yorkshire A Sch. House built here in 1708.
Kingston on Hull, Yorkshire A School or Workhouse, founded by Act of Parliament. The Hospital, where the Children are, cost 600*l.* The Number is at present about 45, who have Meat, Drink, Cloathing and Washing; and are taught to Read, Write, and Spin Jersey, and are every *Sunday* catechized in the Church. The Ch. are so maintained by voluntary Sub. and charitable Gifts.
Kirleatham in Cleaveland, Yorkshire. A School-House, &c. built, which costs about 1000*l.* The School-Master's Salary 100*l.* and the Usher's 50*l. per Annum,* as ordered by the Will of Sir William Turner Knight, not long since Lord Mayor of *London.*
Laberton, Gloucestershire A School erected by a Gentleman, 20*l.* a Year is allowed for 20 Boys by the same Person.
Lanceston, Cornwall 2 Sch. for 48 Ch. The B. are taught to Read, Write, &c. and the G. to Read, Knit, Sew, and make Bone-lace, and they are to have what they earn for their Encouragement. The Subscriptions are about 50*l. per Ann.*
Langham, Rutlandshire 10*l. per Annum* is left by a Gentleman, for teaching the poor Children.
Ledbury, Herefordshire Mrs Hall deceased has built a School, and given

15*l*. a Year to it. The Number of poor Children is 23, 30 more are here taught at the Charge of an unknown Person.

Leeds, Yorkshire A Sch. for 28 B. and 12 G. The Fund is about 208*l*. *per Ann.* namely, 20*l*. *per Annum* of the Collection at the Communion; 20*l*. *per Annum* from the Feoffees for cloathing the Poor of the Town; and the rest is made up of Sub. of the Magistrates and Inhabitants. The Corporation gave a large House for a Sch. and Supplies for repairing and fitting it up. A Gentleman intends to settle on it 6*l*. a Year for ever. A Merchant has given 50*l*. and another Gentleman 50*l*. which has bought 8*l*. *per Ann*, and a Merchant since 100*l*. 8s. *per Annum* will also in time belong to it more. A Dissenter gave by Will to it lately 10*l*.

Leicester 24 B. taught and cl. at the Expence of a private Gentlewoman. And 10 poor G. taught and Cl. at the Expence of 2 others, and 34 Children taught and Cl. at the Expence of 3 others.

Leigh, Worcestershire A School endowed with 13*l*. *per Ann* for ever.

Leighton, Bedfordshire 10*l*. *per Ann.* lately given for the Education of poor Ch. and 7 more are taught at the Expence of a private Person.

Leverpool, Lancashire A School for 50 poor Children taught and cloathed A School-House built, with Lodgings for the Master.

ibid., pp. 28–9

SUBSCRIPTION FORM FOR A CHARITY SCHOOL

Whereas Prophaness and Debauchery are greatly owing to a gross Ignorance of the Christian Religion, especially among the poorer sort; And whereas nothing is more likely to promote the practice of Christianity and Virtue, than an early and pious Education of Youth; And whereas many Poor People are desirous of having their Children Taught, but are not able to afford them a Christian and Useful Education; We whose Names are underwritten, do agree to pay Yearly, at Four equal Payments, (during Pleasure) the several and respective Sums of Money over against our Names respectively subscribed, for the setting up of a Charity-School in the Parish of —— in the City of —— or in the County of —— for Teaching [Poor Boys, or Poor Girls, or] Poor children to Read and Instructing them in the Knowledge and Practice of the Christian Religion, as profess'd and taught in the Church of England; and for Learning them such other Things as are suitable to their Condition and Capacity. That is to say

I, *A.B.*, do subscribe £ s d

An Account of Charity Schools in Great Britain and Ireland, p. 50 (Society for the Promotion of Christian Knowledge, 1711)

BERNARD MANDEVILLE'S *ESSAY ON CHARITY AND CHARITY SCHOOLS*

Bernard Mandeville's essay, published in 1724, mounted a forthright attack on the provision of charity schools, giving expression to views which many of the upper classes would have subscribed to, at least in private if not in public.

Mandeville went against the current acclamation which Charity schools received. Numerous sermons and orations praised them and when the charity school children in their distinctive dress were paraded in London, the rich who had in this way provided for some of the poor, applauded the 'show' with self satisfaction. The following account from Addison's *Guardian*, No. 105, represents the view to which Mandeville ran counter: 'There was no part of the show . . . that so much pleased and affected me as the little boys and girls who were ranged with so much order and decency in . . . the Strand . . . Such a numerous and innocent multitude, clothed in the charity of their benefactors, was a spectacle pleasing both to God and man . . . I have always looked on this institution of charity schools . . . as the glory of the age we live in . . . It seems to promise us an honest and virtuous posterity. There will be few in the next generation, who will not at least be able to write and read, and have not had the early tincture of religion.'

In this first extract Mandeville questions whether charity schools will reduce the criminal population, is sceptical of the 'civility' they will teach to their pupils, and considers that parents and the home environment have a greater effect on the development of children's attitudes than schoolteachers, a view which twentieth-century educationists have re-discovered.

What I have now under consideration leads me naturally to that kind of distraction the nation has laboured under for some time, the enthusiastick passion for charity schools.

The generality are so bewitched with the usefulness and excellency of them, that whoever dares openly oppose them is in danger of being stoned by the rabble. Children that are taught the principles of religion and can read the word of God, have a greater opportunity to improve in Virtue and good morality, and must certainly be more civilized than others, that are suffered to run at random and have no body to look after them. How perverse must be the judgment of those, who would not rather see children decently dressed, with clean linen at least once a week, that in an orderly manner follow their master to church, than in every open place meet with a company of black-guards without shirts or any thing whole about them, that, insensible of their misery are continually increasing it with Oaths and imprecations! Can any one doubt but these are the great nursery of thieves and pick-pockets? What numbers of felons and other criminals have we tried and convicted every session! This will be prevented by charity schools, and, when the children of the poor receive a better education, the society will in a few years reap the benefit of it, and the nation be cleared of so many miscreants as now this great city and all the country about it are filled with.

This is the general cry, and he that speaks the least word against it, an uncharitable, hard-hearted and inhuman, if not a wicked, prophane, and atheistical Wretch. As to the comeliness of the sight, no body disputes it; but I would not have a nation pay too dear for so transient a pleasure, and if we might set aside the finery of the show, every thing that is material in this popular oration might soon be answered.

As to religion, the most knowing and polite part of a nation have every where the least of it; craft has a greater hand in making rogues than stupidity, and vice in general is no where more predominant than where arts and sciences flourish. Ignorance is, to a proverb, counted to be the mother of devotion, and it is certain that we shall find innocence and honesty no where more general than among the most illiterate, the poor, silly country people. The next to be considered, are the manners and civility that by charity schools are to be grafted into the poor of the nation. I confess that, in my opinion, to be in any degree possessed of what I named, is a frivolous, if not a hurtful quality, at least nothing is less requisite in the laborious poor. It is not compliments we want of them, but their work and assiduity. But I give up this Article with all my heart, good Manners we will say are necessary to all people, but which way will they be furnished with them in a charity school? Boys there may be taught to pull off their caps promiscuously to all they meet, unless it be a beggar: But that they should acquire in it any civility beyond that, I cannot conceive.

The master is not greatly qualified, as may be guessed by his salary, and if he could teach them manners he has not time for it: whilst they are at school they are either learning or saying their lesson to him, or employed in writing or arithmetick, and as soon as school is done, they are as much at liberty as other poor people's children. It is precept and the example of parents, and those they eat, drink and converse with, that have an influence upon the Minds of Children: reprobate parents that take ill courses and are regardless of their children, will not have a mannerly civilized offspring though they went to a charity school till they were married. The honest pains-taking people, be they ever so poor, if they have any notion of goodness and decency themselves, will keep their children in awe, and never suffer them to rake about the streets, and lie out a-nights. Those who will work themselves, and have any command over their children, will make them do something or other that turns to profit as soon as they are able, be it ever so little: and such as are so ungovernable, that neither words not blows can work upon them, no charity school will mend; nay, experience teaches us, that among the charity-boys there are abundance of bad ones that swear and curse about, and bar the clothes, are as much black-guard as ever Tower-hill or St. James's produced.

I am now come to the enormous crimes, and vast multitude of malefactors, that are all laid upon the want of this notable education. That abundance of thefts and robberies are daily committed in and about the City, and great numbers yearly suffer death for those crimes is undeniable: But because this is ever hooked in when the usefulness of charity schools is called in question, as if there was no dispute but they would in a great measure remedy, and in time prevent those disorders, I intend to examine into the real causes of those mischiefs so justly complained of, and doubt not but to make it appear, that charity schools, and every thing else that promotes idleness, and keeps the poor from working, are more accessory to the growth of villany, than the want of reading and writing, or even the grossest ignorance and stupidity . . .

It is manifest then that many different causes concur, and several scarce avoidable evils contribute to the misfortune of being pester'd with pilferers, thieves, and robbers, which all countries ever were and ever will be, more or less, in and near considerable towns, more especially vast and overgrown cities. It is opportunity makes the thief; carelessness and neglect in fastening doors and windows, the excessive tenderness of juries and prosecutors, the small difficulty of getting a reprieve and frequency of pardons, but, above all, the many examples of those who are known to be guilty, are destitute both of friends and money, and yet, by imposing on the jury, baffling the witnesses, or other tricks and strategems, find out means to escape the gallows. These are all strong temptations that conspire to draw in the necessitous, who want principle and education.

To these you may add as auxiliaries to mischief, an habit of sloth and idleness and strong aversion to labour and assiduity, which all young people will contract that are not brought up to downright working, or at least kept employed most days in the week, and the greatest part of the day. All Children that are idle, even the best of either sex, are bad company to one another whenever they meet.

It is not then the want of reading and writing, but the concurrence and a complication of more substantial evils, that are the perpetual nursery of abandoned profligates in great and opulent nations; and whoever would accuse ignorance, stupidity and dastardness, as the first, and what physicians call the procatartic cause, let him examine into the lives, and narrowly inspect the conversations and actions of ordinary rogues and our common felons, and he will find the reverse to be true, and that the blame ought rather to be laid on the excessive cunning and subtlety, and too much knowledge in general, which the worst of miscreants and the scum of the nation are possessed of.

BERNARD MANDEVILLE *The Fable of the Bees, or Private Vices, Public Benefits*, vol. I, pp. 199–201, 204 (Edinburgh, 1772)

Here, Mandeville develops his main argument against the increased provision of schools, contending that it will have disastrous economic effects. In particular, he argues that the poor will learn to despise those labouring jobs on which, he considers, society depends. His views of the relation between education and the economy are interesting to compare with those current in the highly industrialized society of the twentieth century.

The whole Earth being cursed, and no bread to be had but what we eat in the sweat of our brows, vast toil must be undergone before man can provide himself with necessaries for his sustenance and the bare support of his currupt and defective nature as he is a single creature – but infinitely more to make life comfortable in a civil society, where men are become taught animals, and great numbers of them have by mutual compact framed themselves into a body politic; and the more man's knowledge increases in this state, the greater will be the variety of labour required to make him easy. It is impossible that a society can long subsist, and suffer many of its members to live in idleness, and enjoy all the ease and pleasure they can invent, without having at the same time great multitudes of people that to make good this defect will condescend to be quite the reverse, and by use and patience inure their bodies to work for others and themselves besides.

The plenty and cheapness of provisions depends in a great measure on the price and value that is set upon this labour, and consequently the welfare of all societies, even before they are tainted with foreign luxury, requires that it should be perform'd by such of their members as in the first place are sturdy and robust and never used to ease or idleness and in the second, soon contented as to the necessaries of life; such as are glad to take up with the coarsest manufacture in every thing they wear, and in their diet have no other aim than to feed their bodies when their stomachs prompt them to eat, and, with little regard to taste or relish, refuse no wholesome nourishment that can be swallowed when men are hungry, or ask any thing for their thirst but to quench it.

As the greatest part of the drudgery is to be done by day-light, so it is by this only that they actually measure the time of their labour without any thought of the hours they are employ'd, or the weariness they feel; and the hireling in the country must get up in the morning, not because he has rested enough, but because the sun is going to rise. This last Article alone would be an intolerable hardship to grown people under thirty, who during nonage had been used to lie a-bed as long as they could sleep: but all three together make up such a condition of life as a man more mildly educated would hardly chuse though it should deliver him from a goal or a shrew.

If such people there must be, as no great nation can be happy without vast numbers of them, would not a wise legislature cultivate the breed of them with all imaginable care, and provide against their scarcity as he would prevent the scarcity of provision it self? No Man would be poor and fatigue himself for a livelihood if he could help it: the absolute necessity all stand in for victuals and drink, and in cold climates for clothes and lodging, makes them submit to any thing that can be bore with. If no body did want no body would work; but the greatest Hardships are looked upon as solid pleasures, when they keep a man from starving.

From what has been said it is manifest, that in a free nation where slaves are not allowed of, the surest wealth consists in a multitude of laborious poor; for besides that they are the never-failing nursery of fleets and armies, without them there could be no enjoyment, and no product of any country could be valuable. To make the society happy and people easy under the meanest circumstances, it is requisite that great numbers of them should be ignorant as well as poor. Knowledge both enlarges and multiplies our desires, and the fewer things a man wishes for, the more easily his necessities may be supplied.

The welfare and felicity therefore of every state and kingdom, require that the knowledge of the working poor should be confined within the verge of their occupations, and never extended (as to things visible) beyond what relates to their calling. The more a shepherd, a plowman or any other peasant knows of the world, and the things that are Foreign to his labour or employment, the less fit he will be to go through the fatigues and hardships of it with cheerfulness and content.

Reading, writing and arithmetic, are very necessary to those, whose business require such qualifications; but where people's livelihood has no dependence on these arts, they are very pernicious to the poor, who are forced to get their daily bread by their daily labour. Few children make any progress at school, but at the same time they are capable of being employed in some business or other, so that every hour those of poor people spend at their book is so much time lost to the society. Going to school in comparison to working, is idleness, and the longer boys continue in this easy sort of life, the more unfit they will be when grown up for downright labour, both as to strength and inclination. Men who are to remain and end their days in a laborious, tiresome and painful station of life, the sooner they are put upon it at first, the more patiently they will submit to it for ever after. Hard labour and the coarsest diet are a proper punishment to several kinds of malefactors;

but to impose either on those that have not been used and brought up to both, is the greatest cruelty, when there is no crime you can charge them with.

Reading and writing are not attain'd to without some labour of the brain and assiduity, and before people are tolerably versed in either, they esteem themselves infinitely above those who are wholly ignorant of them, often with so little justice and moderation as if they were of another Species. As all Mortals have naturally an aversion to trouble and painstaking, so we are all fond of, and apt to over-value those qualifications we have purchased at the expense of our ease and quiet for years together. Those who spent a great part of their youth in learning to read, write and cypher, expect and not unjustly to be employed where those qualifications may be of use to them; the generality of them will look upon downright labour with the utmost contempt, I mean labour performed in the service of others in the lowest station of life, and for the meanest consideration. A Man who has had some Education, may follow husbandry by choice, and be diligent at the dirtiest and most laborious work; but then the concern must be his own, and avarice, the care of a family, or some other pressing motive must put him upon it; but he will not make a good hireling and serve a farmer for a pitiful reward; at least he is not so fit for it as a day-labourer that has always been employed about the plough and dung cart, and remembers not that ever he has lived otherwise.

When obsequiousness and mean services are required, we shall always observe that they are never so cheerfully nor so heartily performed as from inferiors to superiors; I mean inferiors not only in riches and quality, but likewise in knowledge and understanding.

ibid., Vol. I, pp. 214–17

In this last extract, Mandeville argues that the teaching of the Christian faith is a worthy end, but that it could be achieved through the ministry of the Church without building Charity schools.

The only thing of weight then that can be said in their behalf is, that so many thousand children are educated by them in the Christian faith and the Principles of the Church of England. To demonstrate that this is not a sufficient Plea for them, I must desire the reader, as I hate repetitions, to look back on what I have said before, to which I shall add, that whatever is necessary to salvation and requisite for poor labouring people to know concerning religion, that children learn at school, may fully as well either by preaching or catechizing be taught at church, from which or some other place of worship I would not have the meanest of a parish that is able to walk to it, be absent on Sundays.

It is the Sabbath, the most useful day in seven, that is set apart for divine service and religious exercise as well as resting from bodily labour, and it is a duty incumbent on all magistrates to take particular care of that day. The poor more especially and their children should be made to go to church on it both in the fore and afternoon, because they have no time on any other. By precept and example they ought to be encouraged and used to it from their very infancy; the wilful neglect of it ought to be counted scandalous, and if downright compulsion to what I urge might seem too harsh and perhaps impracticable, all diversions at least ought strictly to be prohibited, and the poor hindred from every amusement abroad that might allure or draw them from it.

Where this care is taken by the magistrates as far as it lies in their power, ministers of the gospel may instil into the smallest capacities, more piety and devotion, and better principles of virtue and religion than charity schools ever did or ever will produce, and those who complain, when they have such opportunities, that they cannot imbue their parishioners with sufficient knowledge of what they stand in need of as Christians, without the assistance of reading and writing, are either very lazy or very ignorant and undeserving themselves.

ibid., Vol. I, pp. 232–3

A CHARITY SCHOOL SERMON 1743

The purposes of charity school education as seen by its clerical sponsors are illustrated in the following extracts from a sermon preached by Thomas Secker, Archbishop of Canterbury, on 6 May 1743 to the annual gathering of London Charity school children in the Parish Church of Christ Church, London. Charity school sermons were frequently preached by clergymen throughout the country.

The first extract suggests that the charity schools existed to teach religion, to inculcate obedience to lawful authority and to impose the acceptance of an inferior subordinate social position on the children who were admitted to them.

In the *management* of these children, as teaching them religion is the chief thing proposed, so it ought to employ the chief attention; which it may without hindrance, indeed with advantage, to the other parts of their education. In order to this end, getting by heart their catechism, and their prayers, and select portions of scripture, is a step by no means to be omitted or despised. For experience hath taught the need of fixing thus in their memories at first, what their understandings will afterwards ripen gradually to comprehend. But if this one step be mistaken for the whole, they may be brought up in all the form of religion, with scarce any meaning accompanying it. And though very general and confused sentiments of piety and duty may often be of great use, both in directing and restraining persons, yet sometimes it is possible they may do harm; and more distinct ones cannot fail of being, in proportion, more safe and beneficial. Their teachers, therefore, should very carefully explain to them, as soon and as clearly as they can, everything which they oblige them to repeat; and make proper trials, from time to time, of their apprehending, as well as remembering, what they are taught; in which part of their work they may be greatly assisted, partly by some of the printed expositions, with which they should always be furnished, and partly by informing themselves what methods are taken in the neighbouring schools of best repute. Another very advantageous and very pleasing way of increasing their acquaintance with religion, would be, turning their attention, as they read the Bible, to the more useful parts of its history, by familiar and short remarks upon them; such as their instructors can make, and they can enter into, without difficulty. Nor would it be at all a hard matter, by the help of almost any one of the small pieces written of late in defence of Christianity, to give them so much insight into the grounds and evidences of it, as will furnish them with much better reasons for believing, than they will ever have for disbelieving it. And as this is, at all times, a piece of justice due to reasonable creatures, so it is, at the present time, peculiarly necessary to a most unhappy degree.

The knowledge thus instilled, must be constantly applied to the producing of suitable dispositions. And above all, there must be diligently imprinted on their hearts a deep reverence of God, as the Almighty and all-seeing Ruler of the world; who hath given such laws to men, as he knows are necessary for their good; and will make us everlastingly happy or miserable, as we obey or transgress them . . .

. . . Constant attendance on public worship is one inestimable benefit, which this education secures to children. And to render it as useful to them as possible, they should be diligently taught, and I doubt not but they are, to approach the house of God with the utmost seriousness to hearken reverently to his word read and preached; and perform their part of the liturgy in such a manner as may best engage their own attention, and yet give others no disturbance, by the noise of their responses, or the loudness of their singing: concerning which particulars, express directions have been given by the trustees. The indiscretion of teaching them difficult and unusual tunes is, I hope, nearly corrected every where. But a reasonable degree of skill in the common ones, will be a needful support of the harmony of the congregation, a means of familiarizing good thoughts to their minds, and of making divine service more cheerful and pleasing to them . . .

. . . It must be expected, that we should recommend to these children the faith and worship of our own communion, as all other Christians do; and teach them that respect to the church that they are members of, and the ministers who officiate in it, which the scripture, in very strong terms, requires they should have . . . Tragical fears, it must be owned, were entertained, or pretended, at first, of the immoderate power which the institution of these schools would give us. But time and experience hath thoroughly shewn, how very little reason there was, on any such account, either for us to be fond of the scheme, or the laity jealous of it. The enemies of religion, indeed, will of course exclaim against the greatness of our influence, even whilst they despise us for the smallness of it: but all others may surely see cause to wish, that we had much more than we have, for good purposes; and God forbid we should either desire or use any to promote bad ones.

Next after the duties that we owe to our Maker, Christianity requires obedience to our earthly governors. And the government with which we are now blessed, is so necessary for the preservation of every thing valuable to us, that all persons of all ranks should be habituated from their earliest years to pray for it, and honour it, and live contentedly and thankfully under it; but those of low rank particularly, *to be quiet, and do their own business* (I Thess. iv, 2); *not exercising themselves in matters too high for them* (Ps. cxxxi, 1). And if this rule were either transgressed, or neglected, by the directors or teachers of our charity schools, it would be an insuperable objection, so long as it continued, against encouraging such of them as were thus fundamentally mismanaged. But indeed there hath been found, on repeated inquiry, very good reason to be satisfied, that the faults of this kind, which there might be once, never reached far, and have been long ago reformed. The imputation, therefore, now would be grievously unjust: but there cannot be too strict a caution to avoid all appearance, not only of disloyalty, but of every party regard of every sort, in the whole conduct of this design; for much of its support, and much of its benefit, absolutely depends upon that one thing.

Together with the habits of religion and obedience to lawful authority, these children should be taught every other that is useful and good. Their moral behaviour, a point of vastly more consequence than their learning, should be diligently watched, both in the school, and as much as possible out of it too; for which purpose they are distinguished by a peculiar dress: and their parents should be earnestly warned, not to undo what their instructors are doing. Ill-humour, idleness, indecency, lying, dishonesty, profaneness should be severely punished as often as they are observed: and if any of them corrupts the rest, or appear incorrigible himself, he should be immediately dismissed; and no false tenderness, or mean-spirited fear of disobliging, shewn either by teachers or trustees. For maintaining the credit of a school, is the sure way of providing for the support of it.

But particularly humility should be instilled into them with singular care. They should understand, that the lowest of those whom their own parents maintain, are for that very reason their superiors; and that no education, given as an alms, can be a ground for thinking highly of themselves. Their usage in all respects should be answerable to such lessons. Cleanliness should be required of them, as far as ever their employments allow it: but no extraordinary provision should be made for it, nor the least affection of nicety tolerated in either sex. Their clothes should be no better, if so good, as they may hope to wear all the rest of their lives; no gaiety of colour, no trifling ornaments permitted; nor any distinction between them and other children, in which they can possibly be tempted to take pleasure. If they are fed, their food should be of the coarsest sort, and not more than enough. If they are lodged, it should be in a manner that is suitable to every thing else. For, besides that frugality is a most important branch of faithfulness in the management of charities, *it is good that they should bear the yoke in their youth* (Lam. iii, 27); be inured to the treatment they must expect to receive: and wrong-judged indulgence is the greatest cruelty that can be exercised towards them.

THOMAS SECKER *The Works of Thomas Secker*, Vol. III, pp. 501–5 (Edinburgh, 1792)

In the next extract Secker answers critics like Bernard Mandeville who objected to the teaching of reading on grounds that it encouraged them to leave their labouring jobs. However, Secker also makes it clear that charity school children should be introduced to work of some kind, preferably while still at school, and that on leaving school they should be put into some 'laborious working trade'.

The manner of *disposing* of them, when they come to be dismissed is the next point. And as all education is for the sake of what shall follow it, the trustees for them should interest themselves not a little in their future course of life; and, so far as they can, secure their parents consent when they are admitted, to their being placed out properly . . . Good persons therefore should always be sought out for them to go to. And they should be earnestly entreated, to keep them in the way into which they have been put; especially to see, that they constantly attend on the Lord's day service, and make a proper use of their religious books. For some such should always be given them at their leaving the school, with a solemn charge concerning the main branches of their conduct.

But not only the persons, with whom they are placed, but the employments, in which they are fixed, should be well considered. Great numbers of them have been sent to sea; and it is not the fault of the trustees, but of the parents, that more are not defending or enriching their country on board our ships. Of the rest, those who are bred in this town mostly become either apprentices or household servants; and, it seems, objections are made against each method of disposing of them.

It hath been said, that they are put to retailing shopkeepers, or other easy employments, unsuitable to their original condition; and that more money is required, and given with them, than with other children; all which, I am assured, is absolutely false in fact. They are put, as they undoubtedly ought, to laborious working trades, and no other; with many of them, no money at all is given; with most of them but forty shillings; with some few, five pounds; but more with none. And indeed it is evident, that the friends of such an education will dispose of them as cheap as they can; were it for this reason only, that they may take in as many as they can.

Another suggestion is, that they are put out to worthless persons, in bad circumstances, who take the money, and then break. But neither of this do I find any proof. However, though a groundless assertion, it may furnish a useful warning.

But at least, it is objected further, breeding so many of them to trades occasions a scarcity of servants. Now even in this town, not two thirds of the boys, nor much above one fourth of the girls, have been put apprentices at all; and a great part of these were probably no other than household servants, taken by indenture for a term of years. What the proportion hath been in the country, doth not appear; but in all likelihood it must have been very small, Or were it otherwise, disproportions of this nature will soon rectify themselves. Where apprentices or journeymen are not wanted, and other servants are, these children will of course be sent where the demand is greatest; nor can the trustees have either inclination or power to prevent it.

But whilst one of the writers against our charity schools accuses them of lessening the number of servants, the other charges them with increasing it. Possibly the meaning may be, that they increase the number of the upper and idler sort, and lessen that of the lower and more laborious. Now as to this, the boys, when they come from school, are plainly incapable of the higher services; nor are many of them taken, even for footmen. And yet, what plenty soever there is of livery servants, there is so loud a complaint of the want of sober and honest ones, that I apprehend it would be no inconvenience, but a general advantage, if more of these children were put into the station, in serious and regular families: for in others they would have little chance of doing good, and a great one of being ruined. Then for the girls, as they certainly ought not either to be raised into the easier places, or qualified for them; since it would hurst both others who have a better claim to them, and the public; so I cannot find that they are, but that low business, with low wages of fifty shillings, or three pounds a year at most, is what universally falls to their share, till, by a course of diligence and faithfulness, they can better their condition; which surely then should not be envied them.

ibid., pp. 511–13

LEEDS CHARITY SCHOOL ORDERS FOR THE MASTER AND MISTRESS

Leeds Charity School was founded in 1705. These orders were drawn up by Thomas Wilson, then Master, on 11 July 1750. They show the school hours and emphasize the religious duties of the teachers.

I That they always attend at School in Summer from the first Day of April to the first day of September from Seven to Twelve of the Clock in the Forenoon and from One till Five in the Afternoon, and in Winter from Eight to Twelve and from One to Four.

II That upon common School-Days they shall never suffer to have any Play-Days without the consent of One or more of the Trustees or Subscribers.

III That they form the Children into Upper and Lower Classes, for their Improvement in and Promotion agreeable to their tender Minds.

IV That the Master shall Daily read the Prayers (appointed by the Society for propagating Christian Knowledge) Morning and Evening, then Sing a Psalm, then proceed with the Upper-Class in reading the Psalms and Lessons for the Day, after that the Boys to be set to Writing and Accompts, and the Girls to Sowing and Knitting.

V That the Master shall Catechize the Scholars every Thursday and Saturday in the Forenoon and shall by his own Example, Word of Mouth or by Mr. Lewis's Exposition, Explain to the Children the Sense and Meaning of every Part of the excellent Catechism of the Church.

VI That the Master shall every Forenoon and Afternoon call over the Names of the Scholars and Remark such as are Absent, or misbehave themselves and for the first fault to Exhort and Admonish them to Amend; for the second fault use a little Severity in Reproving, Reprimanding or reasonably Chastising: and for the third fault if (the Parents which is too often the cause or) the Children be incorrigible, then such Children shall be expelled or turned out of the School, with the Consent of One or more of the Trustees or Subscribers.

VII That they shall take care that the Children come Decently to Church on all Sundays and Sermon-Days, and see that they behave themselves with Reverence (as such Charity-Children ought to do) both to God and all Mankind.

Pietas Leodiensis or an Account of the Benefactors, Gifts . . . etc. to the Charity School in Leedes, p. 86 (c. 1735) Leeds City Libraries Archives Department, Ref. No. DB/196/1

LEEDS CHARITY SCHOOL ORDERS FOR THE CHILDREN'S CLOTHES

The following form issued for parental signature shows the kind of clothes distributed by the charity school authorities. The school uniform became an integral part of the charity school movement, indicating to the children themselves, their parents and all who might see them, that they were objects of charity for whom their betters had provided. The uniform was a badge of inferiority, though on the other hand it provided clothing of good quality to children who might otherwise never possess it. The school uniforms of the present have different purposes, though owing their origin to these clothes issued to charity school children.

Whereas at my Request, *A.B.*, my Son (or Daughter) is now admitted into the Charity School of this Town to be instructed and taught to Read and Write and to be cloathed during the pleasure of the Trustees or Committee of Subscribers for the said Charity School and the said *A.B.* both this day received from the Governors the Garments following viz. a New-Coat, Wast-coat, Breeches, Stockings, a Cap, Two New Shirts, a Band, two Check Stocks, a pair of Shoes, a pair of Stockings & Books convenient.

Now I, *C.D.*, in Consideration thereof do hereby promise and undertake to keep all the said Garments in sufficient repair and in case the Committee of the said school, shall for any misbehaviour of the said *A.B.* expell him the said school wthin the space of one year next following or in case the said *A.B.* shall be absent or withdraw himself from the said Charity-School upon any common Schooldays or at the Common Hours or Times of Learning therein not having leave of the Master or any one of the Committee for the time being, All the said Garments shall upon demand to me, my Executors or Administrators be delivered up whole in decent repair unto the Master of the said Charity School or pay money for the value of the said cloaths upon Demand.

Witness my hand

C.D.

Leeds 25 Dec. 17

If a Girl say One New Coat, Petticoat, a pair of Shifts, Apron, a Cap, a Band, Two Hankerchiefs, a pair of Stockings, a pair of shoes.

Pietas Leodiensis or an Account of the Benefactors, Gifts . . . etc. to the Charity School in Leedes, p. 91 (c. 1735) Leeds City Libraries Archives Department, Ref. No. DB/196/1

LEEDS CHARITY SCHOOL ORDERS FOR THE SCHOOL CHILDREN

These orders give additional details about the clothing of the children and the work they had to do in training for their future jobs, perhaps in industry. It also indicates that many Charity School children were sent out of the schools into apprenticeships or into domestic service.

I. Every Person Subscribing Twenty Shillings Yearly shall be a Trustee and Inspector, and may admit such Child or Children at the Age of Eight Years and such as know all the Letters in the Alphabet.

II. The Children to be Cloathed compleatly at every Christmas Day and each a Pair of Shoes every May Day and Michaelmas Day.

III. Such Children as neglect to attend the School at the usual times of Teaching (except in the case of sickness) shall be expelled by the Committee or any one of the Trustees.

IV. Every Child at going out of the School either an Apprentice or to Service shall have a New Bible and a New Hat.

V. If a Child be taken out of the School by the Parents without the Consent of one or more of the Trustees, it loses Benefits in the last Article.

VI. Such child as wilfully Absents from the Working School or hindred by Parents on the Days appointed by the Reading Master (who has a Power to employ what children he thinks proper at Nine Years old, every third half Day, that is Twelve Children at a time, in all Thirty-Six) for such negligence, such child is to be expelled. And every such child is to spin two Hanks of Worsted every half Day when capable.

VII. The Spinning Children are occasionally to spin and Twine Yarn for their own Stockings.

Pietas Leodiensis or an Account of the Benefactors, Gifts . . . etc. to the Charity School in Leedes, p. 85 (c. 1735) Leeds City Libraries Archives Department, Ref. No. DB/196/1

THE CHRISTIAN SCHOOLMASTER 1707

James Talbott, Rector of Spofforth in Yorkshire, wrote *The Christian Schoolmaster* for the guidance of teachers employed in the charity schools established by the Society for the Promotion of Christian Knowledge. It gave comprehensive guidance on the duties of teachers and the curriculum they should follow in the schools. Practical advice on the management of a school and methods of discipline are also covered in detail. The work was reprinted several times.

The following extract gives Talbott's account of that part of the curriculum which is concerned with the 'three Rs'. Particularly noteworthy is the advice given on the teaching of writing and his view of the value of Latin in the teaching of English.

The Third Part of *Instruction*, which is Incumbent upon our *School-Master*; viz. That of Training up the Children under his Care in such necessary Parts of *Learning* as are most suitable to their Condition and Capacity, and will be useful in every State and Circumstance of their Life, which are chiefly these Three.

1. *Reading*. 2. *Writing*. 3. *Arithmetick*.

1. In order to the First of these, after they have gone through the Letters of the *Alphabet*, he must Instruct them in the true Spelling of Words, and the Distinction of Syllables, by the Help of some proper *Spelling Book* for that Purpose. From this they may proceed to the Reading of Words as they are joined together in a Sentence: And great Care must be taken from the Beginning, that each Syllable and every Word may be Pronounced very Plainly, Distinctly, and Audibly, without *Muttering* or *Stammering* (where that Defect is not Natural and Incurable) and without any disagreeable *Tone*, which all Children are very apt to Learn from one another, if it be Suffered or Encouraged in any. They must likewise be Taught the Difference and Use of the Points or Stops; the due Observation of which is very necessary towards their Reading of each Sentence Distinctly and Intelligibly, and also to make them Mind and Understand what they Read.

These Things being thus Premised, it may be very proper to Appoint their first Lessons in such Parts of the *Church Catechism* as they had not Learnt by Heart before they began to Read: That so by frequent Repetition of the Words, while they are thus Practising to Read them, they may become Familiar . . .

2. As soon as the Children can *Read* competently well, they must be entred in the Second Part of *School Learning*, viz. that of *Writing*: the particular Methods of which are so well known by every one who professeth that Art, that it will be needless to say any thing more in this Place, than that the *Master* must take Care to Teach them a Fair, Legible Hand; and that at first it may be somewhat larger than they should ordinarily Write: it being generally observed, that every one comes by Degrees to Write a smaller Hand than he was Taught at first, but never a Bigger.

When they are able to Write Fairly without a Copy, they must Learn both to Improve their Hand and to Gain the Habit of True Spelling and Pointing, by the frequent Practice of Transcribing some useful Sentences of *Scripture*, or some Fable of *Esop;* which they may be required to Compare very carefully with the Original, and to Correct all Mistakes they can find in their Copy, before they shew it to their Master.

3. The Third and Last Part of that Learning which is necessary to be Taught in *Charity Schools*, is *Arithmetick*; I mean so much of it as will be of use in the ordinary Management of *Accounts*; viz. the Five first Rules: wherein every *Scholar* must be very Perfect before he is sent from the *School*.

Thus the whole *School* may be divided into four Classes.

The First, consisting of those that Learn the *Alphabet*, and the first Rudiments of Reading in the *Horn-Book*, *Primer*, and *Spelling-Book*.

The Second, Of those that Read the *Psalter* and the *New-Testament*.

The Third, Of those that Read the *Bible* and such other useful Books as the Master or Governors of the School shall appoint; and who do likewise Learn to *Write*.

The Fourth, Of such as can Write well, and are fit to be Instructed in *Arithmetick*.

Having all along confined this Discourse to such Parts of *Learning* only as are necessary for the *Poor Children*, who are to be Qualified by their Education in these *Schools*, for *Services* and *Apprenticeships*; I shall not so far exceed the Limits and Design of it, as to prescribe any Method for the Teaching of *Latin*, which however by a vulgar Error it has been esteemed very necessary to the Education even of the meanest Children (insomuch that scarce any Husband-Man will venture to take his Son from the *School* to the *Plow*, till he has got some Smattering in this Language) yet upon a due Consideration of all the Ends that such Persons can propose to themselves from it, 'twill be found very Useless and Unprofitable, if not Prejudicial to them.

For *First*, As to that Knowledge of *Latin* which is to be had in Petty *Schools*, whither such Children are usually sent, and which seldom carrys them beyond the first Rudiments of that Language; it is so very little, as to be no way useful to any Purpose of their Education, not so much as to fit them for the lowest Degrees of any Profession that requires a competent Skill in it; which cannot be attained by those whose Parents or Friends are not able to Maintain them in a regular Course of Studies proper to that End. And therefore to what Purpose should these poor Children puzzle their Brains to Conn over and Learn by Heart, (or rather by Rote) a sensless Jargon of hard Words, which must of Course be laid aside and forgotten, when they shall be put out to such Trades or Employments for which they are designed; or which, if they happen afterwards to retain some little Scraps of it, will only serve to make them vain and conceited Pretenders to the Knowledge of what they do not Understand.

Those that fancy a little *Grammar Learning* (as they call it) will be of great Use towards *Orthography*, are widely mistaken, if they imagine that the Spelling, Declining, and (what they value most) the construing of a few *Latin* Words will conduce much to the True Writing of *English*: Which indeed might be more speedily and effectually attained by the Help of some short and plain *English Grammar* digested into a proper Method for the Use of these *Schools*: Though Experience shews, that this may be acquired much sooner and better by frequent Reading and Coppying from *English* Books (according to the Method already proposed under the Article of *Writing*) than by this which is so generally practis'd and so highly extolled by those ignorant Admirers of *Propria quæ Maribus*, &c. who thus preposterously impose a greater Difficulty as the Means of conquering a less.

JAMES TALBOTT *The Christian Schoolmaster*, pp. 78–86 (London, 1707)

The next extract discusses the problem of discipline and suggests various methods for motivating learning and good behaviour. Corporal punishment is seen as a last resort and interesting advice is given as to the method of its administration.

But as *Hope* and *Fear* are the first Principles and Motives of Humane Actions; so *Reward* and *Punishment*, (which are the chief Objects of those Passions) are the surest Sanction of all Laws, and will always be found the most Effectual Means of engaging our Obedience to them. It will therefore be necessary that the *Rules* and *Orders* above-mention'd should be enforced by the just and equal Distribution of such *Rewards* or *Punishments* as shall be suitable to the Occasion . . .

The *Rewards* which are proper to a *School*, are, 1. *Commendation*. 2. *Advancement*, or *Promotion*.

The *Punishments* are, 1. *Reproof*. 2. *Degradation*. 3. *Corporal Correction*. 4. *Expulsion*.

'Tis very truly observed by a Celebrated Writer concerning *Education*, That Children (earlier perhaps than we think) are very sensible of *Praise* and *Commendation*. They find a Pleasure in being Esteem'd and Valu'd, especially by their Superiors, and in the Presence of their Fellows: And on the other Side, they are so naturally Apprehensive of Shame, and of that State of Disgrace and Disesteem, which attends a just *Reproof* from the same Hands; that, I am confident, a discreet and seasonable Use of these Two Methods of *Discipline*, as Occasion shall require, will in many Cases supersede the rest. I say, a Discreet Use of them; because both one and the other must be proportion'd according to the Nature of the Action, which is to be Commended or Blamed: And in the latter Case, especially if the Fault be small, and of no very bad Consequence, the *Reproof* should neither be so Severe, nor so Publick, as when it is Notorious, and of ill Example. Those indeed that offend in this manner, should be *Rebuked before all* (as the Apostle advises) *that others also may fear* to do the like. But in both Cases, as well as in all others, where *Reward* or *Punishment* in any kind are Seasonable, it will be very proper to remind the Children of those Places in the Holy *Scripture*, or in the *Catechism*, where such or such Duties are mention'd as commanded by God, and the contrary Sins forbidden (as has been already Directed in the above-written System of Morality for the Use of Children) and it may be advisable to make them learn by Heart, as Occasion shall offer, such Sentences of the Scripture as are applicable to each respective Head: *All Scripture being profitable for Reproof and Correction*, as well as *for Instruction in Righteousness*; and therefore necessary on these Occasions to be learnt by Children so far at least as is requisite for the Forming of their Manners, *that they may be thoroughly furnished unto all Good Works.*

But forasmuch as Words alone will not always have the same desired Effect upon all Tempers and Dispositions; especially upon the minds of young Children, who are naturally unapt to give that Attention which is due to a serious *Admonition* and *Reproof*: And since even in that tender Age some Sparks of Emulation, and the Desire of Preference and Precedency are very discernable; it will be sometimes convenient to join with the former Methods some other distinguishing Marks of Approbation or Dislike, which may make them and others yet more sensible that they are in such a State of Esteem or Disgrace, as is the just Consequence of that *Commendation* or *Reproof* they have deserved. The most proper means to this End are those of *Promoting* or *Degrading* them, according to their Merit or Demerit. Thus by placing one above or below another, as each shall approve himself better or worse than his Fellows in Virtue, Learning, or Industry; the *Master* will raise in every Ingenuous Mind a Laudable Emulation and Eagerness to Excel in these; or at least, a just Concern not to be out-done in them, much less to Forfeit, by any Neglect or Breach of Duty, the Station which every one holds so long only as he can Maintain it upon the Terms above-mention'd . . .

But after all, it must be confess'd, that in some Cases, and with some Dispositions, the Methods hitherto proposed will be found Ineffectual; and that there are many Faults (to which even Children, by the Bent of Corrupt Nature, are very prone) which require a more severe Kind of Discipline: Especially where they are aggravated by a Wilful Violation of any known Duty, or by a Stubborn Persisting in any (even the least) Misdemeanour. Daily Experience confirms both Parts of the Wise Man's Observation; that *Foolishness is bound in the Heart of a Child, but a Rod of Correction shall drive it far from him.* In such Cases therefore, where *Admonition* and *Reproof* are insufficient; where neither the Sense of the Transgression, nor the Shame that attends it, is of Force to restrain a Child from the Commission of it; *Corporal Chastisement* will be absolutely necessary. Those Faults which seem more especially and indispensably to require it, are chiefly such as are a direct Breach of any Precept in the First or Second Table of the *Decalogue: viz.* of the *Third Commandment*, by taking God's Holy Name in vain; or by Cursing or Swearing: Of the *Fourth*, by the Prophanation of the Lord's Day: Of the *Fifth*, by Disobedience or Undutifulness to their Parents or Superiors: Of the *Sixth*, by Fighting, Quarrelling, *&c.* Of the *Seventh*, by any Unchaste or Immodest Discourse or Behaviour: Of the *Eighth*, by Stealing, Defrauding, or Wronging one another: Of the *Ninth*, by Lying, or Evil-speaking. This sort of Punishment will be likewise necessary in all Notorious Instances of *Idleness* (that being directly contrary to one main End of their Education) such as Loitering, Truanting, and a Wilful Neglect of their Daily Task.

I think indeed there are few other Offences, besides these, which seem to require that harsh and slavish Discipline of the *Rod*: Which, tho' it is generally used in *Schools*, as the shortest way of *Correction* (as indeed 'tis much the easiest to the Master, especially if he does not abound in good Nature) yet it is not always so Effectual in Cases of less Importance, and upon Modest and Ingenuous Tempers, as the Sense of *Shame* for having done amiss, improved by a seasonable and well managed *Reproof*: Which therefore may be very properly join'd with the former on all Occasions where that is requisite: That so the *Mind*, whose Reformation is the only End of all *Punishment*, may have at least an equal Share in it with the *Body*. To this End the *Chastisement* of Both must be govern'd with great Discretion; so as that it may be proportionable to the Nature and Quality of the Offence; and with so much Temper and Impartiality, that the Child may be sensible, before he receives it, that it is not the Effect of Passion or Unkindness in his *Master*, but purely of his own Demerit. Wherefore on all Occasions of *Corporal Punishment*, Care must be taken to convince the Offender that he has deserved what he suffers; that the Fault for which he suffers, is of very bad Consequence in such or such Respects, and especially in that it is a direct Violation of God's Express Command (as he is taught in such or such a Place of the *Holy Scripture*, or of his *Catechism*;) so likewise the *Reprehension* which shall be found necessary, whether it is given alone, or with the Former, must always be delivered in few and plain Words, and with all possible Gravity and Sobriety, rather than with a sharp and hasty Rating, and with that Bitterness and Indecency of Language, which only serves to encrease Passion on both sides, and to lessen the Force of the *Reproof*, as well as the Authority of him that gives it. Where this alone does not work its due Effect, the *Chastisement* that attends it must be inflicted with so much Sedateness, as well as Severity, (intermixing Admonitions betwixt each Blow) that neither one nor the other may seem to proceed from an immoderate Anger and Resentment towards the Person, but rather from a just and tender Sense of his Fault; and that both may appear rather as necessary and unavoidable Remedies for the Prevention of future Mischiefs, than as a furious and passionate Revenge for what is past: Which usually tends more to Exasperate than to Reform the Offender. So that in this Case, it concerns all *Masters* to be as careful as *Parents* are required to be, that they *provoke not their Children to Wrath*: Lest they should be prompted by an unreasonable Severity to conceive a lasting Prejudice, not only against the Persons they ought to Love and Reverence, but even against the Duty which is enforced upon them with some Appearance of Cruelty and ill Humour. On these Occasions therefore, our *School-Master*, who is to *bring up his Children in the Nurture and Admonition of the Lord*, must rather imitate the Example of our *Heavenly Father*, who corrects those he Loves *for their Profit, that they may be Partakers of his Holiness*; than of our *Fathers after the Flesh*, who sometimes *chastened us for their own Pleasure:* Since these do it many times in Anger, to Gratifie their present Passion; but He in Kindness, and purely with a Design to do us Good.

ibid., pp. 96–103

Finally Talbott gives *A Table of Faults* which was in common use in the London Charity-Schools. There is a full explanation of how the teacher should complete the table.

It appears by the Account of the *Charity-Schools*, which was published this last Year, that the *Masters* and *Mistresses* of most of those *Schools in London*, &c. keep a Daily Account of the Faults and Behaviour of the Children under their Care, which they lay before the *Trustees* at their Meetings: Whereby the *Trustees* see at one View the whole Behaviour of each Child since the last Meeting; and by comparing one Account with the other, do better know what Directions to give the *Master* or *Mistress*, and more easily see the Improvement of the Childrens Manners. This Method being found of great Use, it may be proper to insert here the Form of it; which is as follows.

A Table of Faults

JUNE		1	2	3	4	5	6	7	8
1707		*Mon.*	*Tue.*	*Wed.*	*Thur.*	*Fri.*	*Sat.*	*Sun.*	*Mon.*
1	A—								
2	B—							•c /	
3	C—		• /						*Curs.*
4	D—							a /	
5	E—				*L.*				
6	F—						T /		
7	G—								
8	H—								*St.*
9	I—				/ •				
10	K—							pc /	
11	L—			*Sw.*					
12	M—							ac /	
13	N—								

In the first Two Columns from the Left-Hand to the Right, are set down the Month, all the Days of the Month, and the Days of the Week. In the Two Columns downwards, are the Number of the Children in the School, and their Names.

C. signifies *Church.*
P. c. playing at *Church.*
Curs. Cursing.
L. signifies *Lying.*
Sw. Swearing.
St. Stealing.
T. playing *Truant.*

A. when alone, signifies Absence from *School.*

• when alone, signifies coming late to *School.*

When *a.* or the *Dot* is joined with *c.* they signifie coming late, or being absent from *Church.*

Each Square in the Table is taken for the whole Day of the Month and Week under which it is placed; after it's divided, (by the Master) as is the Third Square in the Table under *Tuesday*, the 2nd of *June*, the Upper Part whereof is taken for the Forenoon, and the Lower Part for the Afternoon. And when the Mark is placed on the Upper or Lower Part of the Square, it denotes that the Fault (it signifies) happen'd on the Forenoon or Afternoon.

And the Squares wherein the Marks are set, denote the Child, whose Name is over against it in the Table, to be guilty of such Crime as that Mark signifies, and the Time when. As (*a c*) against *M*. denotes *M*'s having been absent from *Church* on *Sunday* the 7th of *June*, in the Morning. And so of the rest.

ibid., pp. 107–9

An Endowed Grammar School in the Eighteenth Century: Oundle School

In the eighteenth century many of the endowed grammar schools underwent a period of decay, from which some never emerged. Their statutes often limited the curriculum they could offer to Latin and Greek and, as the case of Leeds Grammar School in 1805 showed, this limitation was binding according to Lord Eldon's judgment. Thus these schools offered little attraction to the parents of the newly emerging manufacturing and trading classes who wanted a more modern utilitarian curriculum for their sons and who turned to the private schools and academies to secure it. The endowed schools were often poorly staffed by underpaid masters, and this also led to their loss of pupils.* The following extracts refer to Oundle School, Northamptonshire. It eventually survived its decay and, by taking more boarders, adding modern subjects to its curriculum and increasing its efficiency, it transformed itself in the nineteenth century from a grammar school into a 'public school'. In 1779 – when John Evanson, M.A., of Brasenose College, Oxford, became schoolmaster at Oundle – it had four pupils. He increased the number to twelve, but then, as the extracts show, he lost all his pupils and was eventually dismissed in 1795 by the Court of the Grocers' Company, to whom the founder, Sir William Laxton, had entrusted the school he had endowed in 1556.

Action against John Evanson by the Court of the Grocers' Company began with letters of complaint from parents of pupils at the school. On 25 March 1794 five letters were read to the Court of Assistants of the Grocers' Company, of which three are given here.

The five letters read to the Court of Assistants of the Grocers' Company on 25 March 1794 are as follows:

Mr. Evanson in the year 91 applied to me to let my two Sons go to his School, I sent one of them wholly to him, and my other Son only half Days he perswaided me to let the other go whole days to him, he seemed for a time to bring them forward and took pains with them and the Children made no Complaints some time after my Children had been with him he brought a paper to petition me to sign as he said it being handed by the Childrens ffriends he hoped he shou'd get his salary advanced, I signed his Paper, sometime after my Eldest Son

*For further details of grammar schools at the end of the 18th century the following should be consulted:

N. CARLISLE *A Concise Description of the Endowed Grammar Schools in England and Wales* (London, 1818)
Individual school histories

had cause to complain to his Masters severely of his Master beating him and the rest of the Children unmercifully, and setting them unreasonable tasks, for which he desired that I would not insist upon his going there any more as he declared to me he would rather go to Dung Cart or any hard work than go to Mr. Evansons School, He likewise said that his Master did beat Wm. Kettle in that manner that the Child when he was called up by him wou'd fall a crying, that his Master wou'd knock him down with his fist, so declared Freeman Bradley another of his Scholars whom he has lately us'd very Ill. I saw his back very green eight days after his Ill treatment to him since Freeman Bradley has been taken away Mr. Evanson called on me to beg me not to sign any paper in his disfavor to which I answered him he might depend upon it that I should as I knew too well his severity and negligence to the Children and looked upon him as a very improper Person for a Schoolmaster.

(*signed*) G. Smith
Margt. Smith

Dec. 21, 1793

Respecting the Grammar School Decr 23.93
The common actions of the Master are as follows. Uttering Nonsense Runing about the School Room with his Arms stretch'd out & fits doubled making disagreeable faces so as to cause the Children to smile then sometimes they are to be unlawfully corrected or set more tasks than they are able to get whether from the effect of Liquor or Insanity I am not a Judge but he has been seen in the Street by several People in an undecent manner he seldom attends the School before ten or sometimes eleven o'clock in the morning & makes them holidays whenever he thinks proper so that they are not at school above two or three days in several weeks he charges ten shillings a Quarter for Education three shillings each boy for the Winters fireing 2s&6d twice a year for breaking up five shillings for the first entrance of the School Books Pens Ink & Copies the whole amounts to more than £3 a year we could wish to know the Rules of the School if the honourable Company of Gentlemen will be pleased to inspect a Petition from the Parents of the Children & the Town at Large for a removal of the said Master as thought to be an improper Person through the ill treatment & not bringing them forward in their Learning he has lost all his School on the latter end of August 93 or the beginning of September my Son received a violent Blow on the Loins from the Master with the fist doubled up that was looked over by only telling him of it & on the second of December inst he hit him a violent Blow on the Head with his fist doubled up that occasioned a lump as large as a Walnutt at the

same time recd a bruise on the Loins which was visible a fortnight after and seen by creditable Witnesses & threatened if he told his Parents he should be beat severely had he not been indisposed through the Blows led me to examine him & found the marks of violence John Billing a Scholar was at School the time it happened I took them to Mr. Walcott to be examined they gave him the account of the Master as in the former Page at the time he had a full School which was not more than nine or ten he artfully solicited us to sign a Petition to get his salary augmented which we simply complied with not thinking he would act as he since has done which is plain if the honourable Company will admit to keep him his residence & Salary he wants no Scholars or he would treat them better nor is he never likely to have another sent to him hereafter as their Lives are thought to be in danger he never attends the Church I am not fearful of being brought upon Oath.

(*signed*) Thos. & Katherine Bradley.

I do certify that I placed my Son under the care of Mr. Evanson Master of the Free Grammar School in Oundle but thro' Mr. Evanson's inattention to the few Children he had under his care & his brutal behaviour to my Son, by frequently knocking him down & giving him violent blows on the head which brought his Life in danger, I was under the necessity of taking him away. Mr. Evanson is extremely negligent in attending the School, seldom appearing before eleven o'clock, & when there, his behaviour has so much the appearance of a Man deranged in mind, & that many Persons have entertained an opinion of his being Insane. Altho' the School has been understood to be a free School for the Children whose Parents live in Oundle, yet Mr. Evanson demands £2 a year for tuition & puts the Parents to other unecessary expenses but this wanton cruelty to his Scholars which I can speak to Professionally from my own observations of the blows given to my Son, & to another whose Parents required my assistance render him an improper Person for the conduct of a School; & it is not supposed to anyone in future will venture to put a Child under his care – I conceive the School might be of great benefit to the Inhabitants of Oundle, if well regulated and under the care of a proper Master; at present those who are desirous of giving their Children School Learning are under the necessity of sending them to distant Schools at a great expense.

I am with great respect,
Oundle Yr. most obedt. Servt.
Mar 2. 1794 (*signed*) G. Kettle Surgeon.

Quoted in W. G. WALKER *A History of the Oundle Schools*, pp. 726–8 (London: The Worshipful Company of Grocers, 1956)

This next extract gives the list of charges which the clerk of the investigating committee read out to Evanson when he appeared before them on 13 June 1794.

Mr. Evanson,

In consequence of sundry allegations and complaints which have been exhibited against you by divers inhabitants of the town of Oundle who had placed their children under your care for tuition, which allegations and complaints have been officially transmitted to the Wardens and Assistants of the Company of Grocers in London, we have been deputed as a Committee to visit this town of Oundle and enquire what matters may seem to us amiss in regard to the Free Grammar School and Foundation of Sir William Laxton, and upon such enquiry and examination we find that the inhabitants of the town here have voluntarily come before us and have represented that you have been negligent and inattentive to the School which it is your especial duty to govern in a becoming manner consistent with the regulations of the Statutes and Orders made for the government thereof: that you have been unjustifiably severe in the chastisement of your scholars amounting even to cruelty so as to put them in dread and to hide from going to School: That the children under your care profit but very little in their learning: That you have demeaned yourself unworthily as a Schoolmaster making awkward gestures and running about the School so as to excite the laughter of the children and then that you have wantonly and cruelly chastised them for so laughing: That you have conducted yourself irreverently inasmuch as you have never once for four years past attended divine worship in the Church though by the Statutes you are enjoined to go to the parish Church at least three times by the week: That you have neglected to teach your scholars the Church Catechism or in any other manner to instruct them in the principles of the Christian religion: and lastly we find you have so demeaned yourself in your function of Schoolmaster that the inhabitants of this town will no longer place their children under your care and are thereby deprived of the benefit of the foundation which was designed by the pious donor for no other end than the service of this town of Oundle in the education of the rising generation.

As you have been placed by the Wardens and Assistants of the Grocers' Company during such and so long time as they shall think fit, we shall reluctantly return to represent to them who have delegated us such matters as have come to our knowledge upon this our visitation and by the said Wardens and Assistants you will be called upon, if they think fit, to answer the several complaints alledged against you: but we have thought it right and candid on our part now to make known to you the general heads of the several charges exhibited against you. The rest we submit to the consideration and judgement of the Wardens and Assistants of the Mystery of Grocers in full Court to be assembled.

ibid., pp. 249–50

This extract gives Evanson's reply to the charges.

R. W. Bridgman Esq. Oundle 26th June 1794
Grocers Hall. London.

Sir, Having been apprized that there will tomorrow be a Court of Assistants of the Worshipful Company of Grocers, I shall esteem it a favor, if you will be so obliging as to make known to the Court the following particulars which I take the liberty of sending you relative to the great injustice which has been done me by my enemies at Oundle.

After the prodigious pains taken by my enemies here to prejudice the towns people against me, it would have been extraordinary if in a town noted for scandal as this place certainly is, the late Committee had not heard of many infamous falsehoods which have been industriously circulated about me. But notwithstanding the late numerous complaints against me, not three years are yet elapsed since I not only gave entire satisfaction to all the parents of the children which I then had under my care, but was even popular. I had more than twice the number of boys that I found here at my first coming or than my predecessor had for several years. But popular favor is easily dissipated and often by the means that ought rather to strengthen it. This I am fully convinced of that I have made myself enemies by my anxiety for the improvement of my scholars. If I had been really guilty of that remissness of which I have been accused, I am confident that no petitions would have appeared against me.

The dissatisfaction of the people arose merely from the idle tales of children who, finding their parents inclined to listen to every little imaginary grievance, have represented in a most atrocious light some corrections which I solemnly declare were exceeding slight and trifling, and have also fabricated against me in other respects most abominable falsities. Whatever tales may have reached the ears of the Committee with respect to correction I protest that from a sense of the unreasonable fears of some parents about me in that particular, I have for several years past studiously avoided severity and have been very cautious and sparing in the exercise of correction: and if I had not really been *afraid* of having recourse to such chastisement as is generally thought necessary in schools, for neglect of business and other faults, I am convinced that most of my late scholars would have made much more improvement than they have made: but when independent of that circumstance it is considered that some of them were suffered by their parents to neglect their school so shamefully as not to appear there more than five or six months in the year, surely it would have been extremely surprizing if they had made any rapid progress in their learning.

With respect to that extraordinary charge of my running about the school and using strange gestures, sure no credit can be given by the Court of Assistants to such a ridiculous and improbable tale as this; it can hardly I think be supposed by them that any being endued with reason could act in so preposterous a manner; and the tales of children cannot, I think, induce a belief of my being subject to insanity or intoxication, when a proof of both my sanity of intellect and sobriety can be most easily procured from the testimony of those with whom I have lived and with whom I now live. When I have seen boys laughing in school time without any apparent proper reason, I have several times only reproved them, and when I have at any time had recourse to punishment for such behaviour, the utmost correction I can remember to have ever given for it was a few strokes with a small rod or twig of birch on the back of the hand: and I must confess I know of no mode of correction more unexceptionable than that.

As to charges in the bills, I hope, Sir, that the Court of Assistants cannot think me unreasonable in exacting ten shillings per quarter for English, Writing and Arithmetic, that sum being really much less than what many other masters charge for the same.

With regard to the accusation respecting my not frequenting Church, I answer that the statute, wherein attendance at Church is mentioned, seems to relate to the Master's conducting boarders thither, and superintending their conduct which it is well known I regularly did, when I had boarders.

I shall only add, Sir, that I hope the Court of Assistants will not imbibe prejudice against me from the infamous scandal of this town, with which I have been most grievously oppressed, but that they will weigh all circumstances with candour, making proper allowances for the present low state of the school, for although, through the malicious endeavours of a set of people to prepossess others against me, I have at present but one scholar, I have had more boys even within nine months than I found here at my first coming and may perhaps again have as many in a similar period of time.

I am, Sir, Your most obedient, humble servant, J. Evanson.

ibid., pp. 251–2

Public Schools in the Eighteenth Century

The greater boarding schools of the eighteenth century were in many ways little better than the smaller endowed grammar schools. Their curriculum was equally limited to Latin and Greek, though some French might be taught in a small way, as at Rugby school. The schools were often poorly staffed and conditions for the pupils were primitive, with food scarce and ill-prepared and beating a common means of punishment. Schoolboy revolts were frequent. Winchester, Rugby, Eton and Harrow all had their rebellions and so serious was the rebellion at Rugby in 1797 that the army was called in to quell it.

The state of the schools discouraged many upper class parents from sending their sons to them and instead they relied on private tutors for the education of their offspring. Not until the middle years of the nineteenth century, following the reforms of headmasters like Arnold of Rugby, did the public schools begin to enjoy the prestige which made many wealthy parents, from both the landed and manufacturing classes, turn to the idea of boarding-school education.*

CURRICULUM AT RUGBY SCHOOL

When Samuel Butler went to be Headmaster of Shrewsbury School in 1798 he found it 'with scarcely a single boy'. During his headship (1798–1836) he reformed and built up the school but at the beginning he was influenced by the advice which his own ex-headmaster, Dr James, who had been head of Rugby School from 1780–1794, offered him in various letters.

The following extract is from a letter dated 14 October 1798 and it gives a description of the curriculum – almost wholly classical – in use at Rugby school in the latter part of the eighteenth century.

Fifth and Sixth Forms

Monday, at 7 – Watts' *Scripture History*, sixteen pages, or Goldsmith's *Roman History* (2 vols., 8vo), sixteen pages at a lesson at least, or twenty pages at most; or *History of England* in a series of letters, with geography and chronology of each lesson. Ingles does geography instead of this lesson in its turn, as after *Roman History* finished in one volume; then again after second volume and Watts finished.

Perhaps twelve pages of Watts may be full enough at first.

**Further reading:*

E. C. MACK *Public Schools and British Opinion 1780–1860* (London: Methuen, 1938)

At 10 – Thirty-five lines of the *Iliad*, twice construed and parsed. The next lesson in the same book is always set after doing present lesson. Take *Selecta ex Iliade* by W. Holwell, if it can be got. But at Christmas you may come to Worcester and mark your Homer and Virgil by my books.

At 3 – About fifty lines in *Scriptores Romani*, twice construed. Set Tuesday's translation.

At 5 – Thirty-eight lines in Virgil, or rather *Selecta e Virgilio*. $38 \times 2 = 76$ construed in the week, less fifty repeated Friday, leaving twenty-six (see Friday's lessons at seven and three).

Tuesday, at 7 – Thirty lines of Tully's *Offices* repeated. Themes looked over.

Note. – I should set translation of Tully one week, the next some English to be translated into Latin (as Willymot's *Peculiars*, or my Erasmus Englished), and then translation of Tully or English theme alternately, always rendering English into Latin once a fortnight.

At 10 – Thirty-five lines of *Poetoe Groeci*. Verse theme set and English translation for this day.

Half-Holiday – Absence (i.e. calling over the boys' names to see that they were all there) at three and five, or half after five in summer.

Exercise – One week English theme or English translation. The next week translate English into Latin. This English was Erasmus translated by me, but Willymot's *Peculiars* will do. Lock up at . . . different times between six and eight, according to the season. The earlier Prayers are the better.

Wednesday, at 7 – Translation or English theme looked over. Repeat Tuesday's *Poetoe Groeci*.

At 10 – Thirty-five lines of *Scriptores Groeci*.

At 3 *and* 5 – The same as Monday; but a selection *ex Cicerone*, or his letters (at the end of the book), were construed on Monday, and *Selecta e Livio*, *Tacito* (you may leave out perhaps *e Paterculo*) were construed on a Wednesday.

Exercise Latin Verses – Lowest number of lowest fifth is sixteen.

Note – Tully repeated for themes and Ovid for verses is good, but sometimes Greek grammar must be said, instead of these lessons – at least the principal parts of it.

Thursday, at 7 – Latin verses looked over. Thirty lines of *Selecta ex Ovidio* repeated, or Greek grammar.

At 10 – Homer as on Monday.

Half-Holiday. – In honour of one or even two (perhaps one of these from the fifth form) of the best praepostor's exercises.

Thursday's exercise – Lyrics of various sorts: Iambics, Sapphics, Asclep., Alc., Trochaics. Two upper praepostors make Greek.

Friday, at 7 – Thirty-five lines of Homer repeated (or Thursday's Homer); *or* sometimes twenty-five lines of Homer and twenty-six lines of Virgil have been said, which compleats the repetition of all the Virgil of the week.

At 10 – Sixty lines in Horace's *Satyrs* [sic] and *Epistles* and *Ars Poetica* were construed, or Juvenal, *Sat.* 1, 3, 10, 14, or Persius, *Sat.* 5.

N.B. – Horace and Juvenal are thus finished in two and a half years.

At 3 – Fifty lines of Monday's and Wednesday's Virgil repeated. Horace lesson of the morning construed a second time.

N.B. – If twenty-six lines of Virgil be said on Friday morning, then all the Virgil construed will be said.

At 5 – Thirty lines in Tully's *Offices* once construed, which are to be repeated in the following week, and also thirty lines in *Selecta ex Ovidio* once construed and once hastily read off in English, which are to be repeated *in the next following week*. Ingles's fifth form assistant teaches the fifth form the Tully and *Selecta ex Ovidio*, while he teaches *Funebres Orationes* or Pindar, or etc., for this lesson; but these lessons are perfectly academic, and rather beyond the power of young boys, unless they be already accomplished scholars.

Saturday. – Sixty lines of Friday's Horace repeated. The head-master, having no exercise, examines a lower form. Ingles takes his sixth and fifth form repetition (which is made to an assistant), etc.

At 10 – Fifty lines in Greek play or fifty lines in Demosthenes twice construed; or if time be wanted read it off hastily a second time into English. Latin theme for Monday set now.

Third lesson of Saturday at twelve. Thirty-five lines in select parts of Milton (suppose the printed *Elegant Extracts of Poetry*), by Dr. Knox, were used). This also would be a reading book or a library of poetry to a schoolboy. Now also Mathematics were done, which was my utter ruin at the time; or speeches rehearsed, which I advise you to avoid altogether, as being the most painful and laborious instruction that can be given. Nothing wears a man out so much.

Saturday is a half-holiday, and of course (like other half-holidays) is for writing, dancing, French, drawing, or even fencing – as it is now taught at Rugby.

Sunday – Absence at nine, at breakfast.

SAMUEL BUTLER, *The Life and Letters of Dr. Samuel Butler*, Vol. 1, pp. 25–7 (London: John Murray, 1896)

LIVING CONDITIONS AT CHRIST'S HOSPITAL

The following letter from Samuel Taylor Coleridge to Thomas Poole gives a description of the school of Christ's Hospital at the end of the eighteenth century. Coleridge was there from 1782 to 1791.

Founded in 1553, Christ's Hospital had continued to provide, as this extract shows, education to various standards for boys who through some benefactor secured a place there. Part of the School was at Hertford and the Mathematical School referred to was that founded in 1673 by Charles II with the particular purpose of training entrants in navigation and arithmetic for the navy.

February 19, 1798.

From October, 1781, to October, 1782.

After the death of my father, we of course changed houses, and I remained with my mother till the spring of 1782, and was a day-scholar to Parson Warren, my father's successor. He was not very deep, I believe; and I used to delight my mother by relating little instances of his deficiency in grammar knowledge – every detraction from his merits seemed an oblation to the memory of my father, especially as Parson Warren did certainly *pulpitize* much better. Somewhere I think about April, 1782, Judge Buller, who had been educated by my father, sent for me, having procured a Christ's Hospital Presentation. I accordingly went to London, and was received by my mother's brother, Mr. Bowdon, a tobacconist and (at the same time) clerk to an underwriter. My uncle lived at the corner of the Stock Exchange and carried on his shop by means of a confidential servant, who, I suppose, fleeced him most unmercifully. He was a widower and had one daughter who lived with a Miss Cabriere, an old maid of great sensibilities and a taste for literature. Betsy Bowdon had obtained an unlimited influence over her mind, which she still retains. Mrs. Holt (for this is her name now) was not the kindest of daughters – but, indeed, my poor uncle would have wearied the patience and affection of an Euphrasia. He received me with great affection, and I stayed ten weeks at his house, during which time I went occasionally to Judge Buller's. My uncle was very proud of me, and used to carry me from coffee-house to coffee-house and tavern to tavern, where I drank and talked and disputed, as if I had been a man. Nothing was more common than for a large party to exclaim in my hearing that I was a *prodigy*, etc., etc., etc., so that while I remained at my uncle's I was most completely spoiled and pampered, both mind and body.

At length the time came, and I donned the *blue* coat and yellow stockings and was sent down into Hertford, a town twenty miles from London, where there are about three hundred of the younger Blue-Coat boys. At Hertford I was very happy, on the whole, for I had plenty to eat and drink, and pudding and vegetables almost every day. I stayed there six weeks, and then was drafted up to the great school at London where I arrived in September, 1782, and was placed in the second ward, then called Jefferies' Ward, and in the under Grammar School. There are twelve wards or dormitories of unequal sizes, beside the sick ward, in the great school, and they contained all together seven hundred boys, of whom I think nearly one third were the sons of clergymen. There are five schools, – a mathematical, a grammar, a drawing, a reading and a writing school, – all very large buildings. When a boy is admitted, if he reads very badly, he is either sent to Hertford or the reading school. (N.B. Boys are admissible from seven to twelve years old.) If he learns to read tolerably well before nine, he is drafted into the Lower Grammar School; if not, into the Writing School, as having given proof of unfitness for classical attainments. If before he is eleven he climbs up to the first form of the Lower Grammar School, he is drafted into the head Grammar School; if not, at eleven years old, he is sent into the Writing School, where he continues till fourteen or fifteen, and is then either apprenticed and articled as clerk, or whatever else his turn of mind or of fortune shall have provided for him. Two or three times a year the Mathematical Master beats up for recruits for the King's boys, as they are called; and all who like the Navy are drafted into the Mathematical and Drawing Schools, where they continue till sixteen or seventeen, and go out as midshipmen and schoolmasters in the Navy. The boys, who are drafted into the Head Grammar School remain there till thirteen, and then, if not chosen for the University, go into the Writing School.

Each dormitory has a nurse, or matron, and there is a head matron to superintend all these nurses. The boys were, when I was admitted under excessive subordination to each other, according to rank in school; and every ward was governed by four Monitors (appointed by the *Steward*, who was the supreme Governor out of school, – our temporal lord), and by four *Markers*, who wore silver medals and were appointed by the Head Grammar Master, who was our supreme spiritual lord. The same boys were commonly both monitors and markers. We read in classes on Sundays to our *Markers*, and were catechized by them, and under their sole authority during prayers, etc. All other authority was in the monitors; but, as I said, the same boys were ordinarily both the one and the other. Our diet was very scanty. Every morning, a bit of dry bread and some bad small beer. Every evening, a larger piece of bread and cheese or butter, whichever we liked. For dinner, – on Sunday, boiled beef and broth; Monday, bread and butter, and milk and water; on Tuesday roast mutton; Wednesday, bread and butter, and rice milk; Thursday, boiled beef and broth; Saturday, bread and butter, and pease-porritch. Our food was portioned; and, excepting on Wednesdays, I never had a belly full. Our appetites were *damped*, never satisfied; and we had no vegetables.

E. H. COLERIDGE (ed.) *Letters of Samuel Taylor Coleridge*, Vol. I, pp. 18–21 (London: Heinemann, 1895)

Universities in the Eighteenth Century

The universities of Oxford and Cambridge were neither energetic nor high-powered as centres of learning in the eighteenth century. Many of the Fellows of the Colleges were content to live a life of ease, tutoring their pupils in a pleasant but desultory manner, and with little concern to further the frontiers of knowledge. Professors were often reluctant to lecture in their subjects and 'research' was not yet seen as the main function of the university academic. The undergraduates could survive with a minimum of intellectual effort and though before graduating they had to take part in 'disputations' on medieval lines, these were not very rigorous.

However, it is possible to paint too black a picture of the universities in this period. Some Fellows and Professors were concerned about the advancement of learning and one indication of this is the development of scientific studies which some individual academics pursued. The use of written examinations in the choice of College Fellows which began towards the end of the eighteenth century is a further indication of a more serious approach to learning than might be assumed from merely reading the testimony of Edward Gibbon.*

EDWARD GIBBON ON THE UNIVERSITY OF OXFORD

Edward Gibbon (1737–1794) went up to Oxford in April 1752. He stayed there barely a year and his conversion to Roman Catholicism in June 1753 prohibited his return to his place at Magdalen College. Nevertheless Gibbon saw enough in his short period of residence to make him most critical of the University as a place of learning.

A traveller who visits Oxford or Cambridge is surprised and edified by the apparent order and tranquillity that prevail in the seats of the English muses. In the most celebrated Universities of Holland, Germany, and Italy, the students, who swarm from different countries, are loosely dispersed in private lodgings at the houses of the burghers: they dress according to their fancy and fortune; and in the intemperate quarrels of youth and wine, their *swords*, though less frequently than of old, are sometimes stained with each other's blood. The use of arms is banished from our English Universities; the uniform habit of the academics, the square cap and black gown, is adapted to the civil and

**Further reading:*

D. A. WINSTANLEY *The University of Cambridge in the Eighteenth Century* (Cambridge Univ. Press, 1922)

D. A. WINSTANLEY *Unreformed Cambridge* (Cambridge Univ. Press, 1935)

C. E. MALLET *A History of the University of Oxford*, Vol. III (London: Methuen, 1927) even clerical professions; and from the doctor in divinity to the undergraduate, the degrees of learning and age are externally distinguished. Instead of being scattered in a town, the students of Oxford and Cambridge are united in colleges; their maintenance is provided at their own expense, or that of the founders; and the stated hours of the hall and chapel represent the discipline of a regular, and, as it were, a religious community. The eyes of the traveller are attracted by the size or beauty of the public edifices; and the principal colleges appear to be so many palaces, which a liberal nation has erected and endowed for the habitation of science. My own introduction to the University of Oxford forms a new era in my life; and at the distance of forty years I still remember my first emotions of surprise and satisfaction. In my fifteenth year I felt myself suddenly raised from a boy to a man: the persons, whom I respected as my superiors in age and academical rank, entertained me with every mark of attention and civility; and my vanity was flattered by the velvet cap and silk gown, which distinguish a gentleman-commoner from a plebeian student. A decent allowance, more money than a schoolboy had ever seen, was at my own disposal; and I might command, among the tradesmen of Oxford, an indefinite and dangerous latitude of credit. A key was delivered into my hands, which gave me the free use of a numerous and learned library: my apartment consisted of three elegant and well-furnished rooms in the new building, a stately pile, of Magdalen College; and the adjacent walks, had they been frequented by Plato's disciples, might have been compared to the Attic shade on the banks of the Ilissus. Such was the fair prospect of my entrance (April 3, 1752,) into the University of Oxford . . .

To the University of Oxford *I* acknowledge no obligation; and she will as cheerfully renounce me for a son, as I am willing to disclaim her for a mother. I spent fourteen months at Magdalen College; they proved the fourteen months the most idle and unprofitable of my whole life: the reader will pronounce between the school and the scholar: but I cannot affect to believe that nature had disqualified me for all literary pursuits. The specious and ready excuse of my tender age, imperfect preparation, and hasty departure, may doubtless be alleged; nor do I wish to defraud such excuses of their proper weight. Yet in my sixteenth year I was not devoid of capacity or application; even my childish reading had displayed an early though blind propensity for books; and the shallow flood might have been taught to flow in a deep channel and a clear stream. In the discipline of a well-constituted academy, under the guidance of skilful and vigilant professors, I should gradually have risen from translations to originals, from the Latin to the Greek classics, from dead languages to living science: my hours would have been occupied by useful and agreeable studies, the wanderings of fancy would have been restrained, and I should have escaped the temptations of idleness, which finally precipitated my departure from Oxford.

Perhaps in a separate annotation I may coolly examine the fabulous and real antiquities of our sister universities . . . In the meanwhile it will be acknowledged that these venerable bodies are sufficiently old to partake of all the prejudices and infirmities of age. The schools of Oxford and Cambridge were founded in a dark age of false and barbarous science; and they are still tainted with the vices of their origin. Their primitive discipline was adapted to the education of priests and monks; and the government still remains in the hands of the clergy, an order of men whose manners are remote from the present world, and whose eyes are dazzled by the light of philosophy. The legal incorporation of these societies by the charters of popes and kings had given them a monopoly of the public instruction; and the spirit of monopolists is narrow, lazy, and oppressive: . . . We may scarcely hope that any reformation will be a voluntary act; and so deeply are they rooted in law and prejudice, that even the omnipotence of Parliament would shrink from an inquiry into the state and abuses of the two Universities.

The use of academical degrees, as old as the thirteenth century, is visibly borrowed from the mechanic corporations; in which an apprentice, after serving his time, obtains a testimonial of his skill, and a licence to practise his trade and mystery. It is not my design to depreciate these honours, which could never gratify or disappoint my ambition; and I should applaud the institution, if the degrees of bachelor or licentiate were bestowed as the reward of manly and successful study: if the name and rank of doctor or master were strictly reserved for the professors of science, who have approved their title to the public esteem.

In all the Universities of Europe, excepting our own, the languages and sciences are distributed among a numerous list of effective professors: the students, according to their taste, their calling, and their diligence, apply themselves to the proper masters; and in the annual repetition of public and private lectures, these masters are assiduously employed. Our curiosity may inquire what number of professors has been instituted at Oxford (for I shall now confine myself to my own University)? by whom are they appointed, and what may be the probable chances of merit or incapacity? how many are stationed to the three faculties, and how many are left for the liberal arts? what is the form, and what the substance, of their lessons? But all these questions are silenced by one short and singular answer, 'That in the University of Oxford, the greater part of the public professors have for these many years given up altogether even the pretence of teaching'. Incredible as the fact may appear, I must rest my belief on the positive and impartial evidence of a master of moral and political wisdom, who had himself resided at Oxford. Dr. Adam Smith assigns as the cause of their indolence, that, instead of being paid by voluntary contributions, which would urge them to increase the number, and to deserve the gratitude of their pupils, the Oxford professors are secure in the enjoyment of a fixed stipend, without the necessity of labour, or the apprehension of control. It has indeed been observed, nor is the observation absurd, that excepting in experimental sciences, which demand a costly apparatus and a dexterous hand, the many valuable treatises that have been published on every subject of learning may now supersede the ancient mode of oral instruction. Were this principle true in its utmost latitude, I should only infer that the offices and salaries, which are become useless, ought without delay to be abolished. But there still remains a material difference between a book and a professor; the hour of the lecture enforces attendance; attention is fixed by the presence, the voice, and the occasional questions of the teacher; the most idle will carry something away; and the more diligent will compare the instructions which they have heard in the school, with the volumes which they peruse in their chamber. The advice of a skilful professor will adapt a course of reading to every mind and every situation; his authority will discover, admonish, and at last chastise the negligence of his disciples; and his vigilant inquiries will ascertain the steps of their literary progress. Whatever science he professes he may illustrate in a series of discourses, composed in the leisure of his closet, pronounced on public occasions, and finally delivered to the press. I observe with pleasure that in the University of Oxford Dr. Lowth, with equal eloquence and erudition, has executed this task in his incomparable *Praelectiones* on the Poetry of the Hebrews.

The College of St. Mary Magdalen was founded in the fifteenth century by Wainfleet, Bishop of Winchester; and now consists of a president, forty fellows, and a number of inferior students. It is esteemed one of the largest and most wealthy of our academical corporations, which may be compared to the Benedictine abbeys of Catholic countries; and I have loosely heard that the estates belonging to Magdalen College, which are leased by those indulgent landlords at small quit-rents and occasional fines, might be raised, in the hands of private avarice, to an annual revenue of nearly thirty thousand pounds. Our colleges are supposed to be schools of science, as well as of education; nor is it unreasonable to expect that a body of literary men, devoted to a life of celibacy, exempt from the care of their own subsistence, and amply provided with books, should devote their leisure to the prosecution of study, and that some effects of their studies should be manifested to the world. The shelves of their library groan under the weight of the Benedictine folios, of the editions of the fathers, and the collections of the middle ages, which have issued from the single abbey of St. Germain de Préz at Paris. A composition of genius must be the offspring of one mind, but such works of industry, as may be divided among many hands, and must be continued during many years, are the peculiar province of a laborious community. If I inquire into the manufactures of the monks of Magdalen, if I extend the inquiry to the other colleges of Oxford and Cambridge, a silent blush, or a scornful frown, will be the only reply. The fellows or monks of my time were decent easy men, who supinely enjoyed the gifts of the founder; their days were filled by a series of uniform employments; the chapel and the hall, the coffee-house and the common room, till they retired, weary and well satisfied, to a long slumber. From the toil of reading, or thinking, or writing they had absolved their conscience; and the first shoots of learning and ingenuity withered on the ground, without yielding any fruits to the owners or the public. As a gentleman-commoner, I was admitted to the society of the fellows, and fondly expected that some questions of literature would be the amusing and instructive topics of their discourse. Their conversation stagnated in a round of college business, Tory politics, personal anecdotes, and private scandal: their dull and deep potations excused the brisk intemperance of youth: and their constitutional toasts were not expressive of the most lively loyalty for the house of Hanover. A general election was now approaching: the great Oxfordshire contest already blazed with all the malevolence of party zeal. Magdalen College was devoutly attached to the old interest! and the names of Wenman and Dashwood were more frequently pronounced, than those of Cicero and Chrysostom. The example of the senior fellows could not inspire the undergraduates with a liberal spirit or studious emulation; and I cannot describe, as I never knew, the discipline of college. Some duties may possibly have been imposed on the poor scholars, whose ambition aspired to the peaceful honours of a fellowship (*ascribi quietis ordinibus . . . Deorum*); but no independent members were admitted below the rank of a gentleman-commoner, and our velvet cap was the cap of liberty. A tradition prevailed that some of our predecessors had spoken Latin declamations in the hall; but of this ancient custom no vestige remained: the obvious methods of public exercises and examinations were totally unknown; and I have never heard that either the president or the society interfered in the private economy of the tutors and their pupils.

The silence of the Oxford professors, which deprives the youth of public instruction, is imperfectly supplied by the tutors, as they are styled, of the several colleges. Instead of confining themselves to a single science, which had satisfied the ambition of Burman or Bernoulli, they teach, or promise to teach, either history or mathematics, or ancient literature, or moral philosophy; and as it is possible that they may be defective in all, it is highly probable that of some they will be ignorant. They are paid, indeed, by private contributions; but their appointment depends on the head of the house: their diligence is voluntary, and will consequently be languid, while the pupils themselves, or their parents, are not indulged in the liberty of choice or change. The first tutor into whose hands I was resigned appears to have been one of the best of the tribe: Dr. Waldegrave was a learned and pious man, of a mild disposition, strict morals, and abstemious life, who seldom mingled in the politics or the jollity of the college. But his knowledge of the world was confined to the University; his learning was of the last, rather than of the present age; his temper was indolent; his faculties, which were not of the first rate, had been relaxed by the climate, and he was satisfied, like his fellows, with the slight and superficial discharge of an important trust. As soon as my tutor had sounded the insufficiency of his disciple in school-learning, he proposed that we should read every morning from ten to eleven the comedies of Terence. The sum of my improvement in the University of Oxford is confined to three or four Latin plays; and even the study of an elegant classic, which might have been illustrated by a comparison of ancient and modern theatres, was reduced to a dry and literal interpretation of the author's text. During the first weeks I constantly attended these lessons in my tutor's room; but as they appeared equally devoid of profit and pleasure, I was once tempted to try the experiment of a formal apology. The apology was accepted with a smile. I repeated the offence with less ceremony; the excuse was admitted with the same indulgence: the slightest motive of laziness or indisposition, the most trifling avocation at home or abroad, was allowed as a worthy impediment; nor did my tutor appear conscious of my absence or neglect. Had the hour of lecture been constantly filled, a single hour was a small portion of my academic leisure. No plan of study was recommended for my use; no exercises were prescribed for his inspection; and, at the most precious season of youth, whole days and weeks were suffered to elapse without labour or amusement, without advice or account. I should have listened to the voice of reason and of my tutor; his mild behaviour had gained my confidence. I preferred his society to that of the younger students; and in our evening walks to the top of Headington Hill, we freely conversed on a variety of subjects. Since the days of Pocock and Hyde, oriental learning has always been the pride of Oxford, and I once expressed an inclination to study Arabic. His prudence discouraged this childish fancy; but he neglected the fair occasion of directing the ardour of a curious mind.

EDWARD GIBBON *Autobiography*, pp. 34–43
(Oxford World's Classics, 1950)

RULES FOR HERTFORD COLLEGE, OXFORD, 1747

This extract illustrates various sides of university life; the composition of the academic staff of the college and their salaries, rooms and servants; the religious life of the college; lectures and disputations; and the duties of tutors with regard to their undergraduates.

Rules and *Statutes* for the Government of *Hertford College* in the University of *Oxford*, with *Observations* on particular Parts of them shewing the *Reasonableness* thereof by *R. Newton*, D.D., Principal of *Hertford*-College London: Printed for John Osborn, in Paternoster-Row, 1747. (pp. 162)

The Principal may hold his office for life: the four senior Fellows, *Vice-Principal*, *Catechist*, *Chaplain* and *Moderator* may be Tutors till eighteen years after their matriculation: the eight junior B.A. Fellows may continue in the position of Assistants for three years. There shall be but thirty-two Students, and four Scholars.

One of the four Seniors is to be principal Tutor for a year in rotation; he is to receive the fees and to lecture once a week to all students. Each Tutor to have a class of eight Students and one Scholar who are to continue under his special care for their career of sixteen terms.

The Revenue of the Principal to be 281*l.* 6*s.* 8*d.*
„ „ each Tutor or Senior 93*l.* 11*s.* 8*d.*
„ „ each Junior Fellow 26*l.* 13*s.* 4d.
„ „ each Student 13*l.* 6*s.* 8*d.*
„ „ each Probationer Student 6*l.* 13*s.* 4*d.*
„ „ each Scholar 4*l.* 3*s.* 4*d.*

These stipends are only to be augmented by an allowance of 6*d. per diem* for Commons, for 31 weeks, making an addition of 5*l.* 8*s.* 6*d. per annum* for each member of the foundation.

Any Person of Superior Condition to pay double fees, &c., and to be 'distinguish'd tho' not by a different *Gown* yet by a *Tuft* upon his *Cap*, varying according to the different Rank in which he is Admitted.'

One Tutor is to lodge in the middle Room of the middle Staircase in each Angle of the College Court. [Hence, according to Nic. Amherst (Appendix to *Terrae Filius*, 1726, p. 295, *n.*), they were nicknamed *Anglers*]. Each compartment shall contain an outward Room, a Bed-place, and a Study. One Bed-maker (a Man or elderly Woman), assisted by a Son or Servant, who shall lodge in the tutor's suite and serve him out of the hours of their common service, to have care of each Angle, i.e. of 15 sets of rooms apiece.

§ 2. *Morning* Prayers, on *Common* Days at 6.30 or 7.30 according to the time of year. On Litany Days the Second Service at 9. Fines of 2*d.* for absence or bad behaviour in chapel.

Evening Prayer at 6.30 *p.m.*

Immediately after *First* Service on *Sundays* and *Holidays* in *Term* shall follow a very short *Explication* of some Part of the *Church Catechism*, or *Instruction* in some *Moral Duty*, in a manner Useful to the *Servants.* On Sundays at 8 or 9 *p.m.* a *Catechetical* or *Theological* Lecture for undergraduates. All to communicate on Xmas Day, Easter Day, Whitsunday, the first Sunday in every Term, and at the Admission of a new Principal. Undergraduates to read in course in Chapel on surplice days; and on other days the 2nd lesson for the morning before dinner, and the 2nd lesson for the evening before supper, in Hall, when all shall be present. None to rise from table without leave till the second grace is said. The college officers may examine the reader as to his comprehension of the chapter. He shall write explanations of the difficulties in the lessons instead of his weekly theme, disputation or translation.

§ 3. Oaths on admission. § 4. The Principal to be chosen from the Westminster students of Ch. Ch. by the Chancellor of Oxford.

§ 5. There shall be *Lectures* (1) by the Principal to all Undergraduates on Thursdays; (2) by the Tutors to their respective classes on M. Tuesdays, W.F.; (3) by the Officers or their Assistants at 9 *p.m.* on Tu. Th. Sat. and on Sundays at 8 *p.m.* in winter, 9 *p.m.* in summer.

Disputations 4 to 5 *p.m.*: of Undergraduates (beginning from Easter term in their second year) on M. W. in Philosophy (Logic, Ethics, Physics and Metaphysics): of B.A. on Fridays in Divinity. All persons to take their turn in seniority of being Respondents and Prior Opponents. Notice to be given, a term in advance, of the subjects and persons required in the disputations. And in order to give interest to the proceedings the college moderator is to order the same questions to be disputed in college, as any of the society are intending to take up in their public exercises in the Schools. On these occasions only those of B.A. degree may take part in *philosophical* disputations.

'The *Respondent* and *Opponent* shall each of them, by way of Introduction to the Disputation, premise something relating to them in certain *Speeches* commonly called *Supposition* and *Opposition* Speeches, which shall not be bare *Transcripts* out of Philosophical or Theological Books; but the *Former* a short state of the Question, shewing in what respect the Question is true, in what false, with the Application of such Distinctions as are to be met with in those Books which treat of the Questions to be Disputed upon; the *Latter* an Elusive Speech, treating plausibly of the Other Side of the Question, the known Part of a Declaimant who holds the Wrong Side of the Thesis; unless the Question may be such as may be well supported by good Arguments on *both*

Sides.' [This was probably the original function of the *Terrae Filius* at Oxford, and the *Praevaricator* at Cambridge.]

Undergraduates (even when not in residence) to make a *Theme* or a *Declamation* or a *Translation* every week in full term. Declamations in English during their 2nd and 3rd, and Latin during their 4th year. Translations for Latin into English or English into Latin, or by advanced students into Greek, to be looked over by the Tutors on Saturday at 4 *p.m.*, and corrected in the following week, so as to be ready for reading or recitation the following Saturday morning. Permission may be given to any that has a genius that way, to write English verse instead.

'*Batchelors of Arts* for the 1st *six* Terms which they aim to keep towards their *Master's* Degree, shall read in the *College* as an Exercise of the House the *Six Solemn Lectures* (one every Term) which are afterwards to be read, by those in the Schools as an Exercise of the University for the said Degree; and in every of the Other Terms to be kept for the said Degree, they shall make and publickly Speak or Read a short *Sermon* upon a Text of Scripture assigned them by the *Principal*. Without the Performance of this Exercise they shall neither keep the Term nor receive a *Testimonium* for Orders, nor an Instrument of *Leave* to go to another House.' [A *licet migrare:* still less a *bene discessit.*]

Two Undergraduates a week to deliver *Narration* [cp. p. 119, above. These 'collections' are common-place Beauties, Difficulties, and other noteworthy references, from four classic authors chosen for each student by his tutor, in the way of Elegant Extracts to be recited] instead of their Theme or Translation.

§ 6. The *Principal* is to have the sole nomination of servants, assistants; also of the tutors, only they may not be his own or his wife's relations 'even to the Fourth Remove inclusive,' except at the Visitor's recommendation; he shall be present at all Exercises; shall visit Students in their rooms, reprimand them when necessary, preside over a *Tutor's meeting* fortnightly in his own Lodgings, as *Bursar* shall hold two audits a year. He may take one private pupil only, and that in excess of the statutable number of students (32). If a tutor's place fall vacant within the first year of his Principalship he may take the duties and stipend himself. The Principal shall be removed if he accept any other lectureship, professorship, care of souls, dignity requiring him to break the statutable residence, &c. &c.

§ 7. The *Tutors* shall instruct their classes 1 hour *per diem:* for the first year in classics (composition and translation) and Theology: for the three next 'in *University Learning*, not Exclusive of *Other*: For the Three several Weeks immediately preceding *Christmas*-day, *Easter*-day, and *Whitsunday*, in Divinity *Proper* to that Season: For two several Vacations of the Year, in Whatsoever the *Tutor* shall think *useful* to them.' But as few probably will then stay up, two of the tutors may be absent for either half of each vacation, and only one of the two then in residence need lecture each day. Tutors shall criticize their pupils' themes, &c., see that they do them in good time; shall always commence a lecture by examining them in the last: they shall frequently visit pupils in their Chambers; shall with the Principal's sanction appoint them 'what *Traders* they shall deal with for *Necessaries* . . . shall insist upon it that no *Pupil* . . . do contract any *Intimacies* with Tradesmen or their Families; nor accept of *Invitations* to their Houses, nor introduce them to *Entertainments* at his Chamber.'

C. WORDSWORTH *Social Life at the English Universities in the Eighteenth Century*, pp. 574–7 (Cambridge Univ. Press. 1874)

THE ELECTION OF A FELLOW OF TRINITY COLLEGE, CAMBRIDGE, 1752

In the seventeenth century the election of a fellow often depended more upon party influence and personal interest than the academic ability of the candidates, though there was often a *viva voce* examination. In 1700 when the great classical scholar, Richard Bentley, became Master of Trinity, he changed the system of examining candidates for fellowships, which had formerly been conducted *viva voce* in the college chapel before the Master and seniors, to one in which the candidates were examined by each of the electors in his own apartments, opportunity thus being given for written exercises. The memoirs of Richard Cumberland illustrate how this system worked.

When the day of examination came we went our rounds to the electing seniors; in some instances by one at a time, in others by parties of three or four; it was no trifling scrutiny we had to undergo, and here and there pretty severely exacted, particularly, as I well remember by Doctor Charles Mason, a man of curious knowledge in the philosophy of mechanics and a deep mathematician . . . . He gave us a good dose of dry mathematics, and then put an Aristophanes before us, which he opened at a venture and bade us give the sense of it. A very worthy candidate of my year declined having anything to do with it, yet Mason gave his vote for that gentleman, and against one, who took his leavings. Doctor Samuel Hooper gave us a liberal and well-chosen examination in the more familiar classics . . . .

The last, to whom in order of our visits we resorted to, was the master; he called us to him one by one according to our standings, and of course it fell to me as junior candidate to wait till each had been examined in turn. When in obedience to his summons I attended upon him, he was sitting, not in the room where my grandfather [Bentley] had his library, but in a chamber up stairs, encompassed with large folding screens, and over a great fire, though the weather was then uncommonly warm:

he began by requiring of me an account of the whole course and progress of my studies in the several branches of philosophy, so called in the general, and as I proceeded in my detail of what I had read, he sifted me with questions of such a sort as convinced me he was determined to take nothing upon trust; when he had held me a considerable time under this examination, I expected he would have dismissed me, but on the contrary he proceeded in the like general terms to demand of me an account of what I had been reading before I had applied myself to academical studies, and when I had acquitted myself of this question as briefly as I could, and I hope as modestly as became me in presence of a man so learned, he bade me give him a summary account of the several great empires of the ancient world, the periods when they flourished, their extent when at the summit of their power, the causes of their declension and dates of their extinction. When summoned to give answer to so wide a question, I can only say it was well for me I had worked so hard upon my scheme of General History . . . . This process being over, he gave me a sheet of paper written through in Greek with his own hand, which he ordered me to turn either into Latin or English, and I was shewn into a room containing nothing but a table furnished with materials for writing, and one chair, and I was required to use dispatch. The passage was maliciously enough selected in point of construction and also of character, for he had scrawled it out in a puzzling kind of hand with abbreviations of his own devising: it related to the arrangement of an army for battle, and I believe might be taken from Polybius, an author I had then never read. When I had given in my translation in Latin, I was remanded to the empty chamber with a subject for Latin prose and another for Latin verse, and again required to dispatch them in the manner of an impromptu. The chamber into which I was shut for the performance of these hasty productions was the very room, dismantled of the bed, in which I was born. The train of ideas it revived in my mind were not inappositely woven into the verses I gave in, and with this task my examination concluded . . .

The next day the election was announced, and I was chosen together with Mr John Orde, now one of the masters in Chancery . . . When I waited upon the electing seniors to return my thanks, of course I did not omit to pay my compliments to Dr Mason.

C. WORDSWORTH *Scholae Academicae: Some Account of the Studies at the English Universities in the Eighteenth Century*, pp. 345–6 (Cambridge Univ. Press, 1910)

TRINITY COLLEGE, CAMBRIDGE, FELLOWSHIP EXAMINATION PAPERS 1797

By the end of the eighteenth century the use of written papers in Fellowship examinations was becoming established. The following extract gives an example of this.

Questions at the Fellowship Examination Trinity College Cambridge 1797. (*Set by* W. Collier, *5th wrangler* 1762, *regius professor of hebrew.*)

Questions Historical

1. What were the different forms of Government under which the Jews lived by various names? what were those names? what were the successions of the forms of Government, and at what periods did they appear?
2. What are the four ancient Monarchies? what is their date, succession, and by what means and events did Cyrus establish his empire?
3. Whence proceeded the colonies of the East into the West, or Greece? what were the names of the Colonists? where did they respectively settle, and when?
4. Why was the southern part of Italy called Magna Graecia? and whence in the middle, or more northern parts, did the Etruscans proceed?
5. Whence arose the war between Athens and Sparta?
6. What was the rise of the Punic wars? what was their final event? and what effect did that event produce on the Roman Republic?
7. How many were the families of the Caesars, and with whom did they begin and end?
8. By what Nation was the Roman Empire finally destroyed? and what were the principal causes which brought it to it's fall?

Questions Geographical

1. What is meant by the River and the Sea in the Sacred writings?
2. What is the relative situation of Jerusalem and Samaria? and what the names of the mounts in them, on which the respective temples were built?
3. What are the sources and directions of the principal rivers? and the general directions of the chains of the mountains in Asia, Africa, Europe, and the two Americas?
4. Which are the principal Istmi on the face of the earth?
5. What are the Islands in the Aegean Sea renowned for the birth or habitation of illustrious writers?
6. What is the situation of the Fortunate Islands? what is their modern name? and what is there most distinguished in one of them?

7. What places in the earth appear to have been contiguous to Continents, and are now divided by some great convulsions of nature?

8. What are the principal volcanoes on the surface of the globe?

Questions Grammatical.

1. Is language most probably a gift of the Creator, or an effect of human institution?

2. Whence arises the diversity of languages, and in what manner was it most likely effected?

3. What was the most ancient form of characters to express ideas; and what improvements ensued?

4. What was the most ancient alphabet, the number of the first letters? and the additions afterwards made?

5. What is *βουστροφηδον*, and what instances [of it have been discovered?]

6. What is the digamma? why so called [? and what examples do you know of its] application in Latin from the Greek?

C. WORDSWORTH *Scholae Academicae: Some Account of the Studies at the English Universities in the Eighteenth Century*, pp. 348–9 (Cambridge Univ. Press, 1910)

APPLIED SCIENCE LECTURES AT CAMBRIDGE 1794

Scientific studies were by no means absent from the universities in this period. However, they were the product of individual efforts and as yet neither highly organized nor influential upon either society or education. The following extract gives an account of lectures given by W. Farish of Magdalene College, Professor of Chemistry.

The application of Chemistry to the Arts and Manufactures of *Britain* presented a new and useful field of instruction, which, however, could not be cultivated with effect, without exhibiting whatever else was necessary to the full illustration of the subject. After having taken an *actual* survey of almost everything curious in the manufactures of the Kingdom, the Professor contrived a mode of exhibiting the operations and processes that are in use in nearly all of them. Having provided himself with a number of *Brass Wheels* of all forms, and sizes, such, that any two of them can work with each other, the *Cogs* being all equal; and also with a variety of *Axles*, *Bars*, *Screws*, *Clamps*, &c., he constructs at pleasure, with the addition of the peculiar parts, *working Models* of almost every kind of *Machine*. These he puts in motion by a *Water Wheel*, or a *Steam Engine*, in such a way, as to make them in general do the actual work of the real Machine on a small scale; and he explains at the same time the chemical and philosophical principles, on which the various processes of the arts exhibited, depend.

In the course of his lectures he explains the theory and practice of *Mining* and of *Smelting* metallic Ores – of bringing them to nature – of converting, purifying, compounding, and separating the Metals, and the numerous and various Manufactures which depend upon them, as well as the Arts which are more remotely connected with them, such as *Etching* and *Engraving*. He exhibits the method of obtaining *Coal* and other *Minerals*, the processes by which *Sulphur*, *Alum*, *common Salt*, *Acids*, *Alcalies*, *Nitre*, and other *saline* substances are obtained, and in which they are used; the mechanical process in the formation of *Gunpowder*, as well as its theory and effects. He shews the arts of procuring and working *Animal* and *Vegetable* substances; the great staple manufactures of the country, in *Wool*, *Cotton*, *Linen*, *Silk;* together with the various chemical arts of *Bleaching*, of *Preparing* Cloth, of *Printing* it, of using *adjective* and *substantive* colours, and *Mordants* or *Intermediates* in Dying. He explains in general the nature of Machinery: the moving powers such as *Water-wheels*, *Windmills*, and particularly the *agency* of Steam, which is the *great* cause of the modern improvement and extension of manufactures. He treats likewise on subjects which relate to the carrying on, or facilitating, the commerce of the country, such as *Inland Navigation*, the construction of *Bridges*, *Aqueducts*, *Locks*, *Inclined Planes*, and other contrivances, by which *Vessels* are raised or lowered from one Level to another; of *Ships*, *Docks*, *Harbours*, and *Naval Architecture*. On the whole, it is the great design of these Lectures to excite the attention of persons already acquainted with the principles of Mathematics, Philosophy, and Chemistry to *Real Practice*; and by drawing their minds to the consideration of the most useful inventions of ingenious men, in all parts of the kingdom, to enlarge their sphere of amusement and instruction and to promote the improvement and progress of the Arts.

These Lectures are given in the Schools in the Botanical Garden, alternately with those of the *Jacksonian* Professor, in the *Lent* and *Midsummer* Terms.

C. WORDSWORTH *Scholae Academicae: Some Account of the Studies at the English Universities in the Eighteenth Century*, pp. 190–2 (Cambridge Univ. Press, 1910)

The Grand Tour

Such was the disrepute into which the universities had fallen in the eighteenth century, that many of the wealthy classes preferred to rely on a combination of private tutors and a Grand Tour for the education of their sons. The universities seemed to be 'Schools of Vice' as Lady Leicester of Holkham Hall Norfolk put it and foreign travel under the guidance of a tutor seemed a much better way of finishing off a young man's education. The benefits which it was hoped a foreign tour would give were related to the future employments of a young gentleman. If he was to inherit great landed estates, take a lead in social life, or serve his country in politics, diplomacy or war, then residence in France and Italy could, it was hoped, give him several advantages. He could learn to speak French as a native and French was the language of diplomacy and polite society. In France too he could improve his horsemanship and learn those skills of fencing, dancing and deportment which a rustic English upbringing so often failed to give. In Italy he could acquire a taste in the fine arts and practise the social graces in a succession of parties and balls.

Not everybody was convinced of the value of the Grand Tour as an educational device. Critics were sceptical of the amount of fluency in foreign languages a young man might acquire, and considered that dissipation rather than application and good sense was more likely to be the effect on the characters of those who toured the Continent.*

DIALOGUE ON THE USES OF FOREIGN TRAVEL 1764

In 1764, Richard Hurd, Bishop of Worcester, put the arguments for and against foreign travel as a means to the education of the English gentleman, in dialogue form, imagining a debate between Lord Shaftesbury, who supports foreign travel, and John Locke, who opposes it. The following extract gives some indication of the contemporary debate on the value of the Grand Tour.

Lord Shaftesbury

To put the case at the best, suppose him to have been well whipped through one of our public schools, and to come full fraught, at length, with *Latin* and *Greek*, from his college. You see him now, on the verge of the world, and just ready to step into it. But, good heavens, with what

**Further Reading:*

R. J. WHITE 'The Grand Tour' In A. NATAN (ed.) *Silver Renaissance.—Essays in Eighteenth-Century English History*, pp. 122–41 (London: Macmillan, 1961)

G. C. BRAUER *The Education of a Gentleman: Theories of Gentlemanly Education in England 1660–1775* (New York: Bookman Associates, 1959)

G. TREASE *The Grand Tour* (London: Heinemann, 1967)

PRINCIPLES and MANNERS! His spirit broken by the servile awe of pedants, and his body unfashioned by the genteeler exercises! Timid at the same time, and rude; illiberal and ungraceful! An absurd compound of abject sentiments, and bigoted notions, on the one hand; and of clownish, coarse, ungainly demeanour, on the other! In a word, both in mind and person, the furthest in the world from any thing that is handsome, gentlemanlike, or of use and acceptation in good company! . . .

But now, on the other hand, let a young gentleman, who has been trained abroad; who has been accustomed to the sight and conversation of men; who has learnt his exercises, has some use of the languages, and has read his HORACE or HOMER in good company; Let such an one, at his return, make his appearance in the best societies; and see with what ease, and address, he sustains his part in them! how liberal his air and manner! how managed and decorous his delivery of himself! In short, how welcome to everybody, and how prepared to acquit himself in the ordinary commerce of the world, and in conversation!

I should think, if there were no other advantage of early travel, beside this of *manners*, it were well worth setting against all the other inconveniences, whatever they be, of this sort of Education . . .

You may think as slightly, as you please, of the exterior polish of *manners*, or may even treat as superficial, the *information* that can be acquired in good company. But what say you to that supreme accomplishment, a KNOWLEDGE OF THE WORLD? A science so useful, as to supersede or disgrace all the rest; and so profound, as to merit all the honours, and to fill up all the measures, of the best philosophy? For, by *a knowledge of the world*, I mean that which results from the observation of men and things; from an acquaintance with the customs, and usages of other nations; from some insight into their policies, government, religion; in a word, from the study and contemplation of men; as they present themselves on the great stage of the world, in various forms, and under different appearances. This is that master-science, which a gentleman should comprehend, and which our schools and colleges never heard of.

I know this science is too difficult to be perfectly acquired but by long habit and mature reflexion. I know it is not to be expected from a slight survey of mankind; from a hasty passage through the different countries, or a short residence in the great towns, of *Europe*. All this I am not to be told; but it must be allowed me at the same time, that so important a study cannot be entered upon too soon, and that the rudiments at least of this science cannot be laid too early . . .

You . . . will alow me, I hope, to lay some stress on the LIBERAL ARTS; which adorn and embellish human life; and, where they prevail to some degree of perfection, are among the surest marks of the civility and politeness of any people.

It is notorious enough how backward we have been, and still are, in all these elegant and muse-like applications. There is little or nothing in the way of *picture*, *sculpture*, and the arts of *design* among us, that can stand the test of a knowing and judicious eye. It is but of late we have begun to form ourselves any thing like an *ear* in harmony and the proportions of just music. And whatever magisterial airs our fashionable workmen in the dramatic and poetical kinds may give themselves in their prologues and prefaces, it is no secret to such as have looked into the ancient matters, or have made an acquaintance with the style and manner of the politer moderns, that we are far from possessing a right taste in these things, and that the Muses have hitherto shewn themselves but little indulgent to us . . .

But the likeliest way to quicken the growth of these studies, is to turn our attention from the bad models of our own country, and enter into a free commerce and generous struggle, as it were, with our more advanced neighbours. And it is here again, as in the manners and arts of life, the seeds of good taste cannot be committed to the mind too soon. It were then to be wished, that our young men had right impressions of *art* in their tender years; and that, forming their relish among the ablest proficients in *Europe*, they might afterwards communicate their improvements to their own country.

Thus, it might be hoped, in some convenient time we should have something of our own to oppose to the wit, learning, and elegance of *France;* and that, in the mechanic execution of the fine arts, we should come at length to vye with the *Italian* masters . . .

And, if there be use and value in such things, how shall our ingenuous youth be tinctured with a right sense of them, but by early and well-conducted travel? For what discipline, what examples, what encouragements have we at home? What academies for the genteel exercises? what conferences for the improvement of art or language? what societies for the cultivation of the liberal character?

The contemplation of these defects carries me still further; to the source and fountain of them all . . . the present state of Erudition, as we see it managed in certain sublime seats and authorized nurseries amongst us.

And would you invite our liberal and noble youth to resort thither? Could you expect that their free spirits would stoop to be lectured by bearded boys, or that their minds could ever be formed and tutored by such pedants in a way that fits them for the real practice of the world and of mankind?

Have we not long enough submitted to the inconveniences of this monkish education? Look on the generality of those persons who have had their breeding in those seminaries. What principles in morals, in government, in religion have spouted thence! What dispositions have we known corrupted by their discipline! what understandings perverted by their servile and false systems! Has truth, or liberty, or reason fair play from that quarter? . . .

If such then be the state of our own seats of literature and education, what more needs be alledged in the behalf of FOREIGN TRAVEL; which is the only means left to remedy these mischiefs, or at least to palliate and correct them?

Mr. Locke

Were the subject before us a matter of indifference or curiosity, such as idle men are used to discourse of, I could allow your Lordship to pursue it in this Socratic raillery and declamation. But if ever there was a question, that deserved the examination of a philosopher . . . it is surely this of EDUCATION; and, among the various parts of it, none is more strictly to be inquired into, as none is, perhaps, so big with important consequences, as that which comes recommended to us under the specious name of FOREIGN TRAVEL.

I could not, therefore, but wonder to hear your Lordship enlarge so much, and so long, on I know not what varnish of manners and good breeding; of the knowledge of men and the world; of arts, languages, and other trappings and shewy appendages of education: just as if an architect should entertain you with a discourse on Festoons and Foliage, or the finishing of his Freeze and Capitals, when you expected him to instruct you in what way to erect a solid edifice on firm walls and durable foundations.

What a reasonable man wants to know, is, The proper method of building up *men*: whereas your Lordship seems solicitous for little more than tricking out a set of fine *Gentlemen* . . .

To make this inquiry to purpose, some certain principles must be laid down; some scheme of life and manners must be formed; some idea or model of the character you would imprint on young minds must be described . . .

I begin with this certain Principle, that the business of Education is to form the UNDERSTANDING, and regulate the HEART. If man be a compound of Reason and Passion, the only proper discipline of his nature is that which accomplishes these two purposes.

You have laboured with much plausibility to persuade us, that the only reasonable education is that which prepares and fits a man for the commerce of the world: and I readily admit the notion, provided we first agree about the meaning of this big word, the WORLD. Your

Lordship, it may be, in your sublime view of things, is projecting to make of your Pupil, what is called in the widest sense of the terms, a *Citizen of the world*. A great and awful character, my Lord! But let us advance by just degrees.

First, if you please, let us provide that he be a worthy citizen of *England*; and, by your favour, let me ennoble this small island of our's, with the pompous appellation of the world. It is that world at least, in which our adventurer is to play his part; and for the commerce of which it concerns him most immediately to be prepared.

Now, as your Lordship's chief care is directed, very properly, towards its chief subjects; I mean the men of rank and fortune; whose ample property and noble birth give their country the greatest concern in their education, Let me ask in what manner they are likely to qualify themselves best for the important parts, they are to act in it? . . .

An *English* citizen or, if you will, Senator (for this is the station to which our greater citizens do, and our best should aspire) can never acquit himself of the duties he owes his country, under this character, but by furnishing himself with all those qualities of the *head* and *heart*, which his superior rank and pretentions demand . . .

I require then in our young aspirant to the name and honours of an *English* Senator, that his mind be early and thoroughly seasoned with the principles of virtue and religion: that he be trained, by a strict discipline, to the command of his temper and passions: that his ambition be awakened, or rather directed, to its right object, the *public good*; and, to that end, that his soul be fired with the love of excellence and true honour: above all, that he have a reverence for the legal constitution of his country, and a fervent affection for the great community, to which he belongs . . .

I require . . . in the next place, that our young Senator have a ready and familiar use, at least, of the *Latin* tongue (your Lordship, I know, will add, and of the *Greek*: but in this I am not so peremptory):

That he be competently instructed in the elements of science, as well as what are called polite Letters: that, especially, He be well grounded in the principles of morals, public and private: that he have made a thorough acquaintance with the history of his own country, and with its Constitution, Civil and Ecclesiastical: that he have a general insight into the history of the world, antient and modern: above all, that he have a well-exercised understanding, I mean that he be taught to reason clearly and consequentially upon any subject: and, further, to put all these abilities to use, that he have a ready command of his own language, and the power of expressing himself, whether in writing or speaking, with ease and perspicuity, at least, if not with elegance.

Other ornamental qualities I omit for the present, which will almost certainly come of themselves, if his education be rightly conducted; or may be acquired with little pains, and in the way of diversion only. But these solid accomplishments I hold it necessary for our youth of quality to possess, by the time in which they usually pass out of the hands of their Tutors and Governors, I mean the age of twenty one.

Am I unreasonable in these demands? . . .

Lord Shaftesbury

Without doubt, these accomplishments are no more than may be reasonably required in our young Gentleman, or Senator. But how they are to be come at in our vulgar way of *Education*, I do not easily apprehend.

Mr. Locke

Of that, in due time. At present you accept this as a reasonable idea or sketch of an *English* Gentleman's character; such as the course of his education ought to imprint upon him: And I shall now shew you very clearly that it is not possible to be attained in the way of *foreign travel.*

Consider, *first* of all, the unavoidable WASTE OF TIME; of that time which is so precious in every view; not only as being the most proper for making the acquisitions I speak of; but as being the only period of his life, which he will be at liberty to employ in that manner.

Early youth is flexible and docile: apt to take the impressions of virtue, and ready to admit the principles of knowledge. The faculties of the mind are then vigorous and alert: the conception quick, and the memory retentive. The humble drudgery of acquiring the elements of literature and science is to young minds an easy and a flattering employment . . .

This then, is the season for laying the foundations of knowledge and ability of every kind; and if you let it slip, without applying it carefully to those purposes, you will in vain lament the omission in riper years, when the cares or amusements of life afford little leisure for such pursuits, and less inclination . . . If therefore any considerable part of this precious season be *wasted* in foreign travel, I mean if it be actually *not employed* in the pursuits proper to it, this circumstance must needs be considered as an objection of great weight to that sort of Education.

Your Lordship may consider, *next*, the DISSIPATION OF MIND attending on this itinerant education; while the scene is constantly changing; and new objects perpetually springing up before him, to sollicit the admiration of our young Traveller.

One of the greatest secrets in education is to fix the attention of youth: a painful operation! which requires long use and a steady unremitting discipline; the very reverse of that roving, desultory habit, which is inseparable from the sort of life you would recommend

. . . But were no account to be had of *the loss of time*, or of *this dissipated turn of mind*, which is still more pernicious, I should, nevertheless, object to this travelled Education, on account of the very objects to which our Traveller's APPLICATION is directed.

Instead of those necessary and fundamental parts of knowledge, which I require him to have laid in, his attention, so much of it as can be spared for anything that looks like information, is wasted on things either frivolous or unimportant.

His *first* business is to make himself perfect in the forms of breeding, which he finds in use among those he lives with, or perhaps in their forms of dress only.

His *next* concern, is to acquire a readiness in the languages of *Europe*; or, to shorten his labour as much as possible, at least in the *French* language. The pretence is, that he may fit himself for conversation with his foreign acquaintance; which takes up much time to little purpose as the use ceases, in a good degree, with his return home: and, that he may qualify himself for perusing their best books; which takes him off from the study of those, which are still better, in the learned languages, and I will venture to say, in his own.

If any thing *further* employ his attention, it is perhaps a little virtuoso-ship. He inquires after fine pictures, fine statues, fine buildings. He visits the shops of artificers; gets admission to libraries, cabinets of medals, and repositories of curiosities; and, for some relaxation from these arduous toils, is frequent at Churches, Theatres, and Courts of Judicature, and stares at processions, ceremonies, and other solemn shews.

And, now, when these three points have been duly attended to, I leave your Lordship to guess what leisure he is likely to have for accomplishing himself in those other studies, which you allow me to suppose are of much greater importance.

In one word, my Lord, if he acquires any knowledge, it is only, or chiefly, of such things as he may very well do without, or, at best, are of an inferior and subordinate consideration: while the branches of learning, he must neglect for these, are of the most constant use and necessity to him in the commerce of his whole life.

Till then your Lordship can find a way to reconcile these different pursuits, I must be of opinion that the boasted way of Travel is the worst that can be contrived for the proper instruction of our young countrymen.

Lord Shaftesbury

Without doubt, if these less important points engross all their attention. But can there be a difficulty in carrying on the two designs together?

especially, if a good and attentive Tutor be at hand to direct his pupil's pursuit and quicken his application?

Mr. Locke

Your Lordship, like the friends and parents of a young Traveller, is for exacting wonders at the hands of this important Personage, a Tutor. But the truth is, so many, and so different things cannot be well learned, even with the advantage of the best parts, under the very best direction.

Besides, your Lordship forgets that what we now inquire into, is, whether the generality of our *English* youth of quality should be educated in this form; not, whether two or three young men, of the most uncommon genius and application, may not possibly succeed in it. I demand an education, which may ordinarily produce useful and able men: your Lordship is providing only for, what comes of itself, a Prodigy.

R. HURD *Moral and Political Dialogues*, Vol. III, pp. 40–83 (London, 1765)

ADAM SMITH ON THE GRAND TOUR

Adam Smith in his *Wealth of Nations* (1776) came out quite definitely against the Grand Tour as a fit means of education for the youth of the nation. He takes a typically utilitarian view, contending that foreign travel is likely to corrupt a young man and make him quite unfit for a life of business in an age when industry and trade need to be developed.

In England, it becomes every day more and more the custom to send young people to travel in foreign countries immediately upon their leaving school, and without sending them to any university. Our young people it is said, generally return home much improved by their travels. A young man who goes abroad at seventeen or eighteen, and returns home at one-and-twenty, returns three or four years older than he was when he went abroad; and at that age it is very difficult not to improve a good deal in three or four years. In the course of his travels, he generally acquires some knowledge of one or two foreign languages; a knowledge, however, which is seldom sufficient to enable him either to speak or write them with propriety. In other respects, he commonly returns home more conceited, more unprincipled, more dissipated, and more incapable of any serious application either to study or to business, than he could well have become in so short a time, had he lived at home. By travelling so very young, by spending in the most frivolous dissipation the most precious years of his life, at a distance from the inspection and control of his parents and relations, every useful habit, which the earlier parts of his education might have had some tendency to form in him, instead of being riveted and confirmed, is almost necessarily either weakened or effaced. Nothing but the discredit into which the universities are allowing themselves to fall, could ever have brought into repute so very absurd a practice as that of travelling at this early period of life. By sending his son abroad, a father delivers himself, at least for some time, from so disagreeable an object as that of a son unemployed, neglected, and going to ruin before his eyes.

ADAM SMITH *An Inquiry into the Nature and Causes of The Wealth of Nations*, Bk V, Part III, Article II (London, 1776)

Dissenting Academies

The dissenting academies rose mainly as a result of the Conformity Legislation of the years 1662–5 and the statutes of the Universities of Oxford and Cambridge which together excluded Dissenters from higher education. The effects of this legislation operated in two ways. First, non-conformist ministers and laymen would not let their sons go to universities where they would have to subscribe to the Act of Uniformity and the Thirty-Nine Articles, and consequently there was a demand for schools. Secondly, the ejected clergy provided a supply of teachers who could establish academies and schools and so answer this demand.

As towards the end of the seventeenth century the Clarendon Code legislation was relaxed, dissenting academies increased in number. They became popular with Anglicans as well as Nonconformists as places of higher education for various reasons. They provided more efficient teaching than the universities did. They offered a more utilitarian curriculum in which scientific and commercial subjects figured, together with history, geography, and modern languages, as well as the eternal classics. Finally, they could provide a residential education more cheaply than the universities, and once they had agreed to admit students for a general education in addition to those students for the ministry for whom they had primarily come into existence, their success was assured.*

COURSE OF EDUCATION AT KIBWORTH ACADEMY

Kibworth Academy, Leicestershire, was opened in 1715 by John Jennings, the minister to the Independent congregation at Kibworth. It had a very short life moving to Hinckley in 1722, but then closing in 1723 when Jennings died. It never had more than perhaps half a dozen students at any one time. Nevertheless, it was an important Academy in that it educated Philip Doddridge, who later opened Northampton Academy, perhaps the most famous of all the academies. Kibworth is also important for the historian of education because a full account of the education given there has survived in a letter which Doddridge wrote to the Reverend Thomas Saunders in 1728. This account is given below. It gives a detailed picture of the subjects, textbooks and methods used in preparing men for the ministry.

**Further reading:*

I. PARKER *Dissenting Academies in England* (Cambridge Univ. Press, 1914)

H. MCLACHLAN *English Education Under The Test Acts, Being the History of the Non-Conformist Academies 1662–1820* (Manchester Univ. Press, 1931)

J. W. ASHLEY SMITH *The Birth of Modern Education: The Contribution of the Dissenting Academies* (London: Independent Press, 1954)

N. HANS *New Trends in Education in the Eighteenth Century* (London: Routledge & Kegan Paul, 1951)

Our course of education at Kibworth was the employment of four years, and every half-year we entered upon a new set of studies; or at least changed the time and order of our lectures.

The First half-year we read Geometry or Algebra thrice a week; Hebrew twice, Geography once, French once, Latin prose authors once, Classical exercises once. For Geometry we read Barrow's *Euclid's Elements*; when we had gone through the first book, we entered upon algebra, and read over a system drawn up by Mr. Jennings for our use . . . When we had ended this system, we went over most of the second and fifth books of Euclid's *Elements*, with Algebraic demonstrations, which Mr. Jennings had drawn up and which were not near so difficult as Barrow's geometrical demonstrations of the same prepositions. We likewise went through the third, fourth and sixth books of Euclid; but this was part of the business of the second half-year. We read Gordon's Geography in our closets; the lecture was only an examination of the account we could give of the most remarkable passages in it. For French, we learnt Boyer's Grammar, and read the phrases and dialogues from French into English, without regarding the pronunciation, with which Mr. Jennings was not acquainted. One hour in the week was employed in reading some select passages out of Suetonius, Tacitus, Seneca, Cæsar, and especially Cicero. Our method was, first, to read the Latin, I think according to the grammatical order of the words, and then to render it into as elegant English as we could. We used the same way in reading the classics together the two next half-years. Our academical exercises were translations from some of the Latin authors into English, and from English into Latin. Many passages in the *Spectators* and *Tatlers*, both serious and humorous, were assigned to us upon these occasions. For Hebrew, we read Bythner's Grammar.

The Second half-year we ended Geometry and Algebra, which we read twice a week. We read Logic twice, Civil History once, French twice, Hebrew once, Latin poets once, Exercises once, Oratory once, Exercises of reading and delivery once. For logic, we first skimmed over *Burgersdicius*, in about six lectures, and then entered on a system composed by Mr. Jennings; a great deal of which was taken from Mr. Locke, with large references to him and other celebrated authors, under almost every head. This was the method Mr. Jennings used in almost all the lectures he drew up himself; he made the best writers his commentators. We had a collection of excellent readings on the subject of every lecture, which frequently employed us in our closets for two or three hours, and we were obliged to give an account of the substance of these references at our next lecture. . . . This and the other systems that Mr. Jennings himself composed of Pneumatology, Ethics, and Divinity, were very accurate and elaborate performances. . . . They were thrown into as mathematical a form as their respective subjects would admit of, and consisted of Definitions, Propositions, Demonstrations, Corollaries, and Scholia.

For civil history, we read Puffendorf's *Introduction to the History of Europe*, with Crull's *Continuation*, and his *History of Asia, Africa, and America*. We read these (and afterwards the History of England, Dupin's Compendium, Spanheim's *Elenchus*, King's *Constitution*) and some other printed books just as we did Gordon. . . . For French, we read Telemachus from the original into English, and sometimes select passages out of Bourdeleau's *Sermons*. . . . The Latin poets we made the most frequent use of were Virgil, Horace, and Terence; but we sometimes spent an hour in Lucretius, Juvenal, Plautus, Lucan, etc., with these we generally read a translation. Our oratory was drawn up by Mr. Jennings, and made a part of a volume of miscellanies, which are now printed. . . . Bacon's *Essays* were often used on this occasion, and our exercises were a kind of comment upon some remarkable sentences they contained. . . . For Hebrew, we read Bythner's *Lyra*, and were pretty curious in the grammatical resolution of each word. On Tuesday nights we used to spend an hour in reading the Bible, sermons, or poems, purely to form ourselves to a just accent and pronunciation. . . .

The Third half-year we read Mechanics, Hydrostatics, and Physics twice, Greek Poets once, History of England once, Anatomy once, Astronomy, Globes, and Chronology once, Miscellanies once, and had one Logical disputation in a week. For mechanics, we read a short but very pretty system . . . drawn up by Mr. Jennings; and for hydrostatics, an abridgment of Mr. Eames's lectures. For physics, we read Leclerc's system, exclusive of his first book, of Astronomy, and of the latter part of the fourth, of Anatomy. . . . The Greek poets, which gave us the most employment, were Theocritus, Homer, and Pindar. . . . For the history of England, we read Browne's in two volumes octavo, which we found very good. For anatomy, a system of Mr. Eames's in English, contracted in some places, and in others enlarged. . . We read Jones on the Use of the Globes. Our astronomy and chronology were both Mr. Jennings's, and now printed amongst his Miscellanies. These miscellanies are very short sketches of Fortification, Heraldry, Architecture, Psalmody, Physiognomy, Metaphysics, etc. Our logical disputations were in English, our thesis in Latin, and neither the one nor the other in a syllogistic form. . . .

The Fourth half-year, we read Pneumatology twice a week. The remainder of Physics and Miscellanies once, Jewish Antiquities twice. Our pneumatology was drawn up by Mr. Jennings, pretty much in the same method as our logic. It contained an inquiry into the existence and nature of God, and into the nature, operations, and immortality of the human soul, on the principles of natural reason. There was a fine collection of readings in the references on almost every head. This with our divinity, which was a continuation of it, was by far the most valuable part of our course. Mr. Jennings had bestowed a vast deal of thought upon them, and his discourses from them in the lecture room were admirable. For Jewish antiquities we read an abridgment of Mr. Jones's notes on Godwyn, with some very curious and important additions.

The Fifth half-year, we read Ethics twice a week, Critics once, and had one pneumatological disputation. Our ethics were a part of pneumatology. The principal authors whom Mr. Jennings referred to were Grotius and Puffendorf. . . . Our critical lectures were an abridgment of Mr. Jones's. They were not criticisms on any particular texts, but general observations relating to the most noted versions and editions of the Bible. Our pneumatological and theological disputations were of very considerable service to us. Mr. Jennings was moderator, and many thoughts were often started in them, by which our lectures themselves were improved.

The Sixth half-year, we read Divinity thrice a week, Christian Antiquities once, Miscellanies once, and had one Homily on a Thursday night. Our divinity was conducted in the same method as our pneumatology; and here we had references to writers of all opinions, but Scripture was our only rule, and we had in our written lectures an admirable collection of texts upon almost every head. Our Homilies were discourses delivered from a pulpit; they were confined to subjects of natural religion . . . most of our citations being taken from the ancient poets and philosophers. For Christian antiquities, we read Sir Peter King's *Constitution of the Primitive Church*, with the original Draught in answer to it. . . . We consulted Bingham's *Origines Ecclesiasticæ* for illustration, and sometimes had recourse to Suicer's *Thesaurus*.

The Seventh half-year, we read Divinity thrice, Ecclesiastical History once, had one Sermon, and one Theological Disputation – Our Ecclesiastical History was Dupin's Compendium, which we found in many places very defective. . . . Mr. Jennings examined our sermons himself; we preached them to our own family, and sometimes to the people in his hearing.

The Last half-year we read Divinity once a week, History of Controversies once, Miscellanies once, and had one Theological Disputation. For the history of controversies we read Spanheim's *Elenchus*. These miscellanies were a second volume, they contained a brief historical account of the ancient philosophers, the art of preaching, and the pastoral care, on which heads Mr. Jennings gave us very excellent advice, with some valuable hints on the head of nonconformity. We preached this last half year, either at home or abroad, as occasion required; and towards the beginning of it, were examined by a committee of the neighbouring ministers, to whom that office was assigned at a preceding general meeting.

Mr. Jennings never admitted any into his academy till he had examined them as to their improvement in school learning and on their capacity for entering on the course of studies which he proposed. He likewise insisted on satisfaction as to their moral character and the marks of a serious disposition.

The two first years of our course, we read the Scriptures in the family, from Hebrew, Greek, or French into English. . . . Mr. Jennings expounded about ten lessons in a week, sometimes in the morning and sometimes in the evening. . . . Once a month, on a Friday before the sacrament, we laid aside all secular business to attend to devotion. Those who thought proper, as several did, observed it as a fast. About ten in the morning we all met, and Mr. Jennings gave us a lecture which he had carefully prepared for the purpose. . . . His Two Discourses of Preaching Christ, and Experimental Preaching, were composed and delivered on such an occasion. Every evening an account was taken of our private studies. We repeated to him, immediately after prayer, something which we had met with, which we judged most remarkable; by this means all enjoyed some benefit by the studies of each. . . . We were obliged to talk Latin within some certain bounds of time and place. . . . Every Lord's day evening, Mr. Jennings used to send for some of us into the lecture room, and discoursed with each apart about inward religion. . . . Mr. Jennings allowed us the free use of his library, which was divided into parts. The first was common to all, the second was for the use of the seniors only, consisting principally of books of philosophy and polemical divinity. . . . At our first entrance on each we had a lecture, in which Mr. Jennings gave us the general character of each book, and some hints as to the time and manner of perusing it. We had fixed hours of business and recreation. The bell rang for family prayer at half an hour past six in the summer, i.e., from March to September, and as much past seven in the winter half year. . . . Each lecture began with an examination, by which Mr. Jennings could easily judge of our care or negligence in studying the former. . . . Thursday morning was generally vacant. We had a fortnight's vacation at Christmas, and six weeks at Whitsuntide, when we used to visit our friends, and had no academical business assigned to us. . . .

Quoted in H. MCLACHLAN *English Education under the Test Acts*, pp. 135–40 (Manchester Univ. Press, 1931)

ECCLESIASTICAL ACTION AGAINST NORTHAMPTON ACADEMY

In 1729 Philip Doddridge opened his academy at Northampton. Three years later the Chancellor of the diocese, Dr Reynolds, began litigation designed to force Doddridge to seek episcopal licence for his academy. The extract below gives the citation ordering Doddridge to appear before Dr Reynolds. In the end in 1734 the proceedings were stopped by order of George II who wanted no religious persecution in his reign, but for a time the survival of the Northampton Academy was in jeopardy.

To Philip Dotteridge of the Parish of All Saints, in the Town of Northampton, in the County of Northampton, Gentleman.

By virtue of a Citation under seal herewith shewn unto you I cite you to appear personally before the Reverend George Reynolds Doctor of laws Vicar General Commissary General and Official Principal in spiritual matters of the Right Reverend father in God Robert by Divine Permission Lord Bishop of Peterborough and also official of the Reverend the Archdeacon of the Archdeaconry of Northampton or his lawfull Surrogate or some other competent Judge in this behalfe in the Consistory Court adjoyning to the Parish Church of All Saints in the same town of Northampton on Tuesday the sixth day of November 1733 at the usual time of hearing causes there then and there to answer to certain Articles or Interrogations to be objected and administered to you concerning your soul's health and the Reformation and correction of your manners and excess. And especially your teaching and instructing youth in the Liberal Arts and Sciences not being licensed thereto by the Ordinary of the Diocese touching either your Learning and Dexterity in teaching or your right understanding of God's true religion or your honest and sober conversation at the promotion of and pursuant to a certain Detection or presentment exhibited against you by Thomas Rand and Benjamin Chapman, Churchwardens of the said parish of All Saints in the said town of Northampton. And farther to do and receive according to Law-Justice.

W. M. SPENCER

Quoted in I. PARKER *Dissenting Academies in England*, pp. 80–1 (Cambridge Univ. Press, 1914)

RULES OF DODDRIDGE'S ACADEMY, NORTHAMPTON, 1743

When Doddridge began his academy he conceived it as a training establishment for ministers. However, he was persuaded to open it to laymen on the grounds that otherwise nonconformist parents would have to risk sending their sons to Oxford and Cambridge for a higher or professional education. Such was the reputation of the universities that, rather than force parents into that, Doddridge agreed to widen the admission to the academy. The number of students in residence at the academy at any one time varied greatly – there were forty in 1730, sixty-three in 1743 and twenty-nine in 1747 – but from its founding in 1729 until Doddridge's death in 1751, some two hundred men were educated there, of whom a hundred and twenty were training for the ministry.

In 1740 a system of Rules for the Academy was drawn up and a copy of this, dated 10 December 1743, survives. It was signed by Doddridge, his assistant and sixty-three students. Extracts from it are given below. They give rules about studies, prayers, meals, the library, the office of monitor, leave of absence from the academy and conduct outside it, and the times of closing the gate. Whether the rules were rigorously kept or not, we cannot be sure.

Constitution, Orders and Rules relating to the Academy at Northampton agreed upon by the Tutors and the several members of it in December 1740 and then established as the future conditions of Admission into the Academy or continuance in it.

Section I. Of Academical Studies

1. *1st year.* Translations from Latin into English and vice versa as appointed by the Tutors to be showed them at the day and hour appointed and in the last three months of the year orations are to be exhibited in Latin and English alternately every Thursday which is also to be the time of the following exercises.

2. In first half of second year these orations are to be continued and in the latter part of the year each is in his turn to exhibit a Philosophical Thesis or Dissertation.

3. In third year Ethical Theses or Dissertations are to be exhibited weekly as above and toward the end of this year and during the fourth, Theological.

4. The Revolution of these is to be so adjusted that every student may compose at least six orations, Theses or Dissertations before the conclusion of his fourth year.

5. All subjects to be disputed upon are to be given out with the names of the Respondent and opponent – at least as soon as the Academy meets after the long vacation and at Christmas and, if possible, before the vacation.

6. The absence of the Tutor is not to occasion the omission of any of these exercises . . . etc.

7. Exercises are to be first written in a paper book, then reviewed and corrected by one of the Tutors, after that, fairly transcribed and after they have been exhibited in the manner which shall be appointed a fair copy of them, with the author's name annexed, shall be delivered to the Tutor.

8. Two sermons on given subjects to be composed by every theological student in his eighth half year to be read over by him in the class and having been there corrected to be preached in the family if the student does not propose preaching in public before he leave the Academy, and besides these, at least six schemes of other sermons on given texts are to be exhibited in the class during the fourth year by each student.

9. If any student continue a fifth year he is to compose at least one sermon and exhibit two schemes every quarter whether he do or do not preach in public. Besides which he is this fifth year to exhibit and defend two large Theological theses. . . .

10. Four classics viz.: one Greek and one Latin poet and one Greek and one Latin prose writer as appointed by the Tutor are to be read by each student in his study and observations are to be written upon them to be kept in a distinct book, and communicated to the Tutor whenever he shall think fit.

11. Each student of the upper class may be allowed to propose a difficult scripture to the Principal Tutor every Thursday to be discussed by him the next Thursday. But it will be expected that the person proposing them write some memorandum of the solution . . . etc.

12. . . . each Theological Pupil will be expected to write, either at meeting or afterward. . . . Hints of all the Sermons he hears, to be examined by the Tutor . . . etc.

13. On the four Thursdays preceding the long vacation, the whole Academy is to meet at ten in the morning and all the forenoon is to be spent in the examination of Students . . . And on the first of these days Disputations shall be held by the two upper classes in the Presence of the Juniors that they may learn by example the method of Disputation . . . etc.

14. In case of a total neglect of preparing an appointed exercise sixpence is to be forfeited to the box. . . .

Section II. Of Attendance on Family Prayer and Lecture at appointed times

1. Every Student boarding in the House is to be present at the calling over the names in the great parlour at 10 minutes after six in the morning or to forfeit a penny.

2. Family Prayer is to begin in the morning at eight o'clock and in the evening at seven . . . and every one absenting himself from either . . . is to forfeit two pence.

3. Every student is to be ready for Lecture . . . within five minutes of the Hour fixed for the beginning . . . or to forfeit two pence, and if Lecture be entirely neglected and no reason can be assigned which the Tutor (who is always to be the judge of such reasons) shall think sufficient, he is to be publicly reproved at the next meeting of the whole

Society, and if the neglect be repeated within a month he is to have some extraordinary exercise appointed as the Tutor shall think fit.

4. Each Pupil, after he hath entered on the second half year of his course, shall take his turn at family prayer in the evening . . . etc.

5. . . . nor shall a change of turns be permitted without the Tutor's express leave.

6. If the person whose turn it is to go to Prayer in the evening absent himself and have not procured another to officiate for him he shall forfeit sixpence or take his turn twice together . . . etc.

Section III. Of the Hours, Place and Order of Meals

1. The time of breakfast is to be from the end of family prayer till 5 minutes before Ten.

2. It is to be eaten either in the Hall or the great parlour, a blessing having first been asked by the senior Pupil present at each table if the Assistant Tutor be not at one of them.

3. They that choose tea in the morning may either breakfast with the Tutor in his parlour, or at the other tea board in the great parlour, each, in that case, providing his own tea and sugar in a just proportion as the company shall agree.

4. Dinner is to be set on the table precisely at two when every student is to be in the Hall before the blessing . . . and not to leave the room till thanks be returned.

5. Supper is to be eaten in the Hall between the conclusion of evening prayer and 9 o'clock . . . etc.

6. Neither breakfast, dinner nor supper is to be carried into any room, besides that appointed for the family meal, except in case of sickness . . . etc.

7. As making toasts and butter and toasting cheese has been found to be more expensive than can conveniently be afforded on the usual terms here, that custom is to be disused except by the Parlour boarders.

9. . . . . . .

10. . . . . . .

Section IV. Of shutting up the Gate and retiring to Bed

1. The gate is to be locked every night at ten and the key is to be brought to the Tutor or his Assistant and every Pupil who comes in after that time is to forfeit two pence for every quarter of an hour that he hath exceeded ten.

2. If any one go out of the house without express permission, after the gate is locked, he is to pay One shilling for such offence and should any one get into the house irregularly after the door is locked he and

each person assisting him in such irregular entry must expect that immediate information will be sent to his friends.

3. If any pupil procure a key for the gate he shall not only forfeit it as soon as discovered but be fined two shillings and sixpence.

4. If any one keep a guest beyond half an hour past ten he shall forfeit for every quarter of an hour which such guest stays as if he had stayed abroad himself.

5. If any one stay out all night and do not the next day of his own accord take an opportunity of acquainting the Tutor or assistant with it giving reason for so extraordinary a conduct, he must expect that if it afterward come to the Tutor's knowledge an immediate complaint will be lodged with his friends without any previous notice taken of it to him.

6. An Account is to be brought to the Tutor every Saturday morning by the person who has kept the key the preceding week, of every one who has been let in during that time after ten o'clock.

Section V. Rules relating to the Chambers and Closets

1. That the Chambers and Closets be chosen by persons paying the same price according to the seniority of classes . . . etc.

2. . . . . . .

3. . . . . . .

4. That if Windows be broke, furniture wantonly demolished or any other hurt be done to the House by the fault of any of the pupils the repair . . . be charged to the person by whom it is done. N.B. This extends to the instruments of the apparatus and even to any detriment which may arise to them by the carelessness . . . etc.

5. . . . . . .

6. . . . . . .

Section VI. Rules relating to the Library

1. Every pupil is to pay a guinea to the Library when he enters on the second year of his course if he propose to go through the whole; but if he purpose to stay only two years he is to pay but half a guinea and that from the time he enters on the second half year.

2–10. Ordinary rules for borrowing and returning books.

Section VII. Rules relating to the Office of the Monitor

1. Every Academical student in the Family is to be monitor in his turn excepting only the Senior Class for the time being, and if any of them shall, in his turn, choose to officiate as monitor his assistance shall be thankfully accepted.

2. The monitor is to call up every student at six o'clock in the morning, winter and summer, Vacation times only excepted, and having

rung the bell twice at ten minutes after six is to call over all the names, distinguishing on his bill those who are absent and for every quarter of an hour for which he delays he is to forfeit two pence. He is also to call over his list before morning and evening prayer as above, as also before all Lectures appointed for the whole Academy, together, and if he fail to do it . . . he is to forfeit sixpence for every such failure.

3. He is to review the Library on Saturday at 3 in the afternoon and to call over the catalogue of the books wanting, according to Section VI. No. 7, under a forfeiture of a shilling and he is to see that a pen and ink be left in the Library for public use.

4. He is to lay up the Bibles and Psalm books after prayer in the cupboard . . . and as an acknowledgment for that trouble is to claim one farthing for every one who shall neglect to bring his Psalm book with him at those times, if he choose generally to keep it in his closet.

5. The monitor is to have an eye on the door to see whether any one goes out during divine service and to inform the Tutor of it and is to send the junior pupil present to call the Tutor if in the House as soon as he begins to call over the names.

Section VIII. Rules relating to Conduct Abroad

1. No student is to go into a Publick House to drink there on penalty of a public censure for the first time and the forfeiture of a shilling the second; unless some particular occasion arise which shall, in the judgment of the Tutor, be deemed a sufficient reason.

2. No one is to begin a P.M. at any place in the town without the knowledge and approbation of the Tutor.

3. If any one spread reports abroad to the dishonour of the family or any member of it he must expect a public reproof and to hear a caution given to others to beware of placing any confidence in him.

Section IX. Miscellaneous Rules not comprehended under the former sections

3. When the small pecuniary fines here appointed evidently appear to be despised, they will be exchanged for some extraordinary exercises, which, if they are not performed, must occasion complaint to the Friends of the student in question; for the intent of these laws is not to enrich the box at the expense of those who are determined to continue irregular but to prevent any from being so.

5. Accounts with the Tutor are to be balanced twice a year and all bills from tradesmen, if such there be, are to be delivered in to the Tutor by the persons from whom they are due, at the seasons at which they respectively know their accounts are to be made up.

6. No student is to board abroad unless at the desire and under the

direction of the tutor. And those who do so board abroad are, nevertheless, to attend family prayers and lectures at the appointed times.

7. The news bought for the use of the family is to be paid for out of the box.

8. ......

9. In the absence of the Principal Tutor the Assistant Tutor is to be regarded as his deputy . . . etc.

10. . . . If any gentlemen, not intended for the ministery . . . take up their abode amongst us, whatever their rank in life be, it is expected and insisted upon that they govern themselves by these rules, excepting those which directly relate to exercises preparatory to the ministry . . . etc.

P. Doddridge, D.D. *Dec. 10th*, 1743.
T. Brabant.

We whose names are hereunto subscribed do hereby declare our Acquiescence in these Constitutions, Orders and Rules as the terms of our respective Admission into or continuance in the Academy at Northampton.

Then follow 63 signatures.

Quoted in I. PARKER *Dissenting Academies in England*, pp. 147–53 (Cambridge Univ. Press, 1914)

LETTER HOME FROM A STUDENT AT NORTHAMPTON ACADEMY 1750

This letter is significant in many ways. It illustrates the training in preaching which Doddridge gave his theological students. They were taught English and elocution and sent out in the surrounding villages to preach sermons. At first the sermons need not be their own and in this letter the writer asks for some 'orthodox' sermons to be sent to him, so that he could repeat them. The William Harding who is mentioned had formerly been a student himself at Warrington Academy. The letter also gives some incidental details of student life, the usual bills, student dress and the need for books. The postscript indicates the good relations between teachers and taught which existed at the Academy and in particular the love and esteem which Doddridge inspired in his pupils. It indicates that 'Dames' looked after the students and finally shows that students were able and prepared to act as tutors to the young in their spare time.

Novr. 12, 1750.

Honoured Parents,

I received your last, which I had intended to have answered sooner, had I not had so much business upon my hands, which to have omitted would have been to my disadvantage, etc. As for seeing you and my brother at Northampton I should be extremely glad, but, perhaps, you may think that may be an excuse for my not coming home, for, I will assure you that I cannot go to London along with you, for our vacation will begin the latter end of June, so that if you come it will be unnecessary charges for you to come through Northampton, but I should be very glad if you would send me word in your next letter whether you would have me come home or no, etc.

If I have been extravagant in my expenses I am not sensible of it. You see always all my bills that are of any importance, and as I have sent you some enclosed in this letter, which I hope you will have no objection to. The everlasting which you see is for two pair of . . . waistcoats, one pair of which I have worn out almost; and my gown is so far gone that it will scarce last me till a few weeks longer. I have bought a new wig which I stood in great need of. I wore my old one till it was not worth a penny, and that wig which I had when I first came is almost done. And I have bespoke a new pair of boots, which I cannot possibly do without, for if you knew what I undergo by going into the country towns to repeat sermons and pray. It happened I and another of my fellow pupils were gone out to repeat a sermon and being without boots we were two hours in a storm of rain and wind. We were lost in a country where we did not know nothing at all of, so that I think it is not only useful but necessary to have a pair. I have, according to your desire, bought a quantity of coals, of which I have bought 10 Hund., which cost 12*s.* which I borrow'd of my mistress. I should be very glad to know in particular whether Mr Harding preached from that text and whether he has converted any of the new notioners by preaching. I should be very glad if you would desire Mr Harding to let me have a few of his most orthodox sermons to go to repeat. I wish you would be so good as to ask him that favour, if you think it would not be improper. If he could I hope you would send them immediately. Let me know in your next how the affair is, since sermons of the same kind are so very scarce that we can scarce light on a book to write a good sermon out of, but one or another has heard. Pray let me know in this particular the next letter. And I should be very glad if you would send me my watch and send me a box with a few of your best books, which will be the most convenient for me, as soon as possible. And let me know how my brother Robert goes on, whether he is gone to St Helen's School—and if he is pray don't, and I earnestly beg you would board him at William Claughton's, for if you do, so young as he is, he will certainly be ruined; for I have seen the many dangers and difficulties, and have wondered since how I broke through them; so that for your own happiness and his everlasting happiness, do not send him thither, for if I thought you would send him thither I should never be easy, etc. So I must beg leave to conclude with my respects, as due.

From your very dutiful son

S. Mercer.

P.S. D[r] Father, – I should esteem it not only as a great favour, but as a great honour paid to me, if you would be so good as it is for my interest, to make a present to the doctor of a couple of Cheshire cheeses*, not strong, but mild and fat which will be very acceptable to the doctor, as he provided me a tutor last year, and I do not know whether he will be paid for it, and likewise if you please that I should make a present of something about a crown value to the doctor's Assistant, who, when he should have been taking recreation has been instructing me so that it would be a means of my further improvement, and likewise to send my Dame for she is a widow and she behaves very well to me. I hope, father, you will not forget. And I must beg the favour in particular to send a Cheshire cheese to one of my particular acquaintance, a shop keeper, where I buy my stockings, and where I am positive of it, I am used as if I were almost some of their family, whose son I have under my care to teach Latin, and, who, if it lay in their power, would help me in the greatest extremity, who has made me several handsome presents and sell me their goods, as I have seen with my own eyes – a pair of stockings I have bought 6*d.* cheaper than they have sold to any of our gentlemen – who are very religious people, not those who cant people out of their money, and give them fair words.

Quoted in I. PARKER *Dissenting Academies in England*, pp. 93–5 (Cambridge Univ. Press, 1914)

WARRINGTON ACADEMY: COURSE FOR LAY STUDENTS

Warrington Academy had a short life of some thirty years (1757–86), but in that time educated almost four hundred students, who went into the professions or business, and included on its staff some exceptionally learned tutors among whom the most eminent was Joseph Priestley, who was tutor in Languages and Belles Lettres there from 1761–7.

The academy was notable for the number of non-theological students it admitted, and for these who were 'intended for a life of Business and Commerce' a special three-year course was arranged, as an alternative to the normal five-year course. The following extract gives an outline of this course. Its relevance for young men who are to make their livings in trade and commerce is obvious.

* Samuel's father was Joseph Mercer, a farmer and cheese factor, of Allerton near Liverpool.

First Year:

(1) Elementary Mathematics (Arithmetic, Algebra and Geometry).
(2) French.
(3) Universal Grammar and Rhetoric.

Weekly exercises:

(1) Translations out of French into English.
(2) The composition of an essay on some easy subject in English.
(3) Specimens of letters in the epistolary style to imitate.

Second Year:

(1) Mathematics (Trigonometry; Navigation if desired).
(2) Natural Philosophy, and 'the easier Parts of Astronomy applied to the use of the Globes, and the general system of the Universe.'
(3) French.

Exercises:

(1) Translating out of English into French.
(2) Specimens of French Letters to imitate.
(3) Some English Composition.

Third Year:

(1) Natural Philosophy and 'some of the principal Experiments in the Elements of Chemistry.'
(2) 'A short system of Morality . . . concluding with the Evidences of the Christian Religion.'

Exercises:

(1) Dissertations in some moral, political, or commercial Subjects.
(2) French-English, English-French translations.

Further, lay students were to give attention to pronouncing the English language well, and in this connection attend lectures on Oratory and Grammar, and during 'the whole of their course' they were to learn 'the best methods of Book-Keeping,' 'to improve their Writing,' and 'to make some Progress in the Art of Drawing and Designing.' To this end a special tutor was appointed from time to time to give instruction in Writing, Drawing and Book-keeping. Shorthand would be taught if desired. Finally, 'one or two lectures' were to be given every week on Geography during the whole course in which 'the principal problems upon the Globes will be resolved; the Use of Maps represented; and the Natural History, Manufacturers, Traffick, Coins, Religion, Government, etc., of the several Countries will be enlarged upon.'

Quoted in H. MCLACHLAN *English Education under the Test Acts*, pp. 210–11 (Manchester Univ. Press, 1931)

TIME TABLE, WARRINGTON ACADEMY, C. 1778

The daily life of students at the Academy and the width of the curriculum offered at Warrington is indicated clearly in the extract on the opposite page. Note the inclusion of scientific and commercial subjects in the curriculum, the provision of time for societies and clubs, and the overall religious framework of life in the academy, each day beginning and ending with prayers.

Quoted in H. MCLACHLAN *English Education under the Test Acts*, p. 227 (Manchester Univ. Press, 1931)

TIME TABLE (*c.* 1778).

Hours.	Monday.	Tuesday.	Wednesday.	Thursday.	Friday.	Saturday.	Sunday.
7	Prayers	Prayers	Prayers	Prayers	Prayers	Prayers	Prayers
8	Arithmetic, Bookkeeping	Arithmetic, Bookkeeping	Arithmetic, Bookkeeping	Arithmetic, Bookkeeping	Arithmetic, Bookkeeping	Ancient Geography	—
	Breakfast	Breakfast	Breakfast	Breakfast	Breakfast	Breakfast	Breakfast
9	Algebra	Trigonometry	Algebra	Trigonometry	Algebra	Public Lecture	—
10	Greek Testament	Logic, Ethics, etc.	Theology	Logic, Ethics, etc.	Theology	Scheme Lecture	—
11	Geometry 1	English	Geometry 1	Conic Secs.	Geometry 1		Divine Service
	2	—	2	—	2		
	3	Conic Secs.	3	English	3	Geography	
12	Writing	Drawing	Writing	Drawing	Writing	Theological Society	—
1	Dinner	Dinner	Dinner	Dinner	Dinner	Dinner	Dinner
2	Classics	Classics	Classics	Classics	Classics	—	—
3	French	French	French	French	French	—	—
4	Do.	Do.	Do.	Do.	Do.		
5	Anatomy or Chemistry	—	—	Anatomy or Chemistry	Hebrew	—	—
6	—	—	—	—	—	—	—
7	Composition Society	Speaking Club	Book Club	Classical Club	Divinity Club	—	—
8	Supper	Supper	Supper	Supper	Supper	Supper	Supper
9	Prayers	Prayers	Prayers	Prayers	Prayers	Prayers	Prayers

N.B.—Evening Prayers are now at 7. Several Societies after Supper.

Private Schools

Apart from the dissenting academies many private schools were founded in the eighteenth century. Some offered a classical curriculum only, but many supplemented this with a more utilitarian range of subjects. The number and survival of these schools is hard to determine until more local research is done on the subject. The following selection of local advertisements gives some indication of their nature and activities.*

SCHOOL ADVERTISEMENTS

This advertisement shows the range of 'modern subjects' which many of these private schools offered. There is a distinct emphasis on utilitarian studies, though the stress laid on 'morals and behaviour' is also noteworthy.

AT

Mr PULMAN'S Academy,

IN LEEDS

YOUNG GENTLEMEN

Are Genteely Boarded, and Instructed in,

1. ENGLISH, after a new and approved Method, by which a Youth of a common Capacity may, in a short time, be enabled to speak and write as elegant and grammatical English, as those who have had the Advantage of a Classical Education: An Acquisition well worthy the attention of the Fair Sex, as by this method they may soon attain a thorough Knowledge of the English Language. The Terms are Four Shillings per Quarter, till they enter upon Grammar, and Five Shillings afterwards.
2. LATIN, FRENCH, and most of the Modern Languages. Entrance for French 10s. 6d. and a Guinea per Quarter with Writing and Accounts added.
3. PENMANSHIP in General, with common Accounts, 10s. per Quarter; Grammar and Writing the same per Quarter; Grammar, Writing, and Accounts 13s. per Quarter.

**Further reading:*

N. HANS *New Trends in Education in the Eighteenth Century* (London: Routledge & Kegan Paul, 1951)

4. ARITHMETIC, with all the Latest Improvements; also a very extensive Course of Foreign Exchanges. 13s. per Quarter.

5. MERCHANTS ACCOUNTS, as it is really practised in the best Counting-Houses in LONDON, with all such Precedents and Forms of Business, Letters in Trade, &c. as are fit to qualify Youth for the Counting-House or the Public Offices. The Whole 1*l.* 1s.

6. MENSURATION and GAUGING by Pen and Sliding Rule; EUCLID'S GEOMETRY, and ALGEBRA, with their Application in Gunnery, Optics, Hydrostatics, and other Philosophical Sciences.

7. The Doctrine of MECHANICS, with the Theory and Application of the Mechanic Powers – Plain and Spherical TRIGONOMETRY, with the Orthographic and Sterographic Projections.

8. NAVIGATION in all the Methods of Sailing.

9. ASTRONOMY, founded upon the Discoveries and Philosophical Sentiments of the Illustrious SIR ISAAC NEWTON; in which will be included, the best Methods of calculating Solar and Lunar Eclipses. 1*l.* 1s. per Quarter.

10. GEOGRAPHY, with the USE of the GLOBES. 10s. 6d.

MUSIC and DANCING taught by Masters in Town, esteemed for their respective Abilities.

BOARD and LODGING 12*l.* per Annum,

If under Ten years of age Ten Guineas. Exclusive of Washing, which will be about a Guinea more.

Each Boarder to bring one Pair of Sheets, or pay 7s. 6d. per Annum for the Use of them – Entrance to Boarders 5s.

Those who stay the Vacation Time Must pay 1*l.* 11s. 6d. more.

All proper Regard will be paid to the Morals and Behaviour of the Pupils. Such as are modest and diffident, will be treated with Tenderness and Indulgence; those who, by an honest ambition strive to excell in every Thing that is excellent and praise-worthy, will be regarded with peculiar Marks of Favour and Esteem; and such as are rebellious, obstinate or incorrigible, must be removed from the Academy.

N.B. Land surveyed, and Maps as beautifully drawn as any in the North of England; also Maps wrote or drawn for Surveyors. Likewise Designs wrote for Painters, Engravers, &c. &c.

Leeds Mercury (16 January 1770)

The following notice of a private school at Pontefract shows that it offered a wholly utilitarian curriculum for those who wanted a training for a career in business or trade, in surveying or industry or at sea. There is no attempt to teach the classical languages.

At PONTEFRACT,

Writing; Arithmetic, Vulgar, Decimal and Instrumental; Logarithms, applied to Arithmetical Calculations, and their Use in higher branches of the Mathematics, also their Method of Construction; MERCHANTS ACCOMPTS; ALGEBRA, numerical and in Species, with its Application to various Branches of the Mathematics; GEOMETRY, in Theory and Practice, with its Application to Surveying of Land, Gauging, Mensuration of Artificer's Work, &c. TRIGONOMETRY, both plain and spherical, and their Use in Navigation, Astronomy, Dialling, &c. FLUXIONS, or the new Method of Investigation; and the USE of the GLOBES in Navigation, Geography, Astronomy, &c. as also of all MATHEMATICAL INSTRUMENTS.

Taught by R. WRIGHT, after an easy and plain Method.

N.B. All sorts of Artificer's Work may be survey'd, for either Master or Workman, at reasonable Rates; and the most irregular Parcel of Land may be Survey'd, or Gentlemen taught to Survey it by a new and exact Method founded on the Doctrine of Fluxions.

Also with the said *R. W.* Youth may be boarded.

Leeds Mercury (22 March 1743)

This next notice shows a school which, though primarily offering to teach 'useful Branches of Knowledge', is also prepared to teach Latin. It is noticeable that the proprietor is offering to take unwanted children off their parents' or guardians' hands for the whole year by keeping them at school in the vacations, though pretence is made that such a procedure is really to prevent loss of learning.

EDUCATION AT ABERFORD.

Mr. EPHRAIM SANDERSON continues his SCHOOL as at his first Proposal, for the Boarding and Teaching Youth in the following useful Branches of Knowledge, viz. English Grammar; Writing; Arithmetic, Vulgar, Decimal and Logarithmetical; Geometry; Mensuration of Superficies and Solids; Gauging by the Pen and Slide Rule; Land Surveying and Planning, Trigonometry; Navigation, and other useful Parts of the Mathematics; Book-Keeping after the Italian Method.

Mr. SANDERSON is happy that he has it in his Power to inform his Friends and the Public. That he has built a large New School, in a most pleasant and yet retired Situation, which will be opened after the Christmas Vacation, upon the 7th of January Inst. He hath also engaged an able Assistant to teach the Latin Tongue; his Terms for Latin are Half a Guinea per Quarter.

His Terms for Board, Washing and Learning, are Twelve Pounds per

Annum, for Youth under Fourteen Years of Age; if Fourteen Years of Age, Fourteen Pounds; if Fifteen Years of Age, Fourteen Guineas; and if Sixteen Years of Age and upwards. Fifteen Guineas per Annum; and Half-a-Guinea Entrance.

***ABERFORD is a very healthful Situation, on the great North Road betwixt Ferrybridge and Wetherby.

Mr. SANDERSON proposes to teach no more than Twenty-Four Scholars at one Time, from a Conviction of its not being in his Power to do Justice to a greater Number, except he employ an Assistant, and then not to exceed Thirty-Six.

As long Vacations have a Tendency to alienate the Affections of Youth from their Learning, the usual Term of One Month at Christmas and another at Midsummer will be contracted to a Fortnight at each Time; and those Gentlemen who may chuse to have their Sons remain at School during the Vacations, will only be charged Twelve Shillings more than the above Terms.

Gentlemen who will favour him with the Instruction of their Children, may rest assured of their being treated with the greatest Care and Tenderness, consistent with the Rules of Order and Discipline; and as every Pupil will be under his own immediate Inspection, they will have an Opportunity of making a greater Progress.——The greatest Attention will be paid to their Health and Morals.

Leeds Intelligencer (1 January 1788)

The following school notice obviously indicates that there was a demand from the gentry for schooling for their daughters. The curriculum is suitably domesticated.

Boarding School for young Ladies.

WHereas it has been industriously reported, that Jane Stock and her Daughter Elizabeth Coulston were removed from their late dwelling House in Leeds, this is to certify the Gentry of their Acquaintance, and others, who are desirous to have their Children boarded and taught, That all Sorts of Needle Work, and Patterns drawn on Cloth or Canvas after the newest Fashion, likewise Paistry, Huswifry, Pickling, and Sweet Meats, will be carefully taught as usual, at their School over-against the Vicarage in Leeds, by the abovesaid Teachers,

Jane Stock,
Elizabeth Coulston.

Leeds Mercury (6 March 1739)

Sunday Schools

Robert Raikes (1735–1811) of Gloucester was not the founder of Sunday schools in the sense of being the first to originate teaching the young on the Sabbath Day. Nor was the foundation of Sunday schools in Gloucester his own unaided work, for he had several co-workers in this, particularly the Reverend Thomas Stock, then Headmaster of Gloucester Cathedral School. However, it was Raikes who publicized the movement through his letters and articles in the *Gloucester Journal* which he owned and edited and, as a result, it became a national voluntary enterprise rather than a local activity in a few areas.

It is difficult to assess the effects Sunday schools had in extending literacy but they gave the rudiments of reading and writing to some, together with religious instruction and, to a certain extent, a moral education to many more. Apart from its achievements the Sunday school movement was important in that it pointed the way to universal popular education, and in the nineteenth century the Churches, and eventually the State, sought to achieve this.*

FOUNDATION OF SUNDAY SCHOOLS IN GLOUCESTER

The following letter in the *Gentleman's Magazine* for June 1784 gives Raikes' own account of the foundation of Sunday schools in Gloucester. It was written originally to Colonel Townley of Sheffield who had written to the Mayor of Gloucester for information about Sunday schools. The first school was founded in July 1780, when Raikes and the Reverend T. Stock engaged a Mrs King to hold such a school in her house, at a salary of 1s. 6d. per Sunday.

Gloucester, *November 25th*, 1783.

Sir, – My friend, the Mayor [Mr. Colborne] has just communicated to me the letter which you have honoured him with, enquiring into the nature of Sunday schools. The beginning of this scheme was entirely owing to accident. Some business leading me one morning into the suburbs of the city, where the lowest of the people (who are principally employed in the pin manufactory) chiefly reside, I was struck with concern at seeing a group of children, wretchedly ragged, at play in the streets. I asked an inhabitant whether those children belonged to that part of the town, and lamented their misery and idleness. 'Ah! sir,' said

**Further reading:*

A. GREGORY *Robert Raikes* (London: Hodder & Stoughton, 1877)

the woman to whom I was speaking, 'could you take a view of this part of the town on a Sunday, you would be shocked indeed; for then the street is filled with multitudes of these wretches, who, released on that day from employment, spend their time in noise and riot, playing at "chuck," and cursing and swearing in a manner so horrid as to convey to any serious mind an idea of hell rather than any other place. We have a worthy clergyman (said she) curate of our parish, who has put some of them to school; but upon the Sabbath they are all given up to follow their own inclinations without restraint, as their parents, totally abandoned themselves, have no idea of instilling into the minds of their children principles to which they themselves are entire strangers.'

This conversation suggested to me that it would be at least a harmless attempt, if it were productive of no good, should some little plan be formed to check the deplorable profanation of the Sabbath. I then enquired of the woman, if there were any decent well-disposed women in the neighbourhood who kept schools for teaching to read. I presently was directed to four: to these I applied, and made an agreement with to receive as many children as I should send upon the Sunday, whom they were to instruct in reading and in the Church Catechism. For this I engaged to pay them each a shilling for their day's employment. The women seemed pleased with the proposal. I then waited on the clergyman before mentioned, and imparted to him my plan; he was so much satisfied with the idea, that he engaged to lend his assistance, by going round to the schools on a Sunday afternoon, to examine the progress that was made, and to enforce order and decorum among such a set of little heathens.

This, sir, was the commencement of the plan. It is now about three years since we began, and I could wish you were here to make enquiry into the effect. A woman who lives in a lane where I had fixed a school told me some time ago, that the place was quite a heaven upon Sundays, compared to what it used to be. The numbers who have learned to read and say their Catechism are so great that I am astonished at it. Upon the Sunday afternoon the mistresses take their scholars to church, a place into which neither they nor their ancestors had ever before entered, with a view to the glory of God. But what is yet more extraordinary, within this month these little ragamuffins have in great numbers taken it into their heads to frequent the early morning prayers, which are held every morning at the Cathedral at seven o'clock. I believe there were nearly fifty this morning. They assemble at the house of one of the mistresses, and walk before her to church, two and two, in as much order as a company of soldiers. I am generally at church, and after service they all come round me to make their bow; and, if any animosities have arisen, to make their complaints. The great principle

I inculcate is, to be kind and good natured to each other; not to provoke one another; to be dutiful to their parents; not to offend God by cursing and swearing; and such little plain precepts as all may comprehend. As my profession is that of a printer, I have printed a little book, which I gave amongst them; and some friends of mine, subscribers to the Society for Promoting Christian Knowledge, sometimes make me a present of a parcel of Bibles, Testaments, &c., which I distribute as rewards to the deserving. The success that has attended this scheme has induced one or two of my friends to adopt the plan, and set up Sunday schools in other parts of the city, and now a whole parish has taken up the object; so that I flatter myself in time the good effects will appear so conspicuous as to become generally adopted. The number of children at present thus engaged on the Sabbath are between two and three hundred, and they are increasing every week, as the benefit is universally seen. I have endeavoured to engage the clergy of my acquaintance that reside in their parishes; one has entered into the scheme with great fervour, and it was in order to excite others to follow the example that I inserted in my paper the paragraph which I suppose you saw copied into the London papers.

I cannot express to you the pleasure I often receive in discovering genius, and innate good dispositions, among this little multitude. It is botanizing in human nature. I have often, too, the satisfaction of receiving thanks from parents, for the reformation they perceive in their children. Often I have given them kind admonitions, which I always do in the mildest and gentlest manner. The going amongst them, doing them little kindnesses, distributing trifling rewards, and ingratiating myself with them, I hear, have given me an ascendancy greater than I ever could have imagined; for I am told by their mistresses that they are very much afraid of my displeasure. If you ever pass through Gloucester, I shall be happy to pay my respects to you, and to show you the effects of this effort at civilization. If the glory of God be promoted in any, even the smallest degree, society must reap some benefit. If good seed be sown in the mind at an early period of human life, though it shows itself not again for many years, it may please God, at some future period, to cause it to spring up, and to bring forth a plentiful harvest. With regard to the rules adopted, I only require that they may come to the school on Sunday as clean as possible. Many were at first deterred because they wanted decent clothing, but I could not undertake to supply this defect. I argue, therefore, if you can loiter about without shoes, and in a ragged coat, you may as well come to school and learn what may tend to your good in that garb. I reject none on that footing. All that I require are clean hands, clean face, and their hair combed; if you have no clean shirt, come in that you have on.

The want of decent apparel at first kept great numbers at a distance, but they now begin to grow wiser, and all pressing to learn. I have had the good luck to procure places for some that were deserving, which has been of great use. You will understand that these children are from six years old to twelve or fourteen. Boys and girls above this age, who have been totally undisciplined, are generally too refractory for this government. A reformation in society seems to me to be only practicable by establishing notions of duty, and practical habits of order and decorum, at an early age. But whither am I running? I am ashamed to see how much I have trespassed on your patience; but I thought the most complete idea of Sunday schools was to be conveyed to you by telling what first suggested the thought. The same sentiments would have arisen in your mind, had they happened to have been called forth as they were suggested to me. I have no doubt that you will find great improvement to be made on this plan. The minds of men have taken great hold on that prejudice, that we are to do nothing on the Sabbath day which may be deemed labour, and therefore we are to be excused from all application of minds as well as body. The rooting out of this prejudice is the point I aim at as my favourite object. Our Saviour takes particular pains to manifest, that whatever tended to promote the health and happiness of our fellow creatures, were sacrifices peculiarly acceptable on that day. I do not think I have written so long a letter for some years. But you will excuse me – my heart is warm in the cause. I think this is the kind of reformation most requisite in this kingdom. Let our patriots employ themselves in rescuing their countrymen from that despotism which tyrannical passions and vicious inclinations exercise over them, and they will find that true liberty and national welfare are more essentially promoted than by any reform in Parliament.

As often as I have attempted to conclude, some new idea has arisen. This is strange, as I am writing to a person whom I never have, and, perhaps, never may see – but I have felt that we think alike. I shall, therefore, only add my ardent wishes, that your views of promoting the happiness of society may be attended with every possible success, conscious that your own internal enjoyment will thereby be considerably advanced.

I have the honour to be, Sir, yours, &c.,
R. Raikes

J. HENRY HARRIS (ed.) *Robert Raikes: A Man and His Work*, pp. 305–11 (London and Bristol, 1899)

SOCIAL PURPOSES OF SUNDAY SCHOOLS

The motives behind the founding of Sunday schools were various. Some wanted to preserve the sanctity of the Sabbath, others wanted to protect their property from the vandalism of the young who took the opportunity of a day's freedom from industrial labour to run riot in the streets. This extract from a notice in the *Gloucester Journal* 3 November 1783 makes this point.

Some of the clergy in different parts of this county, bent upon attempting a reform among the children of the lower class, are establishing Sunday schools, for rendering the Lord's day subservient to the ends of instruction, which has hitherto been prostituted to bad purposes. Farmers, and other inhabitants of the towns and villages, complain that they receive more injury to their property on the Sabbath than all the week besides: this, in a great measure, proceeds from the lawless state of the younger class, who are allowed to run wild on that day, free from every restraint. To remedy this evil, persons duly qualified are employed to instruct those that cannot read; and those that may have learnt to read are taught the catechism and conducted to church. By thus keeping their minds engaged, the day passes profitably, and not disagreeably. In those parishes where the plan has been adopted, we are assured that the behaviour of the children is greatly civilized. The barbarous ignorance in which they had before lived being in some degree dispelled, they begin to give proofs that those persons are mistaken who consider the lower orders of mankind incapable of improvement, and therefore think an attempt to reclaim them impracticable, or, at least, not worth the trouble.

ALFRED GREGORY *Robert Raikes*, p. 78 (London: Hodder & Stoughton, 1877)

Raikes himself probably saw Sunday schools as a means to prevent the growth of a criminal population. Since the 1760s he had been a visitor to the county and city gaols of Gloucester and an advocate of prison reform. His work for Sunday schools was an extension of this, as this account in the *Gloucester Journal* of 24 May 1784 suggests.

Whilst the public-spirited exertions of the most distinguished characters in our country are meditating a reform in our Police by rendering our prisons, if possible, the reverse of what they have hitherto been, *seminaries of every species of villainy and profligacy*, several of the clergy in the county are setting forward a model of general instruction for the children of the lower class of the people, by establishing schools for their reception on Sundays, – a day upon which they are given up to follow their wild and vicious inclinations free from restraint.

The promoters of this design seem to concur in the idea that *prevention is better than punishment*, and that an attempt to check the growth of vice at an early period, by an effort to introduce good habits of acting and thinking among the vulgar, is at least an experiment, harmless and innocent, however fruitless it may be in its effect.

J. HENRY HARRIS (ed.) *Robert Raikes: A Man and His Work*, pp. 303–5 (London and Bristol, 1899)

The same notice gives an account of what Sunday schools had already effected in Gloucester.

The good effects of Sunday schools established in this city are instanced in the account given by the principal persons in the pin and sack manufactories, wherein great reformation has taken place among the multitudes whom they employ. From being idle, ungovernable, profligate, and filthy in the extreme, they say the boys and girls are become not only cleanly and decent in their appearance, but are greatly humanised in their manners – more orderly, tractable, and attentive to business, and, of course, more serviceable than they ever expected to find them. The cursing and swearing and other vile expressions, which used to form the sum of their conversation, are now rarely heard among them.

ibid., p. 304

DISCIPLINE IN A GLOUCESTER SUNDAY SCHOOL

Raikes established his second Sunday school in Gloucester under a Mrs Sarah Critchley who taught in it for many years. The following account from a pupil of that school was collected by J. Henry Harris in the 1860s. It gives interesting information about the teaching in the school and the discipline which Raikes himself seems to have enforced.

Another old scholar named BOURNE, who had preserved a copy of the edition of the *Sunday Scholars' Companion*, printed by R. Raikes, 1794, made the following statement with regard to punishment:

'I can speak as to what took place in 1800. The first Sunday I went a boy called "Winkin' Jim" brought a young badger with him and turned it loose. You should have seen old Mother Critchley jump! I laugh now! I shall never forget my first Sunday, nor Winkin' Jim. He went to sea, and was rolled off the yard and drowned. I don't remember if Mr. Raikes was in the room when the badger was "let fly".

'No writing was taught in the school in my time. We used to learn [from a] "Reading-made-Easy" Book, the Collects, Bible and Testament. That is those who could read. Some learnt their letters and A.B.'s.

'Mr. Raikes used always to come to school on Sundays and inquire what the children had learnt, and whether they had been "good boys."

If there had been extra bad boys, or Mrs. Critchley was out of temper and put it on strong, then he would punish them himself.'

Q. 'How did he punish them?'

A. 'The same way as boys were birched. An old chair was the birching stool or horse. The chair was laid on its two front legs, downwards so [describing with chair], and then the young 'un was put on so, kicking and swearing all the time, if he were pretty big and pretty new. Then Mr. Raikes would cane him. I knew a boy he could never draw a tear from – we used to say he couldn't feel. I don't know whether he could or no.

'One boy was a notorious liar. No, I don't remember his name for certain. He was sure to have a nick-name, but I don't remember it. Mr. Raikes could do nothing with him, and one day he caught him by the hand and pressed the tips of his fingers on the bars of the stove or fireplace.'

Q. 'Was he burnt?'

A. 'Blistered a bit. Mr. Raikes would take care that he was not much injured; but he did hate liars! Look at my book. This is what he printed for us to learn: "A thief is better than a man who is accustomed to lie." What I think hurt him most was to hear boys cursing and swearing at each other in church. We were at church one morning and a boy named Philpotts (we called him Mugs) stuck a big shawl-pin into a boy who was nodding. He jumped up into the air with pain, and yelled and swore and flew at "Mugs". The beadles came and turned them out. I saw Mr. Raikes's face and I have never forgotten his look.'

Q. 'Did Mr. Raikes lecture the boys about swearing in church?'

A. 'He must have; it was the only language which some of them knew, and they meant nothing in particular when cursing. Mr. Raikes went down to "Mugs's" father and had him "well leathered". We lived close by and I heard him. "Mugs's" father told mine that he'd strapped Joe well, and didn't know what for except that Mr. Raikes told him he must. He seemed hurt about having to do it. My father said he would see Mr. Raikes —— first. He meant it; for he was a kind man, if rough, and I liked him all the better.'

Q. 'Did you receive any education except what you got in the Sunday school?'

A. 'Not until I grew up.'

Q. 'You are an old man and have had plenty of time for thought. What do you say has been the influence on you of Sunday school teaching?'

A. 'In every way it has been a great blessing to me.'

Q. 'So you have a respect for the memory of Robert Raikes?'

A. 'I love it.'

J. HENRY HARRIS (ed.) *Robert Raikes: A Man and His Work*, pp. 40–3 (London and Bristol, 1899)

RAIKES ON THE SUCCESS OF SUNDAY SCHOOLS

The Sunday school movement continued to grow and in 1785, William Fox, Jonas Hanway and others founded the 'Society for the Establishment and support of Sunday schools throughout the Kingdom of Great Britain.' The following letter from Raikes in reply to one from Fox propounding the scheme for a Society, supports the scheme and points out the success of Sunday Schools and the use of them by adults.

Gloucester, *June 20th*, 1785.

SIR, – You very justly suppose that an apology was utterly unnecessary for a letter like yours. I am full of admiration at the great and noble design of the society you speak of as forming. If it were possible that my poor abilities could be rendered in any degree useful to you, point out the object, and you will not find me inactive. Allow me to refer you to a letter I wrote a week ago to Jonas Hanway, Esq., upon the subject of Sunday-schools. If you ask him for a sight of it, I daresay he will lend it to you. With respect to the possibility of teaching children by the attendance they can give upon the Sunday, I thought with you, in my first onset, that little was to be gained; but I now find that it has suggested to the parents that the little progress made on the Sunday might be improved, and they have therefore engaged to give the teachers a penny a week to take the children once or twice a day during the recess from work at dinner-time or morning to take a lesson every day in the week. To one of my teachers who lives in the worst part of our suburbs I allow two shillings a week extra (besides the shilling I give her for the Sunday employ), to let as many of them as are willing come to read in this manner. I see admirable effects from this addition to my scheme. I find the mothers of the children and grown-up young women have begged to be admitted to partake of this benefit. Sorry I am to say that none of the other sex have shown the same desire. A clergyman from Painswick called upon me this afternoon and expressed his surprise at the progress made there. Many boys now can read who certainly have no other opportunity than what they derive from their Sunday instruction. This he assured me was a fact, but I think they must have applied themselves at their homes. I hear that the people of the Forest of Dean have begun to set this machine in motion among the children of the colliers, a most savage race. A person from Mitcheldean called upon me to report the progress of the undertaking, and observed, 'We have many children who three months ago knew not a letter from a cart wheel' (that was his expression) 'who can now repeat hymns in a manner that would astonish you.'

ALFRED GREGORY *Robert Raikes*, pp. 101–3 (London: Hodder & Stoughton, 1877)

STROUD SUNDAY SCHOOL REGULATIONS

By 1800 the voluntary work of unpaid teachers had extended Sunday schools further and the formation of the Sunday School Union in 1803 gave the movement further impetus. It is difficult to assess the effects Sunday schools had in extending literacy and it seems that the instruction given became increasingly religious in the early years of the nineteenth century.

The following extract of a set of rules drawn up in 1784 for the Stroud Sunday School is typical of many of the early regulations.

I. The master (or dame) appointed by the subscribers shall attend [at his or her own house] every Sunday morning, during the summer, from 8 till 10.30, and every Sunday evening during the summer (except the second in every month), from half an hour after five till eight o'clock, to teach reading, the Church catechism, and some short prayers from a little collection by Dr. Stonehouse; and also to read (or have read by some of those who attend, if any can do it sufficiently) three or four chapters of the Bible in succession, that people may have connected ideas of the history and consistency of the Scriptures.

II. The persons to be taught are chiefly the young, who are past the usual age of admission to the weekly schools, and by being obliged to labour for their maintenance, cannot find time to attend them. But grown persons that cannot read, who are desirous of hearing God's Word, and wish to learn that excellent short account of the faith and practice of a Christian, the Church catechism, are desired to attend, and endeavour to learn, by hearing the younger taught and instructed.

III. Some of the subscribers will in turn visit these schools, to see that their design is duly pursued; and give some little reward to the first, second, and third most deserving in each school.

IV. The subscribers will keep a blank book, in which shall be entered the names of all those parents, and other persons, who, having need of these helps, neglect to send their children, or to attend; and of those who behave improperly when they attend; with intent that they may be excluded from the alms and other charitable assistance of the benevolent. Those who will take no care of their own souls, deserve not that others should take care of their bodies.

V. All that attend these schools shall, as much as may be, attend the public worship both morning and afternoon on Sunday; and shall assemble at church on the second evening of every month, at six o'clock, to be examined, and to hear a plain exposition of the catechism, which the minister will endeavour to give them.

ALFRED GREGORY *Robert Raikes*, pp. 150–1 (London: Hodder & Stoughton, 1877)

SUNDAY SCHOOLS AND INDUSTRY

This next copy of a Church notice issued in 1785 by the Reverend C. Moore, Vicar of Boughton Blaen, Kent, summarizes the aims of Sunday Schools and the attraction, here italicized, of their provision of education without disrupting industry.

Sunday schools supported by voluntary subscriptions in the parish of Boughton Blaen, in Kent, 1785:

The points aimed at in the introduction of Sunday schools, are – to furnish opportunities of instruction to the children of the poorer part of the parish, *without interfering with any industry of the week days;* and to inure children to early habits of going to church, and of spending the leisure hours on *Sunday* decently and virtuously.

The children are to be taught to read and to be instructed in the plain duties of the Christian religion, with a particular view to their good and industrious behaviour in their future character of labourers and servants.

The extent of the plan must be guided by the subscription that may be raised; and all persons willing to encourage the same, even by the smallest donations, are desired to apply to the Rev. C. Moore, Vicar.

J. HENRY HARRIS (ed.) *Robert Raikes: A Man and His Work*, p. 330 (London and Bristol, 1899)

HANNAH MORE AND SUNDAY SCHOOLS IN SOMERSET

In October 1789 Hannah More and her sisters opened a Sunday School at Cheddar, the first of several which they opened and supervised in Somerset. The two following extracts from the letters of Hannah More illustrate her aims and methods.

This first extract shows how, like many of her time, she considered the problem of the poverty of the lower classes as mainly a religious one and not an economic or social problem. Her solution was to teach them to read the Bible as a means of inculcating good morals and, accepting the static society in which she lived, she in no way wanted to educate people above their station.

My plan for instructing the poor is very limited and strict. They learn of week-days such coarse works as may fit them for servants. I allow of no writing. My object has not been to teach dogmas and opinions, but to form the lower class to habits of industry and virtue. I know no way of teaching morals but by infusing principles of Christianity, nor of teaching Christianity without a thorough knowledge of Scripture . . . To make good members of society (and this can only be done by making good Christians) has been my aim . . . Principles not opinions are what I labour to give them.

Quoted in M. G. JONES *Hannah More*, p. 152 (Cambridge Univ. Press, 1952)

This extract from a letter to William Wilberforce shows her methods, including the monetary rewards she gave to children to encourage their learning. The 'Cheap Repository Tracts' referred to were her own works.

In the morning [wrote Hannah to Wilberforce] I open school with one of the Sunday School prayers from the Cheap Repository Tracts. I have a Bible Class – Testament Class – Psalter Class. Those who cannot read at all are questioned out of the first little *Question Book for the Mendip Schools*. Instructing the Bible or Testament class I always begin with the Parables, which we explain to them in the most familiar manner, one at a time, until they understand that one so perfectly that they are well able to give me back the full sense of it. We begin with the three parables in the fifteenth chapter of Luke, first fixing in their minds the literal sense, and then teaching them to make the practical application. When their understandings are a little exercised, we dwell for a long time on the three first chapters of Genesis, endeavouring from these to establish them in the doctrine of the fall of man. We keep them a good while close to the same subject, making them read the same part so often that the most important texts shall adhere to their memories; because on this knowledge only can I ground my general conversation with them, so as to be intelligible. I also encourage them by little bribes of a penny a chapter, to get by heart certain fundamental parts of Scripture, for instance the promises, prophecies and confessions of sin – such as the 9th of Isaiah, 50th of Isaiah, and 51st Psalm – the beatitudes, and indeed the whole Sermon on the Mount – together with the most striking parts of our Saviour's discourses in the Gospel of St John. It is my grand endeavour to make everything as entertaining as I can, and to try and engage their affections; to excite in them the love of God; and particularly to awaken their gratitude to their Redeemer.

When they seem to get a little tired we change the scene; and by standing up and singing a hymn their attention is relieved . . . Those who attend four Sundays without intermission, and come in time for morning prayer [at Church] receive a penny every fourth Sunday, but if they fail once, the other three Sundays go for nothing. They must begin again. Once in every six weeks I give a little gingerbread. Once a year I distribute little books according to merit – those who deserve most get a Bible; second rate merit gets a Prayer Book; the rest [she added with a pleasing touch of humour] Cheap Repository Tracts.

ibid., p. 160

SUNDAY SCHOOLS IN WALES

In Wales the Reverend Thomas Charles of Bala was chiefly responsible for the development of the Sunday School movement in Wales. The following letter written by his grandson, the Reverend David Charles, and dated 24 December 1863, provides an account of his work and its results.

In reference to the Welsh Sunday schools and the part my revered and honoured grandfather had in their formation, &c., I would beg to submit the following observations:

It was the Rev. Griffith Jones, of Llanddowron, in the county of Carmarthen, who gave the first impulse to the work of educating the people by means of catechising his parishioners every Sunday at the public service in the parish church. This was about the beginning of the last century.

Before this time there were no schools in Wales, and the mass of the population were lying in the grossest darkness.

The success that attended his public catechisings led him to the establishment of Circulating Charity Day Schools, which proved very beneficial in the several localities to which they were removed from time to time, and which were the first glimmerings of the dawn of day.

It was in the neighbourhood of Llanddowron that my grandfather was born, and in Llanddowron it was that he received his school instruction, as well as some of his first religious impressions. There lived at Llanddowron at that time an old man of the name of Rhys Hugh, who had lived with Mr. Griffith Jones, and who was the means of infusing Mr. Jones's spirit into Mr. Charles while he was yet a boy; and it appears that this spark of inspiration, first excited by old Rhys Hugh in the mind of his youthful friend, was never extinguished, but broke out into a conflagration which was to embrace Wales and the world.

Mr. Charles in after years, when he went to reside at Bala, in North Wales, established similar circulating charity schools to those of Mr. Griffith Jones; and it was in the working out of these charity schools that Mr. Charles first saw the grand principle of the Welsh Sabbath schools.

The day schools, which survived for about twenty years, were especial means towards preparing teachers for the work of the Sabbath school. For this purpose Mr. Charles himself undertook the instruction of those whom he intended to become Sabbath school teachers, and he composed two catechisms in the Welsh language for the benefit both of the teachers and scholars of the Sunday schools.

These schools Mr. Charles first set up about the year 1785 – about three years, I believe, after Mr. Raikes. Still, we believe we are authorised to say that the *principle* of the Welsh Sabbath school was practically wrought out by Mr. Charles; *and to attribute to him the independent thought of establishing these schools* does not involve the idea that Sabbath schools had not previously existed in other places, but on another and a more inefficient principle.

A reference to a prior institution as evidence that we are not to attribute the originating of the Welsh Sabbath schools to Mr. Charles alone, proves that they who do so do not fully comprehend the nature of the schools which Mr. Charles established.

The distinguishing principle of the Welsh Sunday schools which Mr. Charles incorporated in his institution for the religious instruction of his countrymen was, that the object of the Sabbath school was the instruction not only of children but of adults also, and that it was intended not merely to teach spelling and reading, but to bring all classes together to examine the Word of God and to exchange thoughts upon its all-important truths.

The Welsh Sunday school thus became an institution in which the great doctrines of the Christian religion were learnt, and understood, and practically enforced by men who had themselves experienced their power.

The Church of Christ was taught that it was the duty of every one of its members to care for and instruct the world in the saving precepts of the Gospel; and the Sunday school was put forth as the arena in which the zeal, the love, the knowledge, and the spiritual power of the Church were to be brought to bear upon the masses of their fellow-men. *Thus our Sunday schools were intended to become real missionary institutions for the Church to exert its influence upon all classes of the people.*

This is the distinguishing feature of our Welsh Sunday schools, which is a great advancement upon the ground taken by those which had been previously established in England, and this, we say, was the distinct and original idea of the Rev. Mr. Charles.

He was probably the first also who established regular public meetings in connection with the Sabbath schools – meetings to which the public at large assembled to witness and listen to the regular catechising of several schools which had come together from different localities. On those occasions large multitudes flocked together, and very powerful impressions were generally left on the minds of the audience, as well as upon the Sunday scholars and teachers, and, through them, upon their families.

These meetings afforded opportunities to the people in general to see what kind of instruction was given to their children, and also what the efforts were on the part of the teachers to instruct them in the great truths of religion. *Thus the prejudices of the people against religion were gradually worn down;* their attention was drawn to the Sunday school, and at length they were attracted to place themselves under its fostering care.

In this way the Sunday school wore more the aspect of a church in active operation than a school – prayer and praise being blended with earnest exhortations to all. Instruction was given in every branch of scriptural knowledge, and, at the same time, the teacher exhibited not so much the character of a master as that of a friend and a Christian, who was willing to lecture for the good of others.

The Welsh Sunday schools, are then, to this day well-springs of religious instruction to men of every age, and contain generally more adult members, both male and female, than children. They are speciallly the nurseries of our Churches, both as regards members and ministers.

Trusting the above brief sketch may meet your object, and with Christian regards,

I am, dear Sir,
Yours very faithfully,
David Charles.

J. HENRY HARRIS (ed.) *Robert Raikes: A Man and His Work*, p. 330 (London and Bristol, 1899)

Monitorial Systems of Bell and Lancaster

Independently but almost simultaneously, the Quaker, Joseph Lancaster, and the Anglican, Andrew Bell – the one in London the other in Madras – devised systems for the tuition of large numbers in reading, writing and arithmetic. Bell published his first account of his system in 1797, and Lancaster his in 1803, but both had begun to develop them in the last decade of the eighteenth century.*

The systems were very much alike, both exploiting the principle of self-education by relying on pupils teaching each other under the direction of a single master. Lancaster called his teacher-pupils 'monitors' and Bell referred to his as 'tutors'. Bell had operated his system in India where in 1789 he had been appointed, along with various chaplaincies to regiments, superintendent of the Military Male Asylum at Madras, a charity school for the orphan boys of soldiers. In 1797 he arrived back in England and began to publicize his system, introducing it into various parochial schools, including his own parish school at Swanage, Dorset, where he became rector. Lancaster began teaching in Southwark in 1798 and developed his system in his school at Borough Road, which he was able to finance with the help of subscriptions from well-wishers.

At first there was no element of rivalry between the two men. In 1800 Lancaster read Bell's *An Experiment in Education*, acknowledged his gain from it, later visited Bell at Swanage and the two men interchanged letters on the subject. However, that aggressive Anglican, Mrs Trimmer, published in 1805 a *Comparative View* of the systems and work of the two men, claiming that Lancaster had stolen his ideas from Bell. This provoked a split not only between Bell and Lancaster but also between the respective supporters of these two men which eventually polarized into a religious difference, with Anglicans supporting Bell and nonconformists and interdenominationalists supporting Lancaster.

Many at that time were seeking ways of educating the 'industrious classes', as Lancaster called them, but since State intervention in the provision of education at that time commanded little or no support, private philanthropy was the only means to finance it. The fact that the systems of both Bell and Lancaster offered the chance to educate many at little cost without demanding an increase in the small number of available teachers, commended itself to those wishing to sponsor education. Thus in the early years of the century

**Further reading:*

D. SALMON *The Practical Parts of Lancaster's* Improvements *and Bell's* Experiment (Cambridge Univ. Press, 1932)

C. BIRCHENOUGH *History of Elementary Education in England and Wales from 1800 to the Present Day* (London: University Tutorial Press, 1938)

M. STURT *The Education of the People* (London: Routledge & Kegan Paul, 1967) both Bell and Lancaster enjoyed the support of subscribers of differing views and religious persuasions. However, after Mrs Trimmer's intervention, religion became a dividing line and two societies emerged for the building and management of schools for the poor on the lines of a monitorial system. In 1811 the Church of England formed the National Society for Promoting the Education of the Poor in the Principles of the Established Church, in accordance with the principles of Bell. In 1814, the British and Foreign School Society was formed to manage interdenominational schools. These two societies continued to sponsor schools throughout the nineteenth century, though after 1833 the State helped them with finance and eventually after 1870 began its own system of Local Board Schools.

LANCASTER'S MONITORIAL SYSTEM

Lancaster's main motive in devising his monitorial system was to make the most efficient use of school time – both the teacher's time and the pupil's time. Its basic principle was self-education and to stimulate this Lancaster relied on a system of rewards and punishments, but above all on the fostering of a competitive spirit among his pupils.

In education nothing can be more important than economy of time, even when we have a reasonable prospect of a good portion of it at our disposal; but it is most peculiarly necessary in primary schools, and in the instruction of the poor: – cases wherein the pupil seldom has too much on his hands; and very often a fine genius or noble talents are lost to the state, and to mankind, from the want of it. If we wish to do the best for the welfare of youth, and to promote their interest through life, it will be well for us to study economy of their precious time . . .

As a further proof of the benefit resulting from this mode of instruction, the following instance is remarkable. Several boys, belonging to my school, were in the habit of playing truant continully. This habit was contracted as it usually is, by frequenting bad, idle company. One boy seemed quite incorrigible: his father got a log and chain, chained it to his foot, and, in that condition, beating him all the way, followed him to school repeatedly. Nothing was of any avail – neither was the lad reformed by anything the parent could do. At last he was reformed by a contest about *an old rusty nail.* I am not fond of laying wagers; but, without any other design than the improvement of two classes, by raising a spirit of emulation among them, I betted, with one of my subordinate monitors, a *shilling* against an *old rusty nail,* that another class would excell in writing on the slate, that in which he taught. In case it did, the old rusty nail was to be mine; and the oddity of the thing tickled the fancy of the boys, and served as well for the bone of contention as any thing else. Both classes were disposed to exert all their powers on the ocasion, determined not to be excelled. I lost the wager in the sequel; but if it had been fifty times the value, it could not have had a better effect than it had. The truants, I have been mentioning, were in the two contending classes. The interest they took in the honor of their classes was so great, that instead of playing truant, they came to school, to aid their companions in securing the honour, which was more than the prize. The interest they took in the thing was so great, that they became pleased with school; and, above all, the almost incorrigible boy became reformed, and one of the best proficients in learning in the whole school; and, for two years after, which he remained with me, no more was heard of his playing truant. Thus, a little emulation and mental interest in what he had to do, produced that improvement in conduct, and delight in learning, which neither the log, nor the horse-whip, or any other severe treatment he received from his father could produce . . . It is by the application of this powerful influence, and by controlling and directing the influence lads have over each other, to useful purposes, that, under the *Blessing* which hath rested on my labours, I have been so successful: and, I believe, that others who may wish to establish similar institutions, upon the same principles as mine, must build on the same foundation. The passions of the human heart must be their study; and they will find the system itself answer to the effects, as face to face in a glass.

JOSEPH LANCASTER *Improvements in Education*, pp. 31–4 (London, 1806)

In this next extract, Lancaster summarizes his system, as it worked in his institution for the education of one thousand children, at Borough Road, Southwark. In particular he makes it clear that his 'monitors' were boys who helped in any capacity in the school and the term was not confined to those who assisted in the teaching. In effect it was a method of engaging the co-operation of as many pupils as possible in school life and the value of this principle remains as valid today as it was then.

In establishing this institution, the influence a master has over his scholars, and the influence they have one over another, have been the objects of constant study and practice; it has most happily succeeded in proving, that a very large number of children may be superintended by one master; and that they can be self-educated by their exertions, under his care.

The whole school is arranged in classes; a monitor is appointed to each, who is responsible for the cleanliness, order and improvement of every boy in it. He is assisted by boys, either from his own or another class, to perform part of his duties for him, when the number is more than he is equal to manage himself.

The proportion of boys who teach, either in reading, writing, or arithmetic, is one to ten. In so large a school, there are duties to be performed which simply relate to order, and have no connexion with learning: for these duties, different monitors are appointed. The word monitor, in this institution, means, any boy that has charge either in some department of tuition or of order, and is not simply confined to those boys who teach. The boy who takes care that the writing books are ruled, by machines made for that purpose, is the monitor of ruling. The boy who superintends the inquiries after the absentees, is called the monitor of absentees. The monitors who inspect the improvement of the classes in reading, writing and arithmetic, are called inspecting monitors; and their offices are, indeed essentially different from that of the *teaching monitors*. A boy whose business it is to give to the other monitors such books, &c. as may be wanted or appointed for the daily use of their classes, and to gather them up when done with; to see all the boys do read, and that none leave school without reading, is called the monitor-general. Another is called the monitor of slates, because he has a general charge of all the slates in the school.

ibid., pp. 37–8

Lancaster's system implied 'streaming' and he considered mixed-ability classes inefficient. He knew the value of small group work and the mutual help which pupils could extend to each other but he preferred not to mix up children of differing abilities. In these respects his views provide an interesting comparison to some twentieth-century thinking on this subject.

To promote emulation, and facilitate learning, the whole school is arranged into classes, and a monitor appointed to each class. A class consists of any number of boys whose proficiency is on a par: these may all be classed and taught together. If the class is small, one monitor may teach it; if large, it may still continue the same class, but with more or less assistant monitors, who, under the direction of the principal monitor, are to teach the subdivisions of the class. If only four or six boys should be found in a school, who are learning the same thing, as A, B, C, ab. &c Addition, Subtraction, &c I think it would be advantageous for them to pursue their studies after the manner of a class. If the number of boys studying the same lesson, in any school, should amount to six, their proficiency will be nearly doubled by being classed, and studying in conjunction.

ibid., p. 40

LANCASTER ON THE METHOD OF TEACHING TO READ

This extract illustrates the monitorial system in action. Sand trays are used instead of books in one of the methods recommended, and in the other method the reference to a badge of merit as a learning incentive is notable. Lancaster's acknowledgement of his debt to Andrew Bell over the matter of sand is also noteworthy.

Of the Method of teaching to read

FIRST CLASS

The first, or lowest class of scholars, are those who are yet unacquainted with their alphabet. This class may consist of ten, twenty, or a hundred; or any other number of children, who have not made so much progress as to know how to distinguish all their letters at first sight. If there are only ten or twenty of this description in the school, one boy can manage and teach them; if double the number, it will require two boys as teachers, and so in proportion for every additional twenty boys. The reader will observe, that, in this and in every other class, described in the succeeding plan and arrangement, the monitor has but one plain, simple object to teach, though in several ways; and the scholars the same to learn. This simplicity of system defines at once the province of each monitor in tuition. The very name of each class imports as much – and this is called the first A, B, C, class. The method of teaching is as follows: a bench is placed or fixed to the ground for the boys to sit on; another, about a foot higher, is placed before them. On the desk before them is placed deal ledges, (a pantile lath, nailed down to the desk, would answer the same purpose,) Thus:

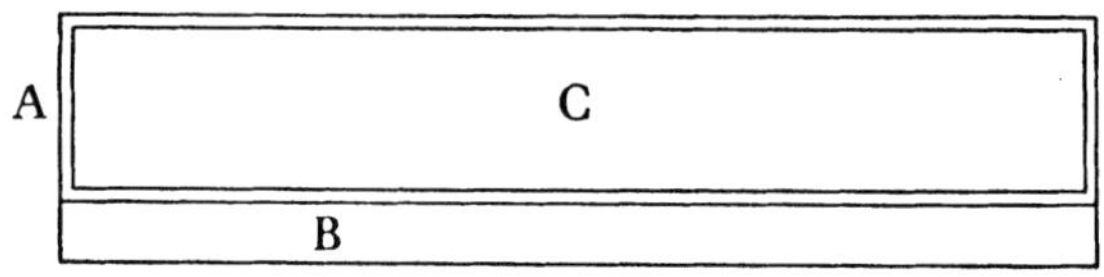

The letter A, shows the entire surface of the desk, which is supported by two, three, or more legs, as usual for such desks, and according to the size. B, is a vacant space, where the boys lean their left arms, while they write or print with the right hand. The sand is placed in the space C. The double lines represent the ledges (or pantile laths) which confine the sand in its place: sand of any kind will do, but it must be dry. The boys print in the sand, with their fingers: they all print at the *command* given by their monitor. A boy who knows how to print, and distinguish some of his letters, is placed by one who knows few or none, with a view to assist him; and particularly, that he may copy the form of his letters, from *seeing* him make them. We find this copying one from another a great step towards proficiency. In teaching the boys to print the alphabet, the monitor first makes a letter on the sand, before any boy who knows nothing about it; the boy is then required to *retrace* over the same letter, which the monitor has made for him, with his fingers and thus he is to continue employed, till he can make the letter himself, without the monitor's assistance. Then he may go on to learn another letter.

The letters are taught in courses: they are arranged in three courses, according to their similarity of form. There are three simple examples, which regulate the formation of the whole alphabet. *First*, a line, as in the letters, I, H, T, L, E, F, i, l: *Second*, depending upon the formation of an angle; as, A, V, W, M, N, Z, K, Y, X, – v, w, k, y, z, x: a circle or a curve; as, O, U, C, J, G, D, P, B, R, Q, S, – a, o, b, d, p, q, g, e, m, n, h, t, u, r, s, f, s, j. These courses of letters are soon acquired, on account of the similarity of form. The greatest difficulty in teaching the letters occur in those, the form of which are exactly alike, and are only distinguished by change of position; p, q, and p, d, are perpetually mistaken for each other; by *making* the two letters at the same time, the children readily learn to distinguish them. Then again, they are all employed printing at once; and it is both curious and diverting to see a number of little creatures, many not more than four or five years old, and some hardly that, stretching out their little fingers with one consent, to make the letters. When this is done they sit quietly till the sand is smoothed for them, by the monitor, with a *flat-iron*, as commonly used for ironing linen. The sand being dry, the iron meets no resistance, and thus, all the letters made in a very short time, by each boy, are, in as short a time, obliterated by the monitor; and the boys again apply their *fingers* to the sand, and proceed as before.

Another method of teaching the alphabet is, by a large sheet of pasteboard suspended by a nail on the school wall; twelve boys, from the sand class, are formed into a circle round this alphabet, standing in their numbers, 1, 2, 3, &c. to 12. These numbers are pasteboard tickets, with number 1, &c. inscribed, suspended by a string from the button of the bearer's coat, or round his neck. The best boy stands in the first place; he is also decorated with a leather ticket, gilt, and lettered *merit*, as a badge of honour. He is always the first boy questioned by the monitor, who points to a particular letter in the alphabet, 'What letter is that?' If he tells readily, what letter it is, all is well, and he retains his place in the class; which he forfeits, together with his number and ticket, to the next boy who answers the question, if he cannot.

This promotes constant emulation. It employs the monitor's attention continually; he cannot look one way, while the boy is repeating his letters another; or at all neglect to attend to him, without being immediately discovered. It is not the monitor's business to teach, but to see the boys in his class or division teach each other. If a boy calls A, by the name of B, or O, he is not to say, it is not B, or O, but it is A; he is to require the next boy in succession to correct the mistakes of his senior. These two methods, of the sand and alphabet card, with their inferior arrangements detailed, are made use of daily in rotation, and serve as a mutual check and relief to each other.

The figures are taught in the same manner. Sand is a cheap substitute for books any where; but more so in those parts of the country where the soil is sandy, than in London. *This* method was taken in outline from Dr. Bell, formerly of Madras; but he did not say, in his printed account of that institution, whether wet or dry sand was used. It, for a long time, involved our minor classes in much difficulty, having begun with the wet sand: we continued it some time. It required great care in wetting: if wetted too much or too little, it was equally useless and inconvenient; it occasioned a deal of trouble to smooth, and took double or treble the quantity of sand which it would have taken dry. All these difficulties, my boys overcame in a short time; but every time we had a change of monitors in the class, we found it a troublesome qualification for him to attain the art of preparing it properly. All these difficulties were obviated by my hearing from Dr. Bell, that it was dry sand. This circumstance fully shows how essential a minute detail is, to the ready practice of any experiment, and will be an apology for the length of this, on the art of teaching the A, B, C.

JOSEPH LANCASTER *Improvements in Education*, pp. 42–7 (London, 1806)

LANCASTER ON THE TEACHING OF ADDITION

This extract gives in painstaking detail the methods by which a monitor could teach simple addition to a class. It also illustrates Lancaster's views of the psychology of learning and in particular his conviction that repetition and written practice are essential in learning arithmetic.

The next is the Simple Addition class. Each boy in every cyphering class, has a slate and pencil; and we may consider, that the subject now before us relates to the best method of conveying the knowledge of arithmetic to those who are unacquainted with it. They usually begin with small sums, and gradually advance to larger; but, boys who have been well instructed in the preceding class, are not only qualified for this, but have a foundation laid for their future proficiency in every branch of arithmetic. As the reader will observe, the whole of this method of teaching is closely connected with writing: it not only unites a mental exertion with itself, but always renders that *mental* exertion, however great or small, visible to the teacher; and enables him to say, with certainty, that his pupils have performed their business. The monitor, or subordinate teacher of the class, has a written book of sums, which his class are to do; and he has another written book, containing a key to those sums, on a peculiar plan, which will be described, and which fully shows how they are to be done.

In the first place, when his class are seated, he takes the book of sums – suppose the first sum is as follows:

	lbs.
(No. 1.)	27935
	3963
	8679
	14327
	54904

He repeats audibly the figures 27,935, and each boy in the class writes them; they are then inspected, and if done correct, he dictates the figures 3,963, which are written and inspected in like manner: and thus he proceeds till every boy in the class has the sum finished on his slate.

He then takes the key, and reads as follows:

First column

7 and 9 are 16, and 3 are 19, and 5 are 24. Set down 4 under the 7, and carry 2 to the next.

This is written by every boy in the class, inspected as before, and then he proceeds.

Second column

2 and 7 are 9, and 6 are 15, and 3 are 18, and 2 I carried are 20. Set down 0 and carry 2 to the next.

Third column

3 and 6 are 9, and 9 are 18, and 9 are 27, and 2 I carried are 29. – Set down 9 and carry 2.

Fourth column

4 and 8 are 12, and 3 are 15, and 7 are 22, and 2 I carried are 24. – Set down 4 and carry 2.

Fifth column

1 and 2 are 3, and 2 I carried are 5.

Total, in figures, 54,904 lbs. Total, in words, fifty-four thousand, nine hundred and four pounds.

The whole of a sum is written in this manner, by each boy in the class: it is afterwards inspected by the monitor, and frequently by the master;

and it is a method, in particular, well adapted to facilitate the progress of the scholars in the elementary parts of arithmetic.

Its good effects are deducible from principle, as well as practice. For youth to be conversant in arithmetic, it is needful that the most frequent combinations of figures which occur in the first four rules, should be familiar to their memory. Now, *the frequent recurring of one idea*, if simple and definite, is alone sufficient to impress it on the memory, without sitting down to learn it as a task; and, in the method of tuition just described, every boy is obliged to repeat it at least twice. First, the impression it makes on his mind, when listening to his monitor's voice, and the repetition of that impression when writing it on the slate. When a certain quota of sums are done, the class begins anew: and thus repetitions gradually succeed each other, till practice secures improvement, and removes boys individually into other classes and superior rules, when each boy has a suitable prize, which our established plan appropriates to the occasion.

Multiplication is easily attained by this method: and the use which is made of the Multiplication table in general, as an auxiliary to the memory in acquiring this rule, is a cogent reason in favour of the method I suggest to public notice.

In the instance of dictating the figures 27,935, and any other variations after the same example, the scholars, by writing, acquire a thorough knowledge of Numeration, expressed both in words and figures, without paying any attention to it as a *separate rule*. In fact, Numeration is most effectually learned by the scholars in my institution, not from the study, but by the practice of it; and I may add, almost every other branch of knowledge, taught in the different classes, is acquired in the same easy and expeditious way.

The boys vie with each other in writing their sums neatly on the slate, and their practice and improvement in writing is greatly increased by this means.

JOSEPH LANCASTER *Improvements in Education*, pp. 69–73 (London, 1806)

LANCASTER ON REWARDS AND PUNISHMENTS

Lancaster was firmly of the opinion that children needed incentives for learning other than the intrinsic interest of the work involved. Consequently he devised an elaborate system of rewards.

Emulation and Rewards

In spelling by writing on the slate, the performances of the scholars are inspected, sometimes by the monitor of their class, often by an inspecting monitor, and occasionally by the master.

Printing in the sand is inspected in the same manner as in the new method of teaching arithmetic. Every boy is placed next to one who can do as well or better than himself: his business is to excel him, in which case he takes precedence of him. In reading, every reading division has the numbers, 1, 2, 3, &c. to 12, suspended from their buttons. If the boy who wears number 12, excels the boy who wears number 11, he takes his place and number; in exchange for which the other goes down to the place and number 12. Thus, the boy who is number 12 at the beginning of the lesson, may be number 1, at the conclusion of it, and *vice versa*. The boy who has number 1, has also a single leather ticket, lettered variously, as, 'Merit,' – 'Merit in Reading,' – 'Merit in Spelling,' – 'Merit in Writing,' &c. this badge of honour he also forfeits, if he loses his place by suffering another to excel him. He has also a picture pasted on pasteboard, and suspended to his breast; this he forfeits to any boy who can excel him. Whoever is in the first place at the conclusion of the lesson, delivers the ticket and picture to a monitor appointed for that purpose. The honour of wearing the ticket and number, as marks of precedency, is all the reward attached to them; but the picture which has been worn entitles the bearer to receive another picture in exchange for it; which becomes his own. This prize is much valued by the minor boys, and regarded by all. Pictures can be made a fund of entertainment and instruction, combined with infinite variety. When a boy has a waggon, a whip-top, or ball, one thing of the kind satisfies him, till it is worn out; but he may have a continual variety of pictures, and receive fresh instruction as well as pleasure from every additional prize. I lament that there is not a series of cheap, regular pictures, that would be fit to put into the hands of children. Nothing can be better adapted to allure their minds into a love of learning. Yet many of the common pictures, of which tens of thousands are printed annually, and sold among the children of the poor, are mere catchpenny rubbish; so badly designed and executed, and on such silly subjects, as to be fit only to debase the minds of youth one with another; he may decide improperly in some instances, at first, but practice will soon make him perfect in discriminating and deciding; and then he will be found a very useful auxiliary in a school. It is as easy to form a number of boys, as one or two, on this plan; and they may be qualified sooner than usual, if required, provided the master renews the same inspection and decision in their presence, after they have done; and shows them every prominent case in which they may have decided wrong, and *why* they have done so. When boys have obtained their tickets for writing the stipulated number of times, they are permitted to choose any prize of the value appropriated to the number on their tickets: and there is a choice variety of prizes, consisting of toys, bats, balls, kites, &c. but the books with prints or pictures are more in request among the children, and generally more useful than any other prizes whatever.

I believe, the emulation I have described as united with my methods of teaching, will be found most useful as a stimulus to the exertions of those scholars who possess no more than common abilities; indeed, it is for this class of learners, who, in general, give the most trouble, that such methods of teaching and encouragement *are most wanting*. The drudgery of teachers is always greater or less, in proportion to the quickness or dullness of their scholars; but, in these modes of teaching all must exert themselves according to their abilities, or be idle. If they exert themselves as well as they can, they will improve accordingly – if they are idle, it is immediately detected, and as rapidly punished; of the method of doing which I shall treat presently. However, where lads of genius and quickness of intellect are found, they will soon show themselves. Indeed, I believe, that many lads of genius are unknown in the schools they attend, even to the masters themselves, because they have no stimulus to exertion, no opportunity of distinguishing themselves – or, that nothing happens to develope their latent powers. Similar to this was the case of the Portuguese in Brazil, who frequently passed diamonds, when in the rough, through their hands, and despised them as pebbles; but, when the mines were discovered, they regretted their ignorance. Whenever superior merit shows itself in schools, it should always be honoured, rewarded, and distinguished: one or two lads of this description influence a whole school by their beneficial example. I generally reward such by gifts of some of the most valuable books and other prizes: silver pens, and sometimes silver medals. The medals are engraved with the name of the youth who obtains them, and for what given. To some of my senior lads I have given *silver watches*, at my own expence; and think the encouragement so given has had its good effect. A regular series of instructive prints might be published at the same expence; but they should be selected or designed by a person acquainted with the minds and manners of youth. The advantage of some prints, as rewards for children, is their cheapness; and others, is their utility: those are printed for sale, at one halfpenny or a penny each; and are sold, wholesale, at a much cheaper rate. Many such prints can be cut into four or six parts. Every part will be a complete subject itself, and fit for a prize: thus, less than a shilling per day will afford prizes, morning and afternoon, for a hundred and twenty children or more, and raise emulation among the whole school. I hope all ladies, who are patrons of schools, will adopt these articles for prizes.

By the foregoing observations it will appear, that emulation and reward are closely united with continual inspection and application to learning. Another method of rewarding deserving boys is by paper tickets, which are numbered, one, two, three, &c. they are given to such boys as distinguish themselves in writing with the pen; which is done about four times a week, by *part* of the school only, in order to accustom them a little to the use of the pen. Each number is to be obtained several times, before the bearer can obtain the prize appropriated to it: as,

Number 1,	three times, to receive	½d.
2,	six times, ...	1d.
3,	eight times, ...	2d.
4,	nine times, ...	3d.
5,	twelve times, ...	6d.

Every time a ticket is obtained, it is booked by a monitor, whose office it is to record tickets, prizes, &c. The tickets are given, according to the evident and various degree of pains the scholar may have taken with his performance. They are given by the monitor or teacher who inspects the written copies, according to his judgment of the performances submitted to his inspection. It requires some discretion in the master to choose a lad for this office, whose eye is capable of at once *discriminating between one performance and another*, and of discerning where exertions have been made by the learner to improve. In small institutions the master may perform this office; in large ones he can only do it occasionally. I have several lads who are capable of this office, and perform it well. The best way to qualify a boy for such a duty, is to accustom him to inspect and compare the performances of boys in writing on the slate,

Another method of encouraging deserving youth, who distinguish themselves by their attention to study, is equally honourable but less expensive. I have established in my institution an order of merit. Every member of this order is distinguished by a silver medal, suspended from his neck by a plated chain. No boys are admitted to this order, but those who distinguish themselves by proficiency in their own studies, or in the improvement of others, and for their endeavours to check vice.

JOSEPH LANCASTER *Improvements in Education*, pp. 89–94 (London, 1806)

On the other hand, Lancaster considered that a system of punishments was also necessary in a school, though as the following extract makes clear he was against excessive punishment of pupils and preferred to encourage learning by more positive means than punishments. The treatment he suggests for the 'frequent transgressor' is noteworthy.

Offences and Punishments

The chief offences committed by youth at school, arise from the liveliness of their active dispositions. Few youth do wrong for the *sake of doing so.* If precedence and pleasure be united with learning, they will soon find a delight in attending at school. Youth naturally seek whatever is pleasant to them, with avidity; and, from ample experience have I found, that they do so with learning, when innocent pleasure is associated therewith. If any misconduct should be punished by severity, vice and immorality are the chief subjects; and, I am convinced that it is not always indispensable in those cases, having known many a sensible boy reformed without, and that, from practices as bad as almost any that usually occur in schools.

That children should idle away their time, or talk in school, is very improper – they cannot talk and learn at the same time. In my school talking is considered as an offence; and yet it occurs very seldom, in proportion to the number of children: whenever this happens to be the case, an appropriate punishment succeeds.

Each monitor of a class is responsible for the cleanliness, order, and quietness of those under him. He is also a lad of unimpeachable veracity – a qualification on which much depends. He should have a continual eye over every one in the class under his care, and notice when a boy is loitering away his time in talking or idleness. Having thus seen, he is bound in duty to lodge an accusation against him for *misdemeanor*. In order to do this silently, he has a number of cards, written on differently: as, 'I have seen this boy idle,' – 'I have seen this boy talking,' &c. &c. This rule applies to every class, and each card has the name of the particular class written thereon: so that, by seeing a card written on as above, belonging to the first or sixth, or any other reading class, it is immediately known who is the monitor that is the accuser. This card is given to the defaulter, and he is required to present it at the head of the school – a regulation that must be complied with. On a repeated or frequent offence, after admonition has failed, the lad to whom he presents the card has liberty to put a wooden log round his neck, which serves him as a pillory, and with this he is sent to his seat. This machine may weight from four to six pounds, some more and some less. The neck is not pinched or closely confined – it is chiefly burthensome by the manner in which it encumbers the neck, when the delinquent turns to the right or left. While it rests on his shoulders, the equilibrium is preserved; but, on the least motion one way or the other, it is lost, and the logs operate as a dead weight upon the neck. Thus, he is confined to sit in his proper position. If this is unavailing, it is common to fasten the legs of offenders together with wooden shackles: one or more, according to the offence. The *shackle* is a piece of wood about a foot, sometimes six or eight inches long, and tied to each leg. When shackled, he cannot walk but in a very slow, measured pace: being obliged to take six steps, when confined, for two when at liberty. Thus accoutred, he is ordered to walk round the school-room, till tired out – he is glad to sue for liberty, and promise *his endeavour* to behave more steadily in future. Should not this punishment have the desired effect, the left hand is tied behind the back, or wooden shackles fastened from elbow to elbow, behind the back. Sometimes the legs are tied together. Occasionally boys are put in a sack, or in a basket, suspended to the roof of the school, in the sight of all the pupils, who frequently smile at *the birds in the cage*. This punishment is one of the most terrible that can be inflicted on boys of sense and abilities. Above all, it is dreaded by the monitors: the name of it is sufficient, and therefore it is but seldom resorted to on their account. Frequent or old offenders are yoked together sometimes, by a piece of wood that fastens round all their necks: and, thus confined, they parade the school, walking backwards – being obliged to pay very great attention to their footsteps, for fear of running against any object that might cause the yoke to hurt their necks, or to keep from falling down. Four or six can be yoked together this way.

When a boy is disobedient to his parents, profane in his language, or has committed any offence against morality, or is remarkable for slovenliness, it is usual for him to be dressed up with labels, describing his offence, and a tin or paper crown on his head. In that manner he walks round the school, two boys preceding him, and proclaiming his fault; varying the proclamation according to the different offences. When a boy comes to school with dirty face or hands, and it seems to be more the effect of habit than of accident, a girl is appointed to wash his face in the sight of the whole school. This usually creates much diversion, especially when (as previously directed) she gives his cheeks a few *gentle strokes of correction* with her hand. The same event takes place as to girls, when in habits of slothfulness. Occasionally, such offenders against cleanliness walk round the school, preceded by a boy proclaiming her fault – and the same as to the boys. A proceeding that usually turns the *public spirit* of the whole school against the culprit.

Few punishments are so effectual as confinement after school hours. It is, however, attended with one unpleasant circumstance. In order to confine the bad boys in the school-room, after school-hours, it is often needful the master, or some proper substitute for him, should confine himself in school, to keep them in order. This inconvenience may be avoided, by tying them to the desks, in such a manner that they cannot untie themselves. These variations in the *modes* of *unavoidable punishment* give it the continual force of novelty, whatever shape it may assume. Any single kind of punishment, continued constantly in use, becomes familiar, and loses its effect. Nothing but variety can continue the power of novelty. Happily, in my institution, there are few occasions of punishment; and this conduces much to the pleasure it affords me.

The advantages of these modes of correction, are, that they can be inflicted, so as to give much uneasiness to the delinquents, without disturbing the mind or temper of the master. The advantage of coolness in correcting of children for misbehaviour, is of so much importance, that it can have no salutary effect on the youthful mind without it. It is in a calm state of mind a master may do real good, by reasoning with his scholars, and convincing them, that, for their good and the order of the institution, such painful regulations are needful. The object of these different modes of procedure is to weary the culprit with a log; or, by placing him in confinement of one kind or another, till he is humbled, and likely to remove the cause by better behaviour in future. When he finds how easily his punishments are repeated – that he himself is made the instrument – and no respite or comfort for him, but by behaving well, it is more than probable he will change for the better. Lively, active-tempered boys, are the most frequent transgressors of good order, and the most difficult to reduce to reason; the best way to reform them, is, by making monitors of them. I have experienced correction of any kind to be only needful, in proportion as boys were under the influence of bad example at home. Nothing is unhappily more common, than for parents to undo, by their bad example at home, all the good their children get at school. This occasions the first trouble to be renewed many times; and many punishments fall to the lot of that child, who, however well regulated at school, is spoiled at home. But, certain it is, that, if punishments must exist, such as those mentioned in the preceding detail are preferable to others more severe, and in common practice. I wish they were never in *sole practice*, without any thing of a more generous nature existing in schools where they are made use of.

ibid., pp. 100–5

BELL'S EXPERIMENT IN EDUCATION AT MADRAS

In 1797 on his return from India, Bell published *An Experiment in Education, made at the Male Asylum of Madras*. Subsequently this first account was expanded and went through four editions between 1797 and 1808, when the fourth edition, from which the following extracts are taken, appeared.

Bell was then Rector of Swanage, Dorset, and a self-confessed enthusiast and publicist for a monitorial system of school education. He was accustomed, he says, to repeat to his friends: 'You will mark me for an enthusiast; but if you and I live a thousand years, we shall see this System of Tuition spread over the world.'

This first extract shows the estimation Bell put on the system. Keen supporter of vaccination though he was, he considered the monitorial system of greater value to the human race.

Even in the mere point of the health of the body, and the preservation of the animal life of man, Vaccination, the most valuable discovery in the physical art, of which this country, or the world, can boast, falls short of this invention; which provides the means of supplying a remedy for the disorders of filth, idleness, ignorance, and vice, more fatal to children than the ravages of the Small-Pox.

ANDREW BELL *The Madras School or Elements of Tuition*, p. vii (London: John Murray, 1808)

In this next extract Bell gives a short account of the origins and advantages of his system. It is notable that, while Lancaster claimed that his method enabled one master to teach a thousand children, Bell considered that one teacher could instruct ten thousand.

The new method of practical Education, which has appeared under different shapes in this country, originated in the Military Male Orphan Asylum, founded at Madras in the year 1789. There it gradually grew to maturity, and, after the experience of several years, was established in all its forms in that school. Hence it was transplanted into England in the year 1797, when it was partially adopted with good success in the oldest charity school in London, that of Aldgate, and in several parts of the kingdom, and is now established at the parochial schools of White Chapel and of Lambeth, and at the Royal Military Asylum, Chelsea.

This sytem rests on the simple principle of tuition by the scholars themselves. It is its distinguishing characteristic that the school, how numerous soever, is taught solely by the pupils of the institution under a single master, who, if able and diligent, could, without difficulty, conduct ten contiguous schools, each consisting of a thousand scholars.

In addition to this general principle, and independent of it, the Madras School furnishes certain individual practices or helps in the art of tuition, by which the pupils are initiated into the elementary processes of reading, spelling, writing, arithmetic, morality, and religion.

ibid., pp. 1–2

In his views on discipline, Bell, like Lancaster, favours the use of praise and emulation as incentives to learning, and he is strongly against corporal punishment.

To attain these ends, to attain any good end in education, the great object is to fix attention, and excite exertion; or, in other words, to prevent the waste of time in school.

Were it required to say, in one word, by what means these primary and essential requisites, attention and exertion, are to be called forth, that word were discipline; a word, which at once conveys a happy illustration of the subject of enquiry. For, as its classical and original meaning is Learning, Education, Instruction, it has come, as often happens, to signify the Means by which this end is attained, whether it be the method, order, and rule observed in teaching, or the punishment and correction employed for this purpose. In the last and common acceptation of the word it has often been termed the Panacea in tuition. 'Praise,' it is said, 'encouragement, fear, threats, and various motives, apply to various descriptions of pupils, but flagellation to all.'

So far from subscribing literally to this opinion, I believe that this last species of discipline may be almost superseded, and other means substituted in its stead, as much more effectual as they are more lenient. But, understanding this word as also comprehending method, order, regulation, it embraces the chief means of education. It is in school as in an army, discipline is the first, second and third essential.

In general, then, the means, by which are elicited the attention and exertion which I have mentioned as the fundamental articles in a school, are arrangement, method, and order; vigilance, emulation, praise and dispraise; favour and disgrace; hope and fear; rewards and punishments; and especially guarding against whatever is tedious, difficult, operose, and irksome, and rendering every talk prescribed to the scholar short, simple, easy, adapted, and intelligible . . . Of these incitements, emulation, praise, rewards, and especially vigilance, along with short and easy lessons, which are never to be dispensed with, deserve to stand in the front, and are entitled to the first trial. Should these prove inefficacious, which, when properly administered, will rarely happen, recourse may be had to confinement between school hours, and on holidays, which will scarcely ever fail: but should it be found necessary, from flagrant climes, or dangerous examples, or with hardened offenders, solitary confinement may be the last resort, as less painful and degrading, and yet more irksome and effectual, than severe flagellation. Besides, corporal punishment, if it had no tendency to degrade and harden the offender, and if its efficacy were less problematical than, from its momentary impression, it is found to be, on the future behaviour of the culprit, does not reinstate him in the immediate possession of what he has forfeited by his idleness; whereas confinement at extra hours is made an instrument of regaining what was lost in past time, as well as of preventing future loss.

ibid., pp. 10–13

In this extract Bell describes the arrangement of his tutorial system and some of its advantages in class – advantages which more recent theorists have claimed for group work in schools.

Each class is paired off into tutors and pupils.

Thus in a class of twenty-four boys, the twelve superior are tutors respectively to the six inferior. Of course in their seats the boys take their places in different order from that in which they stand in their class: as each pupil sits by the side of his tutor.

Mark, at the outset, how many advantages grow out of this simple arrangement.

First, the sociable disposition, both in the tutor and pupil, is indulged by the reciprocal offices assigned to them.

Next, the very moment you have nominated a boy a tutor, you have exalted him in his own eyes, and given him a character to support, the effect of which is well known.

Next, the tutors enable their pupils to keep pace with their classes, which otherwise some of them would fall behind, and be degraded to a lower class, or else continuing attached to their class, forfeit almost every chance of improvement, by never learning any one lesson as it ought to be learned.

This is the reason why so many boys in every school are declared incapable of learning. As often as this was said to me of any of our pupils, in the beginning of my essay, by such ushers as I then had, my reply was, 'It is you, who do not know how to teach, how to arrest and fix the attention of your pupil: it is not that he cannot learn, but that he does not give the degree of attention requisite for his share of capacity.' I then gave an experimental proof . . . This I did by teaching the boy, who was pronounced incapable, the very lesson which, it was declared, he could not learn . . .

Another advantage . . . is that the tutor far more effectually learns his lesson than if he had not to teach it to another. By teaching he is best taught. 'Qui docet indoctos, docet se.'

Still another advantage is, that here is a grand stimulus to emulation; for what disgrace attaches to the boy who, by his negligence, is degraded into a pupil, and falls perhaps to be tutored by his late pupil, promoted to be a tutor!

ibid., pp. 21–3

In the following extract Bell relates the advantages of his system to the economic and social background of his times. He points out that it teaches pupils the virtues of subordination, industry and punctuality, virtues which the upper and manufacturing classes very much wanted to see in the labouring poor whom they employed. He also stresses that it is a mechanical but economical method of instruction, eminently suitable to an age of industrial expansion when workers need at least some elementary education, but when society is unwilling to allow children much time to gain this education, preferring that they should begin work as soon as possible, and also unwilling to pay for enough schools or schoolteachers. His comparison of his system to the steam engine is a very meaningful one.

It is the grand boast of this system . . . that it . . . establishes such habits of industry, morality, and religion, as have a tendency to form good scholars, good men, good subjects, and good Christians.

In a word, it gives, as it were, to the master the hundred hands of Briareus, the hundred eyes of Argus, and the wings of Mercury.

But this scheme lays claim to still higher praise. It is the superlative glory of the system, that, when duly administered, it applies itself to every principle of humanity. It engages the attention, interests the mind, and wins the affection of youth. Their natural love of activity is gratified by the occupation which it furnishes them. They are delighted with being, to every wise and good purpose, their own masters. They are charmed that they see the reason, feel the justice, and perceive the utility of all that is done to them, for them, and by them.

And, still further, this system is to be estimated by the civility, the decorum, the subordination, the regard to good order and good government, which it inculcates and exemplifies; while, by the various offices performed in the different departments of the school, it prepares the disciples for business, and instructs them to act their part and perform their duty in future life with punctuality, diligence, impartiality, and justice; and also cultivates the best dispositions of the heart, by teaching the children to take an early and well-directed interest in the welfare of one another.

Every boy, not totally corrupted and depraved, sees in this system a friend, to whom he is sure to attach himself in the closest bands of amity, and will himself, whenever it is conducted with no interested view, but with impartiality and ability, for the general good, come forward and exert himself in every emergency, for its due support and administration. The policy of your scholars is on your side as well as their heart. Not to forfeit such high privileges, as the system confers on them, they take a deep interest in its support, preservation, and advancement. For should they, by falsehood, perverseness, or ill conduct, disturb its order and harmony, they must expect to revert to other jurisdiction, than that of themselves and their peers; an immunity of which they are no less jealous than every Englishman is of his invaluable privilege, the trial by jury.

By these means, a few good boys selected for the purpose (and changed as often as occasion requires) who have not begun their career of pleasure, ambition, or interest; who have no other occupation, no other pursuit, nothing to call forth their attention, but this single object; and whose minds you can lead and command at pleasure, form the whole school; teach the scholars to think rightly, and, mixing in all their little amusements and diversions, secure them against the contagion of ill example, and, by seeing that they treat one another kindly, render them contented and happy in their condition. . . .

In a word, the advantages of this system, in its political, moral, and religious tendency; in its economy of labour, time, expense, and punishment; in the facilities and satisfaction which it affords to the master and the scholar; can only be ascertained by trial and experience, and can scarcely be comprehended or credited by those, who have not witnessed its productive powers and marvellous effects.

Like the steam engine, or spinning machinery, it diminishes labour and multiplies work, but in a degree which does not admit of the same limits, and scarcely of the same calculations as they do. For, unlike the mechanical powers, this intellectual and moral engine, the more work it has to perform, the greater is the facility and expedition with which it is performed, and the greater is the degree of perfection to which it is carried.

ibid., pp. 32–7

THE NATIONAL SOCIETY

Founded in October 1811 this Society declared its purpose to be 'that the National Religion should be made the foundation of a National Education'. It also proclaimed its adherence to Bell's monitorial system, stating that 'the members of the Establishment are not only warranted, but in duty bound to preserve that system, as originally practised at Madras in the form of a Church of England Education.'

This extract states the aim of the Society more explicitly.

The sole object in view being to communicate to the poor generally, by means of a summary mode of education lately brought into practice, such knowledge and habits as are sufficient to guide them through life in their proper stations, especially to teach them the doctrine of Religion according to the principles of the Established Church, and to train them to the performance of their religious duties by an early discipline.

National Society Annual Report, p. 19 (1812)

THE BRITISH AND FOREIGN SCHOOL SOCIETY

This Society had its origin in a committee formed in 1808 to support Joseph Lancaster in his work, but it was not formally constituted until 1814 and by that time the connection with Lancaster had been severed.

The following extract is from the 'Rules and Regulations' of the Society drawn up in May 1814.

I. This Institution shall be designated 'The Institution for Promoting the Education of the Labouring and Manufacturing Classes of Society of every Religious Persuasion'; and, for the purpose of making manifest the extent of its objects, the title of the Society shall be 'THE BRITISH AND FOREIGN SCHOOL SOCIETY'.

II. This Institution shall consist of a Patron, Vice-Patrons, President, Vice-Presidents, Treasurer, Secretaries, Life and Annual Members; together with such officers as may be deemed necessary for conducting the affairs of the Institution.

III. The Institution shall maintain a School on an extensive scale to educate children. It shall support and train up young persons of both sexes for supplying properly instructed Teachers to the inhabitants of such places in the British dominions, at home and abroad, as shall be desirous of establishing schools on the British system. It shall instruct all persons, whether natives or foreigners, who may be sent from time to time, for the purpose of being qualified as Teachers in this or any other country.

IV. All schools which shall be supplied with Teachers at the expense of this Institution shall be open to the children of parents of all religious denominations. Reading, Writing, Arithmetic, and Needlework shall be taught, the lessons for reading shall consist of extracts from the Holy Scriptures; no catechism or peculiar religious tenets shall be taught in the schools, but every child shall be enjoined to attend regularly the place of worship to which its parents belong.

Quoted in H. B. BINNS *A Century of Education*, pp. 73–4 (London: Dent, 1908)

Index